D1612546

THATCHER, M.

6/93 1/98
264

THE REVIVAL OF BRITAIN.   LAST COPY

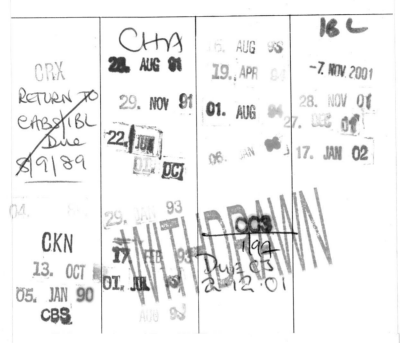

Please return this book on or before the date marked above.
If overdue a fine will be charged in accordance with library regulations.

The period of loan may be extended (once only by post or telephone)
if the book is not required by another reader. To renew, please quote
the AUTHOR, TITLE, the DATE DUE and

▼ ——— THIS NUMBER ——— ▼

1854100467 1 264

NORTH YORKSHIRE COUNTY LIBRARY   C

THE REVIVAL OF BRITAIN

MARGARET THATCHER

The Revival of
BRITAIN

Speeches on Home and European Affairs 1975-1988

Compiled by
Alistair B. Cooke

AURUM PRESS

First published 1989 by Aurum Press Ltd,
33 Museum Street, London WC1A 1LD

British Library Cataloguing in Publication Data

Thatcher, Margaret
    The revival of Britain: Speeches on home
    and European affairs
    1. Great Britain. Social conditions
    I. Title   II. Cooke, Alistair B.
    941.085'8

ISBN 1 85410 046 7

The author and publishers are grateful to
John Murray Publishers Ltd for permission
to reproduce lines from 'The Planster's Vision'
taken from *Collected Poems* by John Betjeman.

The speeches to the Institute of Socio-
Economic Studies (p. 1), to the Conservative
Party Conference (p. 18), to the Institute of
Directors (p. 40) and the Iain Macleod
Memorial Lecture (p. 48) were first published
in *Let Our Children Grow Tall* by the Centre
for Policy Studies in 1977. The speech at
Bruges (p. 256) was first published by the
Conservative Political Centre in 1988.

Typeset by Wyvern Typesetting Ltd, Bristol
Printed in Great Britain by
Biddles Ltd, Guildford and King's Lynn

Contents

CONTENTS

Note: Each speech is preceded by a commentary
by Alistair B. Cooke.

Introduction

From the very moment when she became Leader of the Conservative Party in February 1975, Mrs Thatcher made clear her determination to create the conditions for the revival of Britain. Looking back at the end of the first successful decade of Thatcherism, it is easy to underestimate the magnitude of the task that then faced her. However, the first nine speeches in this collection provide a telling reminder of the scale of the problem which she had to overcome.

Britain's long post-war decline could not be reversed simply by removing Labour from power, vital though that was. From 1975 onwards, therefore, Mrs Thatcher worked out a detailed agenda for radical change which was to break the mould of politics in Britain after her accession to power in 1979. The results have been so profound that Mrs Thatcher has become the first Prime Minister ever to create an 'ism' that is certain to remain a permanent part of the political vocabulary (Beaconsfieldism' flourished briefly in the late 1870s, but as a term of abuse coined by Liberals who wanted to discredit Disraeli's foreign policy).

The speeches which comprise this book provide a unique record of the evolution of Mrs Thatcher's radical Conservative agenda into Thatcherism. She has perhaps gone to greater lengths than any other political leader since Churchill to ensure that her speeches convey her policies and convictions with absolute clarity. Every one designed for a major occasion is prepared with immense care, invariably going through many drafts before Mrs Thatcher is satisfied with it. As is well-known, she had only just completed work on her speech for the Conservative Party Conference in Brighton in 1984 (no. 16 in this collection) when the IRA bomb exploded just before 3 a.m. At each stage of its development Thatcherism is the product of intense work and prolonged reflection and discussion.

Critics of Thatcherism constantly allege that it makes a major departure from Toryism. In fact, one of the most striking features of these speeches is the extent to which they draw on the Conservative tradition. Many of the values and attitudes which Mrs Thatcher has consistently sought to foster in society at large spring directly from it. Edmund Burke, in a famous passage in his *Reflections*, associated Toryism for ever with the encouragement of small, often informal groupings and arrangements: 'To be attached to the subdivision, to love the little platoon we belong to in society, is the first principle (the germ, as it were) of public affections. It is the first link in the series by which we proceed towards a love of our country and to mankind.' Thatcherism promotes exactly that kind of diversity – for instance, by its support for families, voluntary associations and other responsible bodies that unite local communities.

These speeches, therefore, show how Mrs Thatcher has employed radical measures in order to re-create a vision of society based on enduring Conservative values. Very little editorial change has been made to the speeches themselves in preparing them for publication. A small number of short passages containing purely personal remarks have been omitted; and a few brief explanatory comments have been added, mainly to identify individuals mentioned in the text. A few misprints and errors that appeared in the original press releases have been corrected. Punctuation and spelling have been standardized throughout. Otherwise the speeches are printed here in exactly the form in which they were delivered.

I am grateful to Mr William Wellesley for helping me compile the material, and to Mr Nigel Baker for reading the proofs.

The Institute of
Socio-Economic Studies

NEW YORK, 15 SEPTEMBER 1975

Mrs Thatcher made her first visit to the United States as Leader of the
Conservative Party in the autumn of 1975, arriving on 13 September for
an intensive nine-day tour (after which she went on to Canada for another
three days of discussions and meetings). In the United States she had
detailed talks with President Ford, Dr Henry Kissinger and other leading
members of the Administration. She also delivered three major speeches, in
which she expounded at length for the first time many of the ideas and
policies which, when put into practice after 1979, were to create the basis
for the economic revival of Britain. And the coherent philosophy expressed
in these speeches would later be given practical application in the United
States itself.

Nothing emerged more clearly during Mrs Thatcher's American tour
than her conviction that politicians had, above all, to come to grips with the
scourge of inflation. In a lecture at the Roosevelt University in Chicago on
22 September, she said, 'Inflation is a pernicious evil capable of destroying
any society built on a value system where freedom is paramount . . . when
money can no longer be counted on to act as a store of value, savings and
investment are undermined, the basis of contracts is distorted and the
professional and middle-class citizen, the backbone of all societies,
disaffected . . . Yet it is now clear to me that none of the tools for fighting it
which economists offer us can work unless there is the political will to do
so, and public opinion understands what is at stake if we fail.'

In her speech at the Institute of Socio-Economic Studies – the first of the

1

series – Mrs Thatcher highlighted some of the factors (such as 'the progressive consensus', 'bourgeois guilt', over-taxation, and the growth of the State) which had undermined Britain's capacity to grapple seriously with inflation and other economic problems. The speech, which was entitled 'Let the Children Grow Tall', gave a clear indication of the scale of the changes that were needed in Britain, but went on to anticipate confidently a steady recovery when all the lessons, then becoming evident, had been learned: 'In the years to come we shall re-establish, in a form appropriate to tomorrow's world, the foundations on which Britain has flourished.'

Americans appear to be curiously interested in what is happening in Britain today. What you are writing and saying about us we consume avidly, together with the regular flow of self-criticism which is a long-established part of our staple diet. In the spring, Eric Sevareid caused quite a stir when he waved us his fond farewell on television. Indeed, he may have been instrumental in inducing the Prime Minister to occupy our television screens for the best part of an hour. Only a week or two ago Vermont Royster [Pulitzer prize-winner and former editor of the *Wall Street Journal*] wrote that: 'Britain today offers a textbook case on how to ruin a country . . .'

However, the rather morbid and fatalistic tone of much of what is written about Britain by commentators on both sides of the Atlantic is misplaced. So I am extremely grateful to the Socio-Economic Institute for giving me such a splendid opportunity to put the record straight.

Most outside observers have not noticed that amidst our well-publicized difficulties a vital new debate is beginning – or perhaps I should say an old debate is being renewed – about the proper role of Government, the Welfare State and the attitudes on which they rest.

Many of the issues at stake have been debated on countless occasions in the last century or two. Some are as old as philosophy itself. However, the Welfare State in Britain is now at least thirty years old. So after a long period in which it was unquestioningly accepted by the whole of society, we can now do more than discuss its strengths and weaknesses in the hackneyed abstract language of moral and political principles. We can see how it has operated in practice in the light of a substantial body of evidence.

The debate centres on what I shall term, for want of a better phrase, the 'progressive consensus', the doctrine that the State should be active on many fronts in promoting equality; in the provision of social welfare; and in the redistribution of wealth and incomes. This philosophy is well expressed in the following words:

> Since Social Justice is the traditionally Socialist aim, and since it can only be achieved by collective action, this part of the exercise naturally comes to be regarded as the major element in Socialist economic policy . . . It is just because market forces tend towards growing inequality in incomes and property that massive redistribution is necessary if political freedom and other civilized values are to be preserved.
>
> So it should be the aim of the democratic State to re-share out these rewards – to socialize the national income, if you like to call it that . . . There can be no doubt that by far the most effective method has proved to be, and is likely to prove increasingly in the future, the instrument of public finance, and in particular progressive direct taxation and centrally financed public services.

That was written by a former Labour Cabinet Minister in 1962. However, I am not interested in party politics tonight.

Such views are held to varying degrees in all our political parties, in schools and universities and amongst social commentators generally. Interestingly enough, they are now being questioned right across the same broad spectrum.

It is not that our people are suddenly reverting to the ideals of total *laissez-faire*, or rejecting the social advances of recent decades. It is rather that they are reviving a sober and constructive interest in the noble ideals of personal responsibility, because in some respects the concepts of social responsibility have turned sour in practice. They are making an attempt to identify and eliminate errors and fallacies, to consolidate and retrench before advancing further.

It is in that constructive spirit – and as a former Secretary of

3

State for Education and Science myself – that I am speaking to you tonight. I shall concentrate on four issues: What are the facts about the distribution of wealth and incomes? To what extent is greater equality desired in Britain today? Has the economy been strengthened by the promotion of more equality and the extension of the Welfare State? Finally, has it strengthened our political and social framework?

Let us begin then with some facts. Most people say that the distribution of incomes and wealth in Britain is highly inequitable and that it has changed little, despite the steps taken by Government to even it out. From there it is only a short step to two complementary arguments: either that redistribution would greatly swell the incomes of the average man; or that the wealth of the rich is sufficient to finance the substantial extension of the role of the State.

By a fortunate coincidence a major study has just been published (by the newly created Standing Royal Commission) on the distribution of income and wealth.* It gives the first proper statistical picture of the changes that have taken place in Britain between the last war and 1972.

In 1972 incomes after tax were divided up roughly as follows. At the upper end of the scale, the top 1 per cent of income earners got 4 per cent of incomes – four times the average. The top 10 per cent had twice the average and the bottom 10 per cent a bit under half the average. These are not dramatic differences either by the standards of other Western economies or, I suspect, of many countries behind the Iron Curtain. Indeed, research has shown that the distribution of income in Britain is surprisingly similar to that in Poland!

Furthermore, there have been substantial changes over the decades. Taking account of tax, the share of the top 1 per cent of earners went down by half between 1938 and 1949. By 1972 it had fallen by a further one-third.

The share of the *taxable* income of the poor has not increased to so great an extent. But none the less they are markedly better

---

The Distribution of Income and Wealth. A report by the Royal Commission chaired by Lord Diamond (Cmnd 6171: HMSO, 1975).

off in relative (as well as absolute) terms than they were before the war. By 1972 tax-free benefits in cash and kind added about a half to the pre-tax income of a typical household in the bottom 10 per cent. For poor families with many dependants, the gain could be nearer 100 per cent. Today the figures would probably be higher still.

Capital assets have been more unevenly spread than incomes in Britain, as in most other countries. For this reason they have been the chief target of egalitarian critics. In Britain it is almost a received truth that 10 per cent of the population own 80 or 90 per cent of all assets. But that is not the case. The top 10 per cent of the population over eighteen own less than half (45 per cent) of personal wealth when State pension rights are counted as an asset, as they should be.

As you will appreciate, even these figures are rather misleading, since wealth is normally unevenly distributed between husbands and wives, old and young, misers and spendthrifts. If these distorting factors could be properly allowed for, the picture might well look still less extreme.

As with income, there have been big changes over the years. On a narrow definition of wealth which *excludes* pension rights, the top 1 per cent of the population owned:

> 69 per cent of personal wealth in 1911
> 50 per cent of personal wealth in 1938
> 38 per cent of personal wealth in 1960
> 28 per cent of personal wealth in 1972*

*(or 16½ per cent if pension rights are included in wealth holdings.)

So the facts about economic inequality (as opposed to the myths) are these. The rich are getting poorer and the poor are getting richer. This is due both to market forces and the actions of Government through the tax system. And it is no longer the case that taking further money from the rich will make a significant difference to the wealth of the bulk of the population. Nor will taxing them more heavily pay for much more Government spending.

Finally, one notes that it would do little to diffuse economic power more widely. It is already largely in the hands of Government and Labour Unions.

These statistical myths lead directly to the claim that there is a widespread sense of resentment and injustice over the current degree of inequality in our society, and great enthusiasm for its elimination. This political judgement is closely linked in many commentators' eyes with the quite separate proposition that class divisions in Britain are severe and reinforced by economic inequality.

My own experience in politics has always made me doubt this argument, and there is survey evidence which strengthens my view. The following remarks come from the conclusions of a national opinion survey carried out in the early months of this year:

> Our findings show little spontaneous demand for the redistribution of earnings across broad occupational categories and suggest that such redistribution would in itself provide no solution to any problem of pressure on pay. Neither is it necessary to allay any general feelings of injustice in society . . . It may be little consolation to the Government in present circumstances that the chief requirement for maintaining general satisfaction with incomes and earnings is steady economic growth . . . rather than massive redistribution . . . This point is a crucial one to be met by those who suggest that any problem we have is one of distribution rather than of resources or growth.

Whatever ordinary people actually want, there remains in Britain a powerful and vocal lobby pressing for greater equality, in some cases even, it would seem, for total equality. What is it that impels them to do so?

One important pressure is undoubtedly the simplistic desire to help our fellow-men. But often the reasons boil down to an undistinguished combination of envy and what might be termed 'bourgeois guilt'.

Envy is clearly at work in the case of the egalitarian who resents the gap between himself and those who are better off, while conveniently forgetting his own obligations to those poorer than himself.

'Bourgeois guilt' is that well-known sense of guilt and self-criticism that affects people, not only the very rich, when looking the other way, at the position of those poorer than themselves. Far be it from me as an individual to criticize or ridicule their doubts and worries. However, as a politician, I will most certainly criticize the attempts of such people to impose on others a programme of impoverishment through the medium of the State. This brings happiness to no one except to those who impose it.

In a free society, they can give away as much as they want, to whom they want, whenever they want. If they believe in pooling their possessions with others in a commune they are welcome to do so.

There is a far less general desire for equality (as opposed to equity) in Britain today than is often claimed. Even where it does exist the underlying motivation is not always creditable.

But suppose we grant for a moment that greater equality *is* desired. How far is its promotion desirable from the standpoint of the economy?

The promotion of greater equality goes hand in hand with the extension of the Welfare State and State control over people's lives. Universal and usually free social services necessarily transfer benefits in kind and cash from the richer to the poorer members of the community.

So taken together they define rather well the process of 'socializing the national income' which occurs in my first quotation. How far has it strengthened our economy?

The public sector has been a large part of the British economy since the early post-war years. Despite the statistical fog which surrounds all international comparisons, it is clear that the Government's share in GNP has been consistently one of the highest of the OECD countries. And for at least twenty years it has risen faster in the UK than elsewhere. Today the State controls in various ways well over half of our national income.

Naturally the tax bill has risen sharply too, particularly for the private citizen. For the yield of corporate taxes has fallen consistently for twenty years. In the middle Fifties they financed one-sixth of public spending, but by the end of the Sixties they only met one-fourteenth of the total.

In the later Fifties and Sixties, the increase in tax and social security payments in effect knocked about 1 per cent off the growth of private spending each year.

These global figures play down the very serious deterioration in the position of the typical earner that has taken place at the same time. For he has moved, over a few years, from a position of paying negligible taxes and deductions to one in which the burden has become large and onerous. Since 1963, the State has increased its take fivefold from a negligible 5 per cent of disposable incomes to about one-quarter today.

This rising burden of taxation has been one of the major sources of inflationary pressure.

People respond to over-taxation in several equally harmful ways. They press their employers for ever higher wage increases in a vain attempt to sustain a growing standard of living. This has led to a relentless acceleration of cost and price increases since the mid-1950s. (From 2 per cent per annum in 1956–60 to 25 per cent per annum now.) Equally, they press politicians and the Government for faster economic growth and the budgetary policies needed to finance it, without regard for the dangers of an overheated economy and a failing trade balance.

There are many who regard this desire for private spending as irrational, selfish and unworthy. After all, they say, the taxes have financed a substantial growth in the provision of public goods. Any economist will tell one that this is a part of increasing living standards. Unfortunately, any experienced politician or detached observer can also now see that, in practice, people attach peculiar importance to using their own money to buy what they want when they want. Moreover, they cannot relate the tax-man's apparently arbitrary and growing take to the services it finances. These services they regard as an absolute right, a kind of manna from heaven.

While the rising tax burden makes the average worker dissatisfied, a progressive redistributive tax system such as ours has much worse effects on the *executive or professional with a high salary*. You are doubtless all familiar with the arguments about the dulling of personal incentives which this causes. We have that problem. And we have many others as well.

An employer wants to promote his manager in terms of post-tax salary from £8,000 to £12,000 a year – a jump of £4,000. To do so in Britain today (leaving aside the requirements of our current programme of income restraint) he must double the manager's salary from about £15,000 to £30,000 a year. This sort of increase is more than most firms can think of at the best of times. So the cost of rewarding skill or hard work has become almost prohibitive. The whole country therefore loses much of the benefits of competition in the labour market. For the same reasons, it is very easy for employers overseas to hire English executives and professionals. They can offer a vastly higher effective salary at the same, or even lower, cost to themselves than those faced by the English firm. So losses of highly trained manpower through emigration are becoming more serious, despite the depressed state of the world economy.

Steep progressive taxes also hit at the budding businessman, the entrepreneur who has the potential to build up tomorrow's dynamic firm. If he can keep only a fifth or a sixth of the extra profit from some new venture, the odds are that he won't undertake it at all. Or that, if he does, he will have to sell out before long to an established firm to turn his highly taxed income into a less highly taxed capital gain. But as a result he may well lose interest and control, and the firm lose its drive and inspiration. No economy can develop vigorously if it stifles those forces on which it depends for renewal.

The inexorable acceleration of wages, partly in response to over-taxation, has naturally resulted in a wage-price spiral. A spiral with a twist in it. For various reasons, business cannot raise prices far enough or quickly enough to preserve its profits when wage increases are large and accelerating. So profits have fallen for many years on any measure – before tax, after tax, as share in national income or as a rate of return on capital. Since retained profits are the principal source of funds for investment and profit levels, the main incentive, capital expenditure in private industry, has faltered more and more. The upswings have got shorter and the downswings deeper and longer with succeeding cycles of activity. Manufacturing investment next year – 1976 – is likely to be little higher in real terms than it was *ten* years before. It appears, as a natural consequence, that our underlying rate of economic growth has stopped improving after thirty years of modest but perceptible acceleration.

The situation has not been made any easier recently by the curious belief that profits are rather evil and of little economic significance. Both the present and previous Governments have therefore had little choice but to pursue price and profit controls as part of their counter-inflationary policies. The levels of profit emerging from these controls were selected with insufficient regard for their effects on capital spending, employment or growth and they have bitten hard. Our economy has thus been pushed into a loss of profit and therefore an investment recession at a time when the world economy was in serious downturn.

Now the damage has been done, the situation can only be put to rights if considerable price rises can be made and accepted by labour, without any response in the form of wage increases. It is a pretty challenging 'if'.

Two decades of declining profits naturally mean that the saver who invests in equity shares has had a raw deal. The real rate of return has recently been negative even before tax, let alone when changes in the capital value of investments are allowed for. However, Government has made the position worse by taking powers to restrain dividends still further, in the name of fairness and equity, one should note. The case for doing so was simple. Unless profit distribution is restrained, how, it was asked, could one expect unions and workers to acquiesce in a programme of wage restraint?

Now it is bad enough that this seductive little trade-off is based on a very unjust bargain. Savers, and retired people, have already suffered severely from the costs of accelerating inflation, which they have done nothing to cause. Why should they make yet further sacrifices to induce those who have already gained so much at their expense to desist for a while?

What is at stake is more than a painful injustice. Negative real profits and dividend control must, if sustained for any period, have a corrosive effect on the life insurance and pensions institutions. They are put in a position in which it becomes more and more difficult to plan and guarantee the flow of future income which they have promised their beneficiaries. Private employers, for their part, find themselves faced with the sudden need to make enormous payments into their pension funds even to maintain their existing pension obligations in money terms.

I am not suggesting for a moment that these great institutions are dying or dead. But they have a nasty fight on their hands.

Some of the problems I have talked about combine together to create further subtle distortions of the market place which are not immediately evident.

The first is an unbalanced competition for *savings*. The process works like this. The Government increases its spending to fulfil its commitments to extend its activities. The wage earner begins to revolt against the consequent rising tax burden. His resentment leads to higher wages, and lower profits, lower corporate taxes, and ultimately slower growth. It also deters the Government from raising taxes in line with spending. So the Government has a growing deficit and then has to borrow growing sums of money assuming, of course, that it does not resort to the printing press.

In doing so, it competes with the private company and the home-buyer in the savings market. The private company finds it increasingly impossible to bid for funds, since its profits are depressed. The house-buyer may still be able to do so, but even then he is probably subsidized by the savers who lend him the money. At the end of the day, a public spending bill which exceeds the taxable capacity of the economy sucks away money which should be spent on investment in industry or private housing.

The second distortion is an unbalanced competition for *labour*. As wealth increases, spending patterns switch from industrial products towards services in all economies. This will

11

affect the pattern of employment and competition for labour between the private and Government sectors.

Public sector employment in Britain has steadily grown at a substantial rate for more than a decade – about 1 per cent per annum – while the overall working population has contracted. The net effect has been to reduce the pool of labour available to private employers. So when the economy entered its last major upswing in 1972–3, labour shortages were encountered unexpectedly soon. Although the leap in production was as large and sudden as any we have experienced, employment in industry scarcely increased at all. Many of the missing workers had, in effect, been absorbed by Government during the previous period of slack business activity.

The importance of this cannot be overstated, particularly for a trading economy like ours. The private sector creates the goods and services we need both to export, to pay for our imports, and the revenue to finance public services. So one must not overload it. Every man switched away from industry and into Government will reduce the productive sector and increase the burden on it at the same time.

I conclude, therefore, that the persistent expansion of the role of the State and the relentless pursuit of equality has caused, and is causing, damage to our economy in a variety of ways. It is not the sole cause of what some have termed the 'British sickness', but it is a major one.

This brings me to the final issue: the fallacy that extending the role of the State and the correction of inequality will strengthen the political and social framework – that it 'is necessary if political freedom and other civilized values are to be preserved'.

It is obvious that the strains in the economy I have just discussed have affected our political life. This happens in many detailed ways, but now I have only time to touch briefly on certain wider political developments which appear to spring from the 'progressive consensus'.

For many years now there has been a growing awareness of injustice and inequality in our society. In the beginning, much of it was genuine, today some of it is artificial. It has been cultivated by some philosophers, politicians, propagandists in the media and by social commentators. Associated with it is the proposition that it is the job of Government to intervene to put unsatisfactory situations right.

As time passes, more and more groups of people with grievances and common interests combine to press our politicians and institutions for redress and justice. In this process, they are assisted by the growing scope for exploiting grievances through the press and broadcasting, and the new techniques for publicity and protest which the media have nurtured.

These groups frequently have little connection with conventional political parties, and often cannot find any natural niche in our political institutions.

In such cases, the Government is under twin pressures. The first is to treat with pressure groups *outside* Parliament and the democratic framework. The second pressure arises in our attempts to resolve our apparent injustices. Frequently the proper channels are discredited before they are given a chance to work; or, more damaging still, the authorities are induced, sometimes by threat of force, to alter their decisions or even change the law retrospectively. The lesson is quickly learnt. Before long the same tactics are applied by other groups, which previously have been meticulous in their respect for our institutions and the rule of law.

All too often direct action outside the legitimate social and political framework is buoyed up and stimulated by a debased rhetoric of 'fairness' or 'equality'. You know how it goes. It is 'my rights at all costs regardless of who has to pay', or 'society has a duty to me', not 'I have a duty to society', or 'why should I be less well off than he is?' not 'have I earned a right to be better off than my neighbour?' All too often there is no consideration of the consequences which the rest of society must bear. Rarely, if ever, do people notice that in acceding to such pressures a Government is endorsing principles and creating precedents which would be quite disastrous if applied generally – and widespread application is a powerful test of whether a decision is right or wrong. So direct action deals dangerous blows to institutions.

THE REVIVAL OF BRITAIN

The alarming growth of the 'direct action' philosophy has recently led to a growing demand that we should introduce a Bill of Rights in Britain. It is too early to say whether such a fundamental change in our system of Government will in the end turn out to be desirable, or possible. But the fact that the issue is being considered at all is a telling sign of the intense pressures on our constitution and the rule of law. It is a revealing example, too, of the new debate which I referred to earlier.

Finally, it is clear that not only the institutions, but also the civilized values and the moral framework of our political institutions have been put at risk. For the *concepts* of justice and fairness are being distorted by the language and actions of many groups who use them for political advantage.

There are several strands or elements in the concept of justice which are never easy to distinguish. May I explain further by taking two examples.

First, the limit to resources. One of the foundations of modern democracy, one of the main reasons for its success in the last two centuries, has been a growing impatience with the state of our societies, a recognition that much of the misery inflicted by nature on man, or by man on himself, was avoidable and should be avoided. The many advances we have all witnessed have generated a naive unspoken belief and expectation that there are few personal or social ills which cannot now be remedied or mitigated by the State. How easy it is for example, to believe that *a country* like Britain can neutralize the rising cost of imported food and oil by subsidizing their prices. With an apparently omnipotent Government, people forget that the only effective subsidy could come from the oil producers themselves. We do not make ourselves better off by giving ourselves presents of our own money.

How easy it is with a National Health Service to argue, for example, that the State must provide and service artificial kidney machines to all those who need them. With our firm commitment to the sanctity of human life, it is difficult to avoid appearing callous and brutal if we also talk about the limited resources available for saving it. To many it is profane to argue about the cost of saving lives at all. They passionately believe that the moral imperative should be absolute.

So the revolution of expectations can easily lose touch with the real world. As a nation we have perhaps forgotten that human institutions are necessarily imperfect; that they cannot iron out all the wrinkles in the human character, tame the laws of nature, abolish scarcity or bring about heaven on Earth.

The second problem is a closely related one. Suppose that two of us earn the same wages, but you save while I spend them all. When we retire you will be wealthier than I – a classic case of economic inequality, I might claim, but this is not a case of unfairness or injustice, since we both lived our lives as we pleased. Equally, suppose that we have the same intelligence, but that I go to college, work hard and earn a high salary, while you choose to leave school early and coast through life on a modest wage. There will be inequality in our incomes, but not inequality in the gap between the two.

However, were I an egalitarian or a believer in direct action, I might well ask for a share in your savings or as much pay as you, simply because an apparently unfair situation exists, *no matter how it arose*.

To do this is to ignore the fact that society is a living organism resting on processes and changing relationships. We determine justice as much by the way in which things are done as by their consequences, or the state of the world at any given moment. No Government can govern, no society can remain united, justice itself will become meaningless, if each citizen can determine what is fair and just from his own viewpoint and shrug off the rights of others or the decisions of a democratic Government when either displease him.

In Britain today we can already see and demonstrate to our fellow-citizens the dangers and drawbacks of this course. And they are becoming increasingly aware of what is at stake, long before the situation threatens to become critical. In the years to come we shall re-establish, in a form appropriate to tomorrow's world, the foundations on which Britain has flourished in the past.

What lessons have we learnt from the last thirty years? First,

15

THE REVIVAL OF BRITAIN

the pursuit of equality is a mirage. What is more desirable and more practicable than the pursuit of equality is the pursuit of equality of opportunity. And opportunity means nothing unless it includes the right to be unequal. And the freedom to be different. I believe you have a saying in the Middle West: 'Don't cut down the tall poppies – let them rather grow tall.'

Let our children grow tall – and some grow taller than others, if they have it in them to do so. We must build a society in which each citizen can develop his full potential, both for his own benefit and for the community as a whole; in which originality, skill, energy and thrift are rewarded; in which we encourage, rather than restrict, the variety and richness of human nature.

Second, we must strike a proper balance between the growing demands and powers of the State and the vital role of private enterprise. For private enterprise is by far the best method of harnessing the energy and ambition of the individual to increasing the wealth of the nation; for pioneering new products and technologies; for holding down prices through the mechanism of competition; above all, for widening the range of choice of goods and services and jobs.

Government must therefore limit its activities where their scope and scale harm profits, investment, innovation and future growth. It must temper what may be socially desirable with what is economically reasonable.

Finally, we must measure the economic and political demands of some of our people against their consequences. We must have regard to their effect on our political and social framework. We must devote ourselves to a greater understanding and more realistic pursuit of true justice and liberty, and the maintenance of the free institutions on which these values depend.

In the coming months we shall all be thinking particularly of the achievements of the United States in the two hundred years of its existence, and of the lessons your country can still teach the rest of the world. May I conclude with the modest hope that you will also spare a few moments to learn from our recent experience. It shows, in my view, how essential it is to escape from the facile arguments which both our countries have experienced. And to reaffirm, before it is too late, those true values which both our countries traditionally have shared.

Those values have never been more important than they are today.

The Conservative Party Conference

BLACKPOOL, 10 OCTOBER 1975

In her first speech to the Conservative Party Conference as Leader, Mrs Thatcher showed that she had already placed her stamp firmly on Conservative policy. It was obvious that a new approach had been forged – an approach which was to be established ever more thoroughly and convincingly in the years ahead. The essence of that new approach was, of course, a strong reaffirmation of the economic and moral case for free enterprise – with Government setting the framework to enable it to flourish.

The speech posed starkly the choice Britain faced – between a reinvigorated Conservatism dedicated to liberating the talents of the British people, and a decaying Socialism which now constituted the chief obstacle to Britain's progress and recovery. In presenting the choice in these terms, Mrs Thatcher created a new mood of determination and confidence in the Conservative Party. The Times *(11 October 1975) commented:*

> *She reopened the attack on Socialism across a broad front with a vigour and wit of phrase that gave her party new hope. She gave many proofs of her personal commitment to capitalism and individual freedom, and she left her followers convinced, as she put it, that Britain faces not a crisis of capitalism but a crisis of Socialism.*

The enthusiasm with which the speech was received – with 'rolling breakers of cheers, shouts and foot-stamping' – showed how strongly the Party endorsed the Thatcherite vision of Conservatism.

18

The first Conservative Party Conference I ever attended was in 1946 and I came to it as an undergraduate representing Oxford University Conservative Association (I know our Cambridge supporters will not mind). That Conference was held in this very hall and the platform then seemed a long way away and I had no thought of joining the lofty and distinguished people sitting up there, but our party is the party of equality of opportunity, as you can see.

I know you will understand the humility I feel at following in the footsteps of great men like our Leader in that year, Winston Churchill, a man called by destiny to raise the name of Britain to supreme heights in the history of the free world; in the footsteps of Anthony Eden, who set us the goal of a property-owning democracy – a goal we still pursue today; of Harold Macmillan whose leadership brought so many ambitions within the grasp of every citizen; of Alec Douglas-Home whose career of selfless public service earned the affection and admiration of us all; and of Edward Heath, who successfully led the Party to victory in 1970 and brilliantly led the nation into Europe in 1973.

During my lifetime all the Leaders of the Conservative Party have served as Prime Minister and I hope the habit will continue. Our Leaders have been different men with different qualities and different styles, but they all had one thing in common: each met the challenge of his time.

Now, what is the challenge of our time? I believe there are two: to overcome the country's economic and financial problems, and to regain our confidence in Britain and ourselves.

The economic challenge has been debated at length this week in this hall. Last week it gave rise to the usual scenes of cordial brotherly strife. Day after day the comrades called one another far from comradely names and occasionally, when they remembered, they called us names too. Some of them, for example, suggested that I criticized Britain when I was overseas. They are wrong. It was not Britain I was criticizing, it was Socialism, and I will go on criticizing Socialism and opposing Socialism because it is bad for Britain. Britain and Socialism

19

are not the same thing, and as long as I have health and strength they never will be.

Whatever could I say about Britain that is half as damaging as what this Labour Government has done to our country? Let us look at the record. It is the Labour Government that has caused prices to rise at a record rate of 26 per cent a year. They told us the Social Contract would solve everything, but now everyone can see that the so-called Contract was a fraud – a fraud for which the people of this country have had to pay a very high price. It is the Labour Government whose past policies are forcing unemployment higher than it need ever have been. Thousands more men and women are losing their jobs every day, and there are going to be men and women, many of them youngsters straight out of school, who will be without a job this winter because Socialist Ministers spent last year attacking us instead of attacking inflation.

It is the Labour Government that brought the level of production below that of the three-day week in 1974. We have really got a three-day week now, only it takes five days to do it. It is the Labour Government that has brought us record peace-time taxation. They have the usual Socialist disease: they have run out of other people's money. It is the Labour Government that has pushed public spending to record levels. How have they done it? By borrowing and borrowing. Never in the field of human credit has so much been owed.

Serious as the economic challenge is, the political and moral challenge is just as grave and perhaps even more so, because economic problems never start with economics. They have much deeper roots in human nature and roots in politics, and they do not finish at economics either. Labour's failure to cope, to look at the nation's problems from the viewpoint of the whole nation, and not just one section of it, has led to a loss of confidence, and to a sense of helplessness; and with it goes a feeling that Parliament, which ought to be in charge, is not in charge, and that the actions and decisions are taken elsewhere.

It goes even deeper than that, to the voices that seem anxious not to overcome our economic difficulties, but to exploit them, to destroy the free enterprise society and put a Marxist system in its place. Today those voices form a sizeable chorus in the parliamentary Labour Party, a chorus which, aided and abetted by the many constituency Labour Parties, seems to be growing in numbers. Mind you, anyone who says this openly is promptly accused of seeing Reds Under the Beds, but look who is seeing them now. On his own admission, Mr Wilson has at last discovered that his own party is infiltrated by extreme left-wingers or, to use his own words, it is infested with them. When even Mr Wilson gets scared about their success in capturing key positions in the Labour Party, should not the rest of us be? Should not the rest of us ask him, 'Where have you been while all this has been going on, and what are you doing about it?' The answer is nothing.

I sometimes think the Labour Party is like a pub where the mild is running out. If someone does not do something soon all that is left will be bitter, and all that is bitter will be Left.

Whenever I visit Communist countries their politicians never hesitate to boast about their achievements. They know them all by heart; they reel off the facts and figures, claiming this is the rich harvest of the Communist system. Yet they are not prosperous as we in the West are prosperous, and they are not free as we in the West are free.

Our capitalist system produces a far higher standard of prosperity and happiness because it believes in incentive and opportunity, and because it is founded on human dignity and freedom. Even the Russians have to go to a capitalist country – America – to buy enough wheat to feed their people – and that after more than fifty years of a State-controlled economy. Yet they boast incessantly, while we, who have so much more to boast about, for ever criticize and decry. Is it not time we spoke up for our way of life? After all, no Western nation has to build a wall round itself to keep its people in.

So let us have no truck with those who say the free enterprise system has failed. What we face today is not a crisis of capitalism but of Socialism. No country can flourish if its economic and social life is dominated by nationalization and State control.

The cause of our shortcomings does not, therefore, lie in

private enterprise. Our problem is not that we have too little Socialism. It is that we have too much. If only the Labour Party in this country would act like Social Democrats in West Germany. If only they would stop trying to prove their Socialist virility by relentlessly nationalizing one industry after another.

Of course, a halt to further State control will not on its own restore our belief in ourselves, because something else is happening to this country. We are witnessing a deliberate attack on our values, a deliberate attack on those who wish to promote merit and excellence, a deliberate attack on our heritage and our great past, and there are those who gnaw away at our national self-respect, rewriting British history as centuries of unrelieved gloom, oppression and failure – as days of hopelessness, not days of hope. And others, under the shelter of our education system, are ruthlessly attacking the minds of the young. Everyone who believes in freedom must be appalled at the tactics employed by the far Left in the systematic destruction of the North London Polytechnic – blatant tactics of intimidation designed to undermine the fundamental beliefs and values of every student, tactics pursued by people who are the first to insist on their own civil rights while seeking to deny them to the rest of us.

We must not be bullied or brainwashed out of our beliefs. No wonder so many of our people, some of the best and the brightest, are depressed and talking of emigrating. Even so, I think they are wrong. They are giving up too soon. Many of the things we hold dear are threatened as never before, but none has yet been lost, so stay here, stay and help us defeat Socialism so that the Britain you have known may be the Britain your children will know.

These are the two great challenges of our time – the moral and political challenge, and the economic challenge. They have to be faced together and we have to master them both.

What are our chances of success? It depends on what kind of people we are. What kind of people are we? We are the people that in the past made Great Britain the workshop of the world, the people who persuaded others to buy British, not by begging them to do so but because it was best.

We are a people who have received more Nobel Prizes than any other nation except America, and head for head we have done better than America, twice as well in fact.

We are the people who, among other things, invented the computer, the refrigerator, the electric motor, the stethoscope, rayon, the steam turbine, stainless steel, the tank, television, penicillin, radar, the jet engine, hovercraft, float glass and carbon fibres, et cetera – and the best half of Concorde.

We export more of what we produce than either West Germany, France, Japan or the United States, and well over 90 per cent of these exports come from private enterprise. It is a triumph for the private sector and all who work in it, and let us say so loud and clear.

With achievements like that who can doubt that Britain can have a great future, and what our friends abroad want to know is whether that future is going to happen.

Well, how can we Conservatives make it happen? Many of the details have already been dealt with in the Conference debates. But policies and programmes should not just be a list of unrelated items. They are part of a total vision of the kind of life we want for our country and our children. Let me give you my vision: a man's right to work as he will, to spend what he earns, to own property, to have the State as servant and not as master – these are the British inheritance. They are the essence of a free country and on that freedom all our other freedoms depend.

But we want a free economy, not only because it guarantees our liberties, but also because it is the best way of creating wealth and prosperity for the whole country, and it is this prosperity alone which can give us the resources for better services for the community, better services for those in need.

By their attack on private enterprise, this Labour Government has made certain that there will be next to nothing available for improvements in our social services over the next few years. We must get private enterprise back on the road to recovery, not merely to give people more of their own money to spend as they choose, but to have more money to help the old and the sick and the handicapped. And the way to recovery is

23

through profits, good profits today leading to high investment, leading to well-paid jobs, leading to a better standard of living tomorrow. No profits mean no investment and that means a dying industry geared to yesterday's world, and that means fewer jobs tomorrow. Other nations have recognized that for years now, and because they have recognized it they are going ahead faster than we are; and the gap between us will continue to increase unless we change our ways. The trouble here is that for years the Labour Party has made people feel that profits are guilty unless proved innocent.

When I visit factories and companies I do not find that those who actually work in them are against profits; on the contrary, they want to work for a prosperous concern, a concern with a future – their future.

Governments must learn to leave these companies with enough of their own profits to produce the goods and jobs for tomorrow. If the Socialists will not, or cannot, there will be no profit-making industry left to support the losses caused by fresh bouts of nationalization. If anyone should murmur that I am preaching *laissez-faire*, let me say I am not arguing, and have never argued, that all we have to do is to let the economy run by itself. I believe that, just as each of us has an obligation to make the best of his talents, so Governments have an obligation to create the framework within which we can do so – not only individual people, but individual firms and particularly small firms. If they concentrated on doing that, they would do a lot better than they are doing now. Some of the small firms will stay small, but others will expand and become the great companies of the future. The Labour Government has pursued a disastrous vendetta against small businesses and the self-employed. We will reverse its damaging policies.

Nowhere is this more important than in agriculture, one of our most successful industries, made up almost entirely of small businesses. We live in a world in which food is no longer cheap or plentiful. Everything we cannot produce here must be imported at a high price. Yet the Government could not have destroyed the confidence of the industry more effectively if they had tried deliberately to do so with their formula of empty promises and penal taxation.

So today what is the picture? Depressed profits, low investment, no incentive, and, overshadowing everything, Government spending, spending, spending far beyond the taxpayers' means.

To recover, to get from where we are to where we want to be – and I admit we would rather not be here – will take time. 'Economic policy,' wrote Maynard Keynes, 'should not be a matter of tearing up by the roots but of slowly training a plant to grow in a different direction.'

It will take time to reduce public spending, to rebuild profits and incentives, and to benefit from the investments which must be made. But the sooner that time starts, the better it will be for Britain's unemployed and for Britain as a whole.

One of the reasons why this Labour Government has incurred more unemployment than any Conservative Government since the war is because they have concentrated too much on distributing what we have and too little on seeing that we have more.

We Conservatives hate unemployment. We hate the idea of men and women not being able to use their abilities. We deplore the waste of natural resources and the deep affront to people's dignity from being out of work through no fault of their own. It is ironic that we should be accused of wanting unemployment to solve our economic problems by the very Government which has produced a record post-war unemployment and is expecting more.

The record of Mr Wilson and his colleagues on this is unparalleled in the history of political hypocrisy. We are now seeing the full consequences of nearly twenty months of Labour Government. They have done the wrong things at the wrong time in the wrong way, and they have been a disaster for this country.

Now let me turn to something I spoke about in America. Some Socialists seem to believe that people should be numbers in a State computer. We believe they should be individuals. We are all unequal. No one, thank heavens, is quite like anyone else, however much the Socialists may pretend otherwise. We believe that everyone has the right to be unequal. But to us, every human being is equally important. Engineers, miners, manual workers, shop assistants, farmworkers, postmen, housewives – these are the essential foundations of our society, and without them there would be no nation. But there are others with special gifts who should also have their chance, because if the adventurers who strike out in new directions in science, technology, medicine, commerce and industry are hobbled, there can be no advance. The spirit of envy can destroy; it can never build. Everyone must be allowed to develop the abilities he knows he has within him, and she knows she has within her, in the way they choose.

Freedom to choose is something we take for granted until it is in danger of being taken away. Socialist Governments set out perpetually to restrict the area of choice, and Conservative Governments to increase it. We believe that you become a responsible citizen by making decisions for yourself, not by having them made for you. But they are made for you by Labour all right!

Take education: our education system used to serve us well. A child from an ordinary family, as I was, could use it as a ladder, as an advancement, but the Socialists, better at demolition than reconstruction, are destroying many good grammar schools. Now this is nothing to do with private education. It is opportunity and excellence in our State schools that are being diminished under Socialism. Naturally enough, parents do not like this, but in a Socialist society parents should be seen and not heard.

Another denial of choice is being applied to health. The private sector helps to keep some of our best doctors here, and so available part-time to the National Health Service. It also helps to bring in more money for the general health of the nation; but under Labour, private medicine is being squeezed out, and the result will be to add to the burden of the National Health Service without adding one penny to its income.

Let me make this absolutely clear: when we return to power we shall reverse Mrs Castle's stupid and spiteful attack on hospital pay beds. We Conservatives do not accept that because some people have no choice, no one should have it. Every family should have the right to spend their money, after tax, as they wish, and not as the Government dictates. Let us extend choice, extend the will to choose and the chance to choose.

I want to come now to the argument which Mr Wilson is trying to put across to the country: namely, that the Labour Party is the natural party of Government because it is the only one that the trade unions will accept. From what I saw on television last week, the Labour Party did not look like a party of Government at all, let alone a natural one.

But let us examine the argument, because it is important. If we are told that a Conservative Government could not govern because certain extreme leaders would not let it, then general elections are a mockery, we have arrived at the one-party State, and a parliamentary democracy in this country will have perished. The democracy for which our fathers fought and died is not to be laid to rest as lightly as that.

When the next Conservative Government comes to power many trade unionists will have put it there. Millions of them vote for us at every election. I want to say this to them and to all of our supporters in industry: go out and join in the work of your unions; go to their meetings and stay to the end, and learn the union rules as well as the far Left knows them. Remember that if parliamentary democracy dies, free trade unions die with it.

I come last to what many would put first, the rule of law. The first people to uphold the law should be Governments, and it is tragic that the Socialist Government, to its lasting shame, should have lost its nerve and shed its principles over the People's Republic of Clay Cross,* and that a group of the Labour Party should have tried to turn the Shrewsbury pickets

*The militantly left-wing council at Clay Cross in Derbyshire refused to implement the Housing Finance Act 1972 which required them to increase their rents. Their action was endorsed by the Labour Party Conference, and special legislation was passed by the Labour Government in 1975 to cancel the surcharges which the councillors would otherwise have had to pay.

into martyrs.* On both occasions the law was broken and on one violence was done. No decent society can live like that, and no responsible party should condone it. The first duty of Government is to uphold the law, and if it tries to bob, weave and duck round that duty when it is inconvenient, the governed will do exactly the same thing, and then nothing will be safe, not home, not liberty, not life itself.

There is one part of this country where, tragically, defiance of the law is costing life day after day. In Northern Ireland our troops have the dangerous and thankless task of trying to keep the peace and hold a balance. We are proud of the way they have discharged their duty. This party is pledged to support the unity of the United Kingdom, to preserve that unity and to protect the people, Catholic and Protestant alike. We believe our Armed Forces must remain until a genuine peace is made. Our thoughts are with them and our pride is with them, too.

I have spoken of the challenges which face us here in Britain – the challenge to recover economically and the challenge to recover our belief in ourselves – and I have shown our potential for recovery. I have dealt with some aspects of our strength and approach and I have tried to tell you something of my personal vision and my belief in the standards on which this nation was greatly built, on which it greatly thrived and from which in recent years it has greatly fallen away. I believe we are coming to yet another turning point in our long history. We can go on as we have been going and continue down, or we can stop and with a decisive act of will say 'Enough'.

Let all of us here today, and others far beyond this hall who believe in our cause, make that act of will. Let us proclaim our faith in a new and better future for our party and our people; let us resolve to heal the wounds of a divided nation, and let that act of healing be the prelude to a lasting victory.

*In December 1973 three pickets were jailed for offences committed during an industrial dispute at Shrewsbury. In February 1975, eighty-eight Labour MPs signed a Commons motion calling for 'the immediate release from jail of the Shrewsbury trade unionists'. The Government rejected their demand.

Surrey Conservative Rally

DORKING, 31 JULY 1976

At no time was Mrs Thatcher concerned solely with Britain's domestic and economic affairs. She has always recognized that no hard and fast distinction can be made between home and foreign affairs. Britain's freedom could not be strengthened, nor its prosperity firmly rebuilt, without vigilance and resolution abroad. That has been one of the consistent themes of Thatcherism from the early days. It was underlined firmly in this speech delivered to mark the first anniversary of the Helsinki Declaration which, it was hoped, would produce a new spirit of understanding and accord between East and West. One year later there were few grounds for optimism. Mrs Thatcher clearly identified the extent of the threat which the West faced – a threat which would increase, not diminish, if Britain reduced its defences (as it was then doing). Mrs Thatcher stressed, 'I believe it is only when they see that the West is militarily prepared that the Soviet leadership will begin to realize that their own massive investment in armaments is leading nowhere.'

The major arms reductions – both nuclear and conventional – announced by Mr Gorbachev in 1987–8 vindicated Mrs Thatcher's approach in the clearest possible fashion. The consistency with which Mrs Thatcher has maintained this approach emerges forcefully in her subsequent major speeches on defence and foreign affairs (published by Aurum Press in 1986 under the title In Defence of Freedom).

Tomorrow is the first anniversary of the Helsinki Declaration, the Final Act of the Conference on Security and Co-operation in Europe.

Signed by thirty-five countries from the East and the West, this Declaration was the product of two years' work by some 600 officials who produced, on behalf of their Governments, a text of some 30,000 words. The text I take today is very much shorter than that. It comes from a remarkable interview that reached out of the television screens to grip millions of hearts and minds more compellingly than any other I can remember: Alexander Solzhenitsyn's *Warning to the Western World*.

It was a testament of experience, courage, conviction and challenge. It had a concentrated alchemy that few of us will ever forget.

And the warning to the West?

Let me repeat some of the words:

'I am not a critic of the West . . . for nearly all our lives, we worshipped it . . . I am a critic of the weakness of the West. I am a critic of a fact which we can't comprehend . . . how can one lose one's spiritual strength, one's will-power, and possessing freedom not value it – not be willing to make sacrifices for it . . . ?'

Solzhenitsyn's questions are the ones we need to ask ourselves every waking hour. They go to the heart of any analysis of the balance between Russia and the West, one year after the Helsinki Declaration.

Are we in the West losing our spiritual strength? How strong *is* our will-power, in the face of Soviet might? *Do* we value our freedom? *Are* we, truly, willing to make sacrifices for it? One of the first requirements of spiritual strength is clarity.

That is why, in trying to assess our relations with the Soviet Union, we need to clear our minds of all delusions. Delusions can be comforting. But in international affairs they are dangerous.

A genuine search for peace is impossible on the basis of misunderstandings about the true nature of one's adversaries.

Let us therefore be done with the delusion, much cultivated since Helsinki, that the Soviet system differs from ours only in style and degree; that its leaders, though Marxist in outlook, are basically much the same as the rest of us.

Solzhenitsyn's most eloquent warning was that there is a quite fundamental separation between our ideas and ideals and those of the Soviet Union.

Again I quote his words: 'The most important aspect of *détente* today is that there is no ideological *détente*. You Western people, you simply can't grasp the power of Soviet propaganda; today you still remain "British imperialists" who wish to strangle the whole earth . . . You are shown up as villains who can't be tolerated; well, maybe for one more day.'

That part of Solzhenitsyn's message was strangely similar to one given many years ago – 1946, to be precise, by Arthur Koestler, printed, of all places, in *Tribune*. Koestler said, 'The Soviet Government has achieved, for the first time in history, a complete State monopoly not only over the production and distribution of goods, but also over the distribution of ideas, opinions and customs.'

Koestler went on to say that world peace could only become a reality if suspicion is abolished, and that suspicion could only be abolished if the Soviet Government could be induced to turn off the master-switch of their propaganda factory.

Here, then, is another delusion that we in the West must be rid of. It does not help to pretend that all the world's problems can be solved if only both sides will look at them from the other person's point of view.

The danger is our Western tendency to assume that other people will apply our own standards and values. When considering international matters, the important thing is not to look at other nations as if *we* were standing in their shoes, but as if *they* were standing in *their* shoes.

We need to make the effort, the intellectual and imaginative effort, to penetrate what Winston Churchill, in describing the Soviet Union, called the 'riddle wrapped in mystery inside an enigma'. It's no good pretending that the Soviet leaders mean the same things as we do when they use the same words. They are the products of an entirely different history, and of profoundly different ideas. Their lives have followed a course quite alien to anything we have experienced.

31

So if we want real *détente*, as all reasonable people do, we must have a clear grasp of the problem. The Soviet regime makes no secret of the fact that it is in principle hostile to everything we stand for. That is a fact we must face.

Indeed, the question of how to change that hostility becomes one of the central problems of foreign affairs. The most striking measure of Soviet hostility is the war footing on which the Soviet economy is run.

Solzhenitsyn identified this and it will not be outside this audience's recollection that one or two politicians here have sounded a similar warning. At the same time some of those who preferred comfortable delusion to uncomfortable reality derided these warnings as alarmist. Since then we, and they, have learnt more.

Indeed, our own Ministry of Defence has issued to the Atlantic Council a pretty sombre memorandum on the vulnerability of Western defences. The Warsaw Pact countries have 40 per cent more front-line troops than NATO. Their tanks, field guns and aircraft outnumber NATO by 5:2. In the Eastern Atlantic, where our sea-lanes converge, NATO is outnumbered 2:1 in surface ships and 3:2 in submarines and aircraft. And whereas we had thought that Russia spends 7 per cent of her GNP on arms, the Ministry of Defence now acknowledges that the true figure is nearer 11 to 12 per cent. By comparison, the United States figure is 6.7 per cent, and the NATO average 4.5 per cent.

It was against this background that on August 1 last year, the UK, the USA, Canada, our European friends and allies, with the Soviet Union and its allies and the neutral states, signed the Helsinki Declaration.

These countries declared themselves, in the words of the Final Act, to be: 'Motivated by the political will . . . to improve and intensify their relations and to contribute in Europe to peace, security, justice and co-operation.'

All responsible men are bound to applaud those objectives. Nor can any right-thinking person quarrel with the words in which they are expressed. If only those words became deeds, a whole new era of peace in Europe would begin. It is still too soon to judge whether this will happen eventually or not. But twelve months is long enough to make a first assessment.

The question is whether the Soviet Union genuinely wants to relax tension or whether they are using *détente* to lull the West into a false sense of security, so that *we* lower our guard and become an easier prey to Soviet expansion or blackmail. And the test is to what extent the Soviets so far have observed the letter and the spirit of the Helsinki Accords.

So let us look at what has happened. The first part of the Declaration deals with security in Europe: each State undertook to 'refrain from any intervention, direct or indirect, individual or collective, in the internal or external affairs falling within the domestic jurisdiction of another participating State, regardless of their mutual relations.'

The signatures were hardly dry on the Declaration before the Soviet Union was flagrantly interfering in the internal affairs of Portugal – one of the participating States in the Helsinki Conference. Even more serious was the extension of Soviet activity into Angola, including the provision of weapons and advisers.

True, the Russians may claim that *they* have no actual troops operating in Southern Africa – but what were the Cubans doing? Would they, could they, have invaded Angola except at the instigation of the Russians and with their support? Angola itself was not a participating State in the Helsinki Conference, and therefore, strictly speaking, was not covered by the Declaration, but the presence of 15,000 regular Cuban troops and the projection of Soviet military power into Southern Africa can scarcely be held to be consistent with – what was the phrase? – refraining from any intervention, direct or indirect, in other people's internal affairs. In another section of the Declaration dealing with co-operation in humanitarian and other fields, the Helsinki signatories agreed 'to facilitate the improvement of the dissemination in their territory of newspapers and printed publications, periodical and non-periodical, from the other participating States.'

Once again an admirable sentiment. Yet still there is no free circulation of Western newspapers or periodicals in the Soviet

Union. If the Russians want news of the West, the only English newspaper they can get it from is that monument to political objectivity – the *Morning Star*. Similarly, at Helsinki there were binding undertakings about human rights and personal freedom. The Final Act stated flatly that, 'The participating States recognize the universal significance of human rights and fundamental freedoms, respect for which is an essential factor for the peace, justice and well-being necessary to ensure the development of friendly relations and co-operation among themselves as among all States.'

To these propositions Mr Brezhnev 'solemnly' – such was the word employed – bound his country. But what have they actually *done*? We are not alone in finding it difficult to discern, let alone to monitor, progress.

Nine brave people in the Soviet Union, led by Dr Yury Orlov, a nuclear physicist, banded themselves together to check how far their Government was honouring the Helsinki Accords. The KGB questioned Dr Orlov and the group was promptly advised to desist from what the Soviets called 'unconstitutional' activity, on pain of being arrested. How's that for 'respecting human rights and fundamental freedoms'?

Despite the clear endorsement at Helsinki of freedom of thought and freedom of religion, the persecution of intellectual dissidents, and of religious minorities – Jews and Baptists in particular – continues. It appears to be no easier for people to leave the Soviet Union either permanently or temporarily than it was a year ago. Many people are even refused permission to reunite with their families outside the Soviet Union.

So much for that part of the Declaration which says, 'The participating States will deal in a positive and humanitarian spirit with the applications of persons who wish to be reunited with members of their family.'

Mrs Sakharov, the wife of the scientist who won the Nobel Peace Prize, said a few weeks ago, 'Our life is proceeding in such a way that you can't even call it life in the human sense of the word.'

In spite of Helsinki, the Soviet Union remains a closed and repressive society. The significance of this for the West can hardly be overestimated. It means that the men in the Kremlin can, and do, suppress not only unwelcome ideas, but unwelcome facts too. Their 'freedom of information' consists of their absolute right to tell their subjects what they should believe and what they should hear. There is no free press, no free Parliament, no free courts of law, no free trade unions to insist on respect, or even regard, for the wishes of the Russian people. Consequently there is virtually no restraint by an informed public opinion on the actions of the Soviet regime.

Perhaps the most important undertaking of the Helsinki Declaration was that relating to disarmament. In this the participating States recognized 'the interest of all of them in efforts aimed at lessening military confrontation and promoting disarmament'. Yet far from promoting disarmament and lessening confrontation, the year which has passed has seen the progressive growth of Soviet armed strength which confronts both Western Europe and China. Only yesterday we learnt from the United States that Russia has started to equip her 600 nuclear missiles aimed at Western Europe with multiple warheads (MIRVs).

On the oceans of the world we have seen the continued expansion of the Soviet fleet. We have seen the first Soviet aircraft carrier, the *Kiev*, complete her trials in the Black Sea, and pass through the Turkish Straits to the Mediterranean. Meanwhile two, or maybe more, sister ships have been laid down.

We have learnt that the Soviet Union has continued to build up a highly sophisticated civil defence system in its major cities. She now locates her new industrial plant away from urban areas. All of this is of great significance, in the interpretation of her nuclear strategy.

The question we have to ask ourselves is whether the Soviet Union has concluded that if she implements her full civil defence programme, she has the capacity to fight a nuclear war and still survive. The only honest assessment that can be made of the results from the past twelve months since Helsinki is that they have been a profound disappointment

Whatever we may have hoped, it would seem that the

realities of Soviet foreign and military policy have not changed. There is still repression at home. There is still a powerful thrust to expansion abroad. Let us hope that things will have improved by the time of the review conference in Belgrade next year.

It is one thing to make an assessment of the Helsinki Agreement, to conclude that the objectives of Soviet foreign policy haven't changed and to identify the dangers to our freedom. But the important question is – what can we do about it? Of course we must go on striving for a confident and true peace with the Soviet Union. It is the greatest need and greatest prize of our time. But wishing won't make it so.

There are, however, a number of things that we *can* do – in politics the cards are never stacked all on one side. I see some encouraging signs of a clearer vision and firmer resolve on the part of the Western Alliance. Certainly in the last year there has been a new awareness of the military threat posed by the Soviets and a new determination to meet it. The Americans, without whom the West could have no effective defence, are stepping up their defence expenditure. France is reported to be increasing her defence budget substantially over the next six years. West Germany too is putting up her defence spending.

But what of Britain? What is the strategic judgement of the British Labour Government, and what are they doing about it? The Secretary of State for Defence has admitted that Soviet military expenditure has been growing at the rate of 4 per cent a year in real terms. He has acknowledged that the Soviet Union is devoting a much higher share of its resources to defence than any NATO country and that the Soviet Union's military spending is greater than their spending on health and education combined. 'The real danger,' he told the National Defence College, 'is that if the military power of the Warsaw Pact was allowed to become overwhelmingly greater than ours in the West, the mere threat of military force might be enough to persuade us to bend our policies in directions desired by the Pact.'

So much for the Government's assessment. But are Mr

36

Mason and the Labour Government following the example of our friends and allies, and strengthening the British contribution to our own and the West's defences? Not a bit of it. They are doing the opposite. They have cut, cut and cut again.

They have cut our defence spending three times in two years. Only in June, Mr Mason was saying, 'The question most people are asking themselves is "Have we cut too much?" rather than "When are we going to cut some more?" ' And he was right to pose the question, because on his own figures he had already cut, or planned to cut, defence spending by the massive total of £7,400 million.

But he was forgetting his own left wing. For them even those cuts aren't enough. So now a further cut of £100 million is to fall on defence expenditure. But the National Executive Committee of the Labour Party are calling for an additional cut of £1,000 million which, as Mr Mason has admitted, would result 'at best in a policy of neutrality, at worst it would be surrender'.

The Conservatives will fight these latest cuts in every way we can. If necessary we will strengthen our defences when we return to power, because we believe that the first and overriding responsibility of any Government is the security of its own people. And we regard it as a grave reflection on Britain that we should be cutting down on our contribution to the Western Alliance just when our partners are strengthening theirs.

But defence is not the whole of our relationship with the Soviet Union. We trade with her – and on subsidized terms too! The remarkable thing about the Soviet economy is that after sixty years of Marxist planning it still has to rely significantly on the West for advanced technology, and even for food.

In Britain, we have provided large-scale credit facilities to help the Soviets to buy our goods at terms far more favourable than those on which we could borrow. Facilities such as these have enabled the Soviets to divert resources from their industries to build up their already massive military establishment.

Now trade brings great advantages – and Britain lives by

trade. But if the Kremlin continues to pour such huge resources into armaments directed against the West; if she refuses to act in accordance with the Helsinki Agreement, then shouldn't we in the West consider carefully how we can ensure that our commercial relations with the Soviet Union don't damage our own long-term security interests? Certainly we must see that they do not directly contribute to the capacity of the Soviet Union to sustain a policy of imperialist expansion.

Perhaps once again I shall be called the Iron Lady for daring to voice these things. Iron? I know not. But I do know that the one thing that has meant more than anything else in my life is that my children and their generation have not had to risk everything in war as their fathers did before them. And why? Because we have learnt the lesson of weakness and resolved that it must not happen again. Because we have based our actions not just on hope, but on looking at the facts; on judging other nations not by what they said, but by what they did, and making our decisions accordingly.

We must not fail now. I believe it is only when they see that the West is militarily prepared that the Soviet leadership will begin to realize that their own massive investment in armaments is leading nowhere. And then, and only then, will we have a real prospect of mutually agreed disarmament as part of a general movement towards peace and stability in the world.

To keep up our defence is vital. To practise the skills of commerce with foresight and perception is essential. But these alone are not enough. In all our dealings, we must demonstrate that we have the will and determination sufficient to guarantee that our way of life will survive; that we shall overcome whatever assault may be made upon it.

So much depends on our confidence in ourselves; on our knowledge that liberty and prosperity alike are to be found in our system as in no other; on the steadfastness of our belief in the great traditional values of Western society.

Those who have lived for a time without freedom know

its true worth even better than we do. It is part of our birth-
right . . .

> *Dear-bought and clear, a thousand year,*
> *Our fathers' title runs.*
> *Make we likewise their sacrifice,*
> *Defrauding not our sons.*

The Institute of Directors

ROYAL ALBERT HALL, 11 NOVEMBER 1976

From the outset it was one of Mrs Thatcher's principal aims to roll back the frontiers of the State, which the Labour Government extended significantly in this period. By the late 1970s the State-owned industrial sector in Britain accounted for no less than 11½ per cent of Gross Domestic Product; the number of major industries in Government hands was at its highest peacetime level. And under Labour the number working in the public service rose to some 4½ million. The presence of such a leviathan had an extremely damaging effect on the economy of the country, as Mrs Thatcher explained in this speech. Above all, it led to massive Government borrowing and contributed to inflation.

If the recovery of the country was to proceed, leviathan had to be curbed. It was not possible to reach final decisions in Opposition, but Mrs Thatcher indicated clearly in this speech the criteria which she would seek to apply in reducing the role of the State in economic affairs. And once it had been removed from spheres into which it should not have intruded, Government would be in a position to discharge more effectively the tasks that it alone could undertake on behalf of society as a whole. 'The private sector should then operate alongside the substantial but clearly defined areas of central and local Government, and public authority activity.'

Over the years politicians have paid lip-service to 'the mixed economy'. It has become one of those innocent and rather warming phrases that is supposed to be the hallmark of the intelligent and wordly élite that crowd the middle ground in British politics. Isn't it really time that we allowed the scales to fall from our eyes? The mixed economy has become a nonsense phrase.

It has been used to justify the extension of Government into almost every aspect of business.

It has produced a situation where the investment, pricing and wages policies of private enterprise are formed in response to political, rather than economic, considerations.

It has led to a substantial extension of Government itself.

It has required a dramatic growth of the bureaucracy within private industry to comply with the demands of new statutes and the demands for new statistics.

The growth in Government has resulted in a substantial rise in public spending. Public ownership has been extended, and more and more taxpayers' money has been pumped into companies that no prudent banker could go on supporting for long.

Government spending is now so high that we have penal levels of direct taxation, and a system that discriminates savagely against income from private savings. And yet, despite these levels of taxation, the Government still needs to borrow on a massive scale. It has been obliged to pitch interest rates at a record post-war level. Even this has not been enough, and the Government has resorted to printing money to try to pay for its own spending.

The consequences have been confusion and demoralization as traditional standards and disciplines have been swept away by the floodtide of inflation. Taxation and inflation have damaged the stability and framework of order necessary to accommodate genuine economic expansion and social change. Traditional values have been assaulted with a growing dis-respect for authority. The living standards of entrepreneurs, managers and skilled workers have been squeezed by the impact of taxation, salary controls and inflation. There is a sense of despair and hopelessness amongst our wealth creators. They perceive the increasingly political character of the busi-ness world while they, along with many others, bear the

41

personal cost of financing more Government. The matter can be put quite simply. There is a vendetta against success. That is the tragic truth.

How, then, should we proceed to remedy this miserable situation which otherwise can only end with an exodus of talent from these shores? My first point is that we should be more precise about what 'the mixed economy' really means. It should not be the alibi for endless political intervention. It should, however, define the respective roles of the State and the individual. The true characteristic of 'the mixed economy' is the recognition that Government has a considerable but limited role: and the larger private sector should flourish and expand in response to the choice of the consumer within the framework of public law. On the Government side this involves setting priorities.

First, there is the overriding commitment to external and internal security. Second, there is a long British tradition of community provision for education and welfare. Third, successive British Governments have assumed a responsibility for the financing, and ultimately the management, of a range of public utilities. Some, like the major roadways and postal services, have been under Government ownership over generations, but the nationalized sector was much extended immediately after the Second World War, and again now.

The role of Government that I have just outlined is substantial. It gives rise to large-scale public purchasing that obviously spills over into the private sector, although that purchasing should be essentially commercial in character. The private sector should then operate alongside the substantial, but clearly defined, areas of central and local Government, and public authority activity. In that sense we should have 'a mixed economy', where a large profit-motivated private sector co-exists alongside a substantial, but defined, area of Government activity.

There is now an imperative need to stop the growth of Government and to re-establish urgently just what the functions of Government are. It is a bitter irony that as Government has aspired to do more and more, it is unable to discharge its

basic functions. There is deep unease about the state of our
defences and about the lack of success we are having in
containing domestic lawlessness. The Government has been
quite unable to manage the currency so as to provide a stable
financial framework for the economy. Yet Government alone
can fulfil these functions. The Government needs to return to
these priority and unavoidable obligations to ensure that we
have reasonable security at home and abroad and monetary
stability. Thereafter, Government can consider the other functions where it has a traditional, but not necessarily a monopoly,
role. In this area politicians need a healthy dose of humility.
There is a great and growing desire for improved educational
standards and for a welfare system that equitably identifies and
generously relieves real poverty.

The way in which some of the present welfare schemes
operate with their disincentive to work, particularly in areas
where wages and salaries are below average, has lost them the
confidence of the people.

There is also a growing realization that, while the finances of
the nationalized industries must be restored, those industries
with their monopoly powers must not take a cost-plus attitude
to their captive customers. In the absence of competition, the
consumer must not be held to ransom for inefficiency.

The tendency to use public funds to subsidize everything and
to enlarge the range of State activity has cast a political blight
on the capacity to make commercial decisions in this country.
And yet our very prosperity depends upon taking the right
decisions in world markets. The mixed economy has become a
mixed-up economy, where the Government has departed from
its valid and essential role and has become hopelessly en-
tangled in the everyday business and personal decisions that
are the normal processes of a free society.

My first call, therefore, is for a defined role for Government.
There should be a demarcation between public and private
sectors so that both can contribute productively to 'the mixed
economy'.

Second, I believe the restored and proper role for Government would mean there was then the prospect of fashioning a

budget that could honestly finance the role of the State. The present role and expenditure of Government has produced unacceptable taxation and a horrendous borrowing requirement. A reduction in the borrowing requirement is a first essential. It is needed in order to reduce interest rates, and secondly to counter the scourge of inflationary money printing.

Of course, there is some expenditure by Government that is perfectly legitimate to finance by borrowing. I have in mind the creation of productive assets such as power stations or coal mines. The broad strategic objective of Government, however, should be to balance its budget by matching expenditure with taxation and keeping borrowing to a strictly limited and manageable proportion. Let our political opponents abandon the phoney argument that you can spend your way out of difficulties. Rather let the political debate concern the desirable level of public spending and the taxes deemed appropriate to finance such expenditure. That will give us more than enough to argue over and present the British people with a political choice.

I have no doubt that the role I have defined for Government would permit some reduction in the burden of our taxation: although it would be wrong to promise that this can be done immediately. Nevertheless, morale would be markedly lifted if there was an inkling that a new Government has a spending, borrowing and taxation strategy that would guide it through a Parliament and lead to a reduction in the rates of direct taxes.

I need hardly remind an audience such as this that direct taxation is now a major handicap. It operates disadvantageously at two levels. Senior and middle management and entrepreneurs bear a heavier burden than their counterparts elsewhere in the Western world. Differentials have been dangerously narrowed: we are stumbling into a fringe benefit economy on an increasing scale, as means are sought to find a way of simulating the monetary rewards necessary to attract and retain skill and talent. Our forebears would rub their eyes in disbelief if they could witness the present. They would recall how they had fought to abolish the system of payments in kind – the system of 'truck payments' – only to discover that in modern Britain the company benefit is often the only chance of retaining employees. What a tragic nonsense this has become: and what a case it makes for a tax package designed to deal with the higher income brackets. There is, further, a similar and powerful case for tax changes that affect lower incomes. One of the astonishing features of British society today is the extent to which a large number of people are materially better off in receipt of social security and related benefits than remaining in, or taking, employment.

This is well understood by the general public. It is little wonder that we politicians are regarded as woefully out of touch with shop-floor realities when such a situation develops. The present absurdities challenge the raising of revenue from direct and indirect taxation respectively. We have to judge anew the extent to which we tax the earning and spending of income. Expenditure tax catches up with even the most audacious moonlighter. There is, then, throughout the national economy a powerful and irrefutable case for financing a balanced budget with a more equitable system of taxation designed to promote, rather than impede, success and wealth creation.

What then would be the major gains of this strategic approach to the role and cost of Government and the necessary supporting structure of taxation? It would impart hope. Hope is a precious commodity in today's circumstances. The strategy I have outlined offers the prospect of reduced government involvement in the pricing, investment and marketing policies of industry and commerce. Management could then return to its essential economic function, namely to provide the wealth not only to sustain our general living standards but also to finance the legitimate objectives and responsibilities of Government. There would be a clearer demarcation between the respective fields for private endeavour and for public action.

One might even dare to hope that the quality of Government would improve as it concentrated upon areas where it alone has the authority to act. The highest national interest to be pursued by private industry is the creation of wealth. The most dubious pursuit of national interest is when the private sector has to put aside its long-term wealth-creating role in order to conform with the wishes of transitory politicians.

Politics is essentially about the law: and where business activities need the constraint of law it should be openly and generally applied. The developing habit of Government by 'invitation', or by sub-contract to extra parliamentary industrial agencies, is a dangerous slide towards collectivism and general inefficiency. It is a prescription for the manufacture of goods without markets and for a reduced standard of prosperity for the future.

The tax consequences of such a redefined role for Government would also impart hope. There would be a chance of giving at least some encouragement for work, for skill, for effort and, above all, for success. In a very profound sense we are witnessing a great loss in national self-confidence and in self-respect. Such defeatism owes its origins to a complex of factors, by no means wholly economic. None the less a Britain where individuals have a chance to savour the rewards of success is a Britain that will re-emerge as a self-respecting nation.

The success will be won on the shop floor, in the boardrooms, and above all in the market place – at home and the world over. It is a success that will be founded upon wealth creation – something that cannot be anticipated or simulated by politicians and their advisers, however distinguished and decorated.

It is a policy that imparts hope because it recognizes that a revitalization of Britain proceeds from the nation's most precious asset – the people. It argues that it is human resources, even more than raw materials, that provide the key to our future.

Our mineral wealth, on land and offshore, provides much that is welcome: but it pales into insignificance when considered alongside the wealth-creating skills of people. The world around us tells us that it is human ingenuity, and not natural resources, that determine economic success.

However, what I say is not only a philosophy of hope, but it is also a policy of challenge. It totally rejects the concept of Britain living in the nostalgic glories of a previous industrial revolution based upon manufacturing techniques and products which may have little relevance to our future pattern of wealth.

We are not ready for the dust sheets of a Museum Economy. Of course such a challenge has social implications. It demands policies designed to see through their difficulties those individuals and their families who are the temporary victims of economic change. A truly far-sighted social policy will seek to identify and aid those people, rather than resist economic change itself. To resist that would be to convert large sections of British industry into a subsidiary of the Welfare State.

Is this aim beyond the capacity of the British people? No – it should be well within our reach. There is nothing in my description of a mixed economy which would offend the great majority of social democrats in the Western world. It could become part of the common currency of British politics if our own social democrats would stand their ground. There is a widespread and popular disenchantment with ever larger Government. Education, social welfare and the health and hospital services are testaments to the inability of top-heavy and centralized Government to identify and remedy the problems of contemporary society. State control of industry has yielded a harvest of bureaucracy and constant political lobbying.

The Western world is at an economic watershed. Many of the popular conceptions about the protective role of the State are being re-examined. A politician can help generate and guide public discussion. That debate will be the precondition for action. The profound mood of scepticism that exists towards Government and politicians today can be guided to a constructive end. It can produce a situation where Government is compelled to re-assess its role and priorities and also to judge the levels of taxation that can be borne by a society with a healthy prejudice for freedom.

I have campaigned to promote a partnership of Government and individual which alone holds hope for the dynamic evolution of the Free World, rather than its decline and decay in the face of disciplined totalitarian regimes. I shall not cease from that campaign. The penalty of failure has never been more sombre, but the prize of success has never been greater.

The Iain Macleod
Memorial Lecture

CAXTON HALL, 4 JULY 1977

One of the most intriguing and instructive features of modern Conservatism is the manner in which it adjusts and adapts its old, long-standing values and assumptions in the light of changing circumstances. Mrs Thatcher described this process, which prevents Conservatism from ossifying but nevertheless preserves its basic continuities, in the lecture, entitled 'The Dimensions of Conservatism', which she delivered to commemorate the life and work of Iain Macleod, one of the Party's greatest post-war orators and a guardian of Tory values.

As she pointed out, Conservatism had to define itself afresh to meet the challenges of the 1970s, just as Iain Macleod and his generation had reinterpreted it in order to equip it for the post-war world. The Tory tradition, stretching back through Disraeli and Burke, is both continuous and evolutionary, resting on a set of values that stem clearly from British culture and, in particular, from its Christian heritage. That is its greatest strength, enabling it to make proper provision for individual endeavour within a well-ordered but flexible social framework – in sharp contrast to Socialism, which tries to fit individuals into a preconceived mould.

In a key passage of this lecture, Mrs Thatcher states, 'Our religion teaches us that every human being is unique and must play his part in working out his own salvation. So whereas Socialists begin with society, and how people can be fitted in, we start with Man, whose social and economic relationships are just part of his wider existence.'

There is no reason to believe that the State has a unique capacity to help

48

those whose social and economic relationships are unsatisfactory or insufficient to provide for their needs. To illustrate that point, Mrs Thatcher referred to the spectacular growth of voluntary service and philanthropy in nineteenth-century Britain. Victorian values – which Mrs Thatcher was to praise on subsequent occasions – have an enduring significance, particularly for Tories, because they instil a proper sense of responsibility in society and foster feelings of mutual human obligation which a Socialist State will be inclined to sweep away.

We honour the memory of Iain Macleod by continuing his life's work, the restoration of the Conservative heritage. Some of you here today will remember him, some will have come into politics after he was taken from us. So I shall begin by trying to sum up for you the essence of his contribution to Conservative politics. He was a great pragmatist, in the true meaning of the word; he saw practice as the acid test, and principles as the motivating force.

He was the practical man *par excellence* precisely because his every thought and act were so firmly rooted in principle. So when we ask, as all of us do, what would Iain have done in these circumstances, it is to his underlying principles that we must turn first.

He was a Tory in that he saw himself as part of a continuous and growing Tory tradition, going back three whole centuries to the dawn of parliamentary Government in the aftermath of the civil war, and forward into a future, presaging changes and challenges of equal magnitude. He was a Christian, for whom Tory politics were a part – a subordinate part – of a great commitment to the Good Life and service of God.

He was a national politician, who thought in terms of Britain's needs, ways, and wider contribution to the world, drawing ideas and solutions from the British context, and seeing the statesman's task as finding political solutions for urgent British problems.

It is to these dimensions of Conservatism, which he exemplified for us, that I shall devote this talk.

Every generation must restate its values in the light of present challenges, but also in the light of past experience.

There has never been greater need for us Conservatives to do so than there is today. For we have been in danger of allowing our thinking to be dominated by Socialism to a point where we even define our own position in terms of how, where and why we differ from Socialism and Socialists – as though Conservatism was primarily an alternative to Socialism. This is a compliment that I for one refuse to pay this recent creed. For we are not just anti-Socialists, nor primarily anti-Socialists; our opposition to Socialism is just one corner of our vision, in which what we are *for* sets the tone, not what we are against. What we are against stems from what we are for.

The Tory tradition long antedates not only Socialism, but also what the Socialists call capitalism and I prefer to call free economy. To describe us as the party of free enterprise, as opposed to State ownership, would be misleading, although we believe in the vital contribution of free enterprise to a free and prosperous Britain and have good cause to fear the deadening effect of State ownership and control. For to pose our commitment to free enterprise as our main purpose and distinguishing mark would be to describe the whole in terms of one of its many parts.

Free enterprise has a place, an honoured place, in our scheme of things, but as one of many dimensions. For Tories became Tories well before the modern concept of a free market economy meant anything, well before it became a matter of political controversy.

Conservatism will, I believe, continue to be a living, growing creed long after economic controversy gives way to other issues, long after Socialism comes to be seen as one of the many blind alleys of history, of interest to the historian alone.

The Conservative Party is an integral part of the British tradition, not to be explained in abstract terms, but as part of the living flesh of British life over the generations. So let me begin today, as I learnt to do with Iain's help, from a sense of shared history; not just Tory history, but British history.

For we are essentially *a British party*. We try to the best of our ability to understand Britain's problems and do what is good for Britain, while fulfilling our obligations as members of the world community. We observe what happens elsewhere, and draw lessons from it, but aware that different national traditions, experience and religious values must affect the social, political and economic solutions.

We know that there are certain human needs and values, not simply material needs but human rights, dignity, freedom from fear. These should be accorded everywhere. But the further we proceed from these fundamentals to political and economic arrangements, the less competent we feel to do much more than pronounce success or failure.

Our sense of history imparts caution and humility to us. You will have noted how the Socialist is happy to lay down the law for all mankind, past, present and future, giving marks, usually bad ones, convinced that he could have done much better. You will have noticed how they claim solidarity with Socialist parties and regimes everywhere, in the name of human solidarity, while preaching hatred towards fellow-British citizens of differing background or views.

You will have noted too how Socialists consider themselves qualified to lay down what is good for all countries and societies, for the Chinese and the Chileans, Uruguayans and Paraguayans, South African and South Vietnamese, Anguillans and Angolans – and never does a shadow of self-doubt cross their closed little minds.

We beg to differ from them. First, I think it arrogant to claim that our generation is any wiser than previous generations. We are here, they are gone. We can stand on their shoulders, as I hope succeeding generations will be able to stand on ours. But we should not be too hasty in judging them, not simply because we shall be judged in turn, but because to judge requires so much knowledge, such an effort of imagination to put ourselves into their shoes that could well be spent – barring the professional historian – on understanding our own pressing problems.

Least of all do we feel qualified to offer advice to more successful nations, on whose bounty this Government's spendthrift measures have made us dependent.

But we are more than just a British party. The Tories began

as a Church party, concerned with the Church and State, in that order, before our concern extended to the economy, and many other fields which politics now touches.

Religion gives us not only values – a scheme of things in which economic, social, penal policy have their place – but also our historical roots. For through the Old Testament our spiritual roots go back to the early days of civilization and man's search for God. The New Testament takes us on through Greek philosophy, Roman law, the Church Fathers and the great flowering of a specifically Christian civilization in the Middle Ages from which our own characteristic way of life emerged.

Our religion teaches us that every human being is unique and must play his part in working out his own salvation. So whereas Socialists begin with society, and how people can be fitted in, we start with Man, whose social and economic relationships are just part of his wider existence.

Because we see man as a spiritual being, we utterly reject the Marxist view, which gives pride of place to economics. However much the Marxists and their fellow-travellers, new and old, may try to wriggle and explain away, this was Marx's stated view and a linchpin of his whole system.

The religious tradition values economic activity – how we earn our living, create wealth – but warns against obsession with it, warns against putting it above all else. Money is not an end in itself, but a means to an end.

The letters to the Archbishop of Canterbury, received in reply to his 'call to the nation', were recently published. One of them was from a country vicar. 'I am concerned,' he wrote:

> that I haven't enough to do my job properly. I am concerned because my parishioners, some of them at least, are not receiving what I ought to be able to provide and be glad to give them, that is, a visit in emergencies, just because there is no petrol in the tank and no money in the pocket to buy more; or that there is petrol only sufficient to provide transport for my wife to work.

That vicar knew that he needed money, not for itself, but for what he could do with it.

The increased involvement of Government with economic life has coincided with a marked worsening of economic performance. It has heightened tensions between different groups of workers, some struggling to keep differentials, others trying to override them; between producers and consumers, landlords and tenants, public services and the public.

To observe these things is not to deny a role to Government in economic life; it is not to preach *laissez-faire*. That was preached two centuries back when manufacture and commerce were fighting to free themselves from State monopoly and interference which were holding back their development. There is much that the State should do, and do much better than it is doing. But there are also proper limits which have long since been passed in this country.

To understand the reason and how these limits can be adduced, we must come back to the nature of man. This is a matter where our understanding and our case, based on religion and common sense, is so much sounder than that of the Socialist doctrine. Yet the Socialist travesty has succeeded in gaining wide acceptance by default, even among our own people. I refer to the question of self-interest as against the common good. The Socialists have been able to persuade themselves and many others that a free economy based on profit embodies and encourages self-interest, which they see as selfish and bad, whereas they claim Socialism is based on, and nurtures, altruism and selflessness.

This is baseless nonsense in theory and in practice. Let me explain why. Let us start from the idea of self. There is not, and cannot possibly be, any hard-and-fast antithesis between self-interest and care for others, for man is a social creature, born into family, clan, community, nation, brought up in mutual dependence. The founders of our religion made this a cornerstone of morality. The admonition: love thy neighbour as thyself, and do as you would be done by, expresses this. You will note that it does not denigrate self, or elevate love of others above it. On the contrary, it sees concern for self and responsibility for self as something to be expected, and asks only that this be extended to others. This embodies the great truth that self-regard is the root of regard for one's fellows. The child learns to understand others through its own feelings; at first its immediate family; in course of time the circle grows.

Our fellow-feeling develops from self-regard. Because we want warmth, shelter, food, security, respect and other goods for ourselves, we can understand that others want them too. If we had no desire for these things, would we be likely to understand and further others' desire for them?

You may object that saintly people can well have no personal desires, either material or prestigious; but we do not legislate for saints.

Now since people in their day-to-day lives are motivated by this complex of attitudes – self-regard and fellow-feeling, group and sectional interests, personal and family responsibility, local patriotism, philanthropy – an economy will be effective only in so far as it can contain and harness all these drives. Perhaps Archbishop Temple had it right when he said, 'The art of Government, in fact, is the art of so ordering life that self-interest prompts what justice demands.'

Adam Smith, who came to economics via philosophy (socio-logy, as we should now call it) and history, described how the interplay between the self-interest of many can further the mutual interest of all. I urge you to read him, both for what he said and for what he did not say, but is often ascribed to him. He did not say that self-interest was good *per se*; he saw it as a major drive which can be a blessing to any society able to harness it and a curse to those who cannot harness it. He showed how the market economy obliges and enables each producer to serve the consumer's interest by serving his own.

People must be free to choose what they consume in goods and services. When they choose through the market, their choice is sovereign. They alone exercise their responsibility as consumers and producers. To the extent that the fruits of their efforts are appropriated by the State, or other coercive bodies, they not only have responsibility taken away from them, but the ability to make their wishes felt. Power accrues more and more to the politician, the bureaucrat; and the State-owned or subsidized providers of goods and services.

Choice in a free society implies responsibility. There is no hard-and-fast line between economic and other forms of personal responsibility to self, family, firm, community, nation, God. Morality lies in choosing between feasible alternatives. A moral being is one who exercises his own judgement in choice, on matters great and small, bearing in mind their moral dimension, that is, right and wrong. In so far as his right and duty to choose is taken away by the State, the Party or the union, his moral faculties, that is, his capacity for choice, atrophy, and he becomes a moral cripple in the same way as we should lose the faculty of walking, reading, seeing, if we were prevented from using them over the years.

In a letter from a person who responded to the Archbishop of Canterbury's 'call to the nation', this point was beautifully put:

> We wish to be self-reliant and do not want to be dependent on the State, nor do we want the State to take so great a proportion of our money in rates and taxes to decide for us what we shall have and not have . . . I may be wrong, but I think it weakens character when little by little our freedom of choice is taken from us.

And another person said:

> I am a middle-aged woman, wife of a lower-paid worker. We have struggled through the years to buy our own house, old though it may be. We have asked for nothing. We only had one child, so no child allowance. What we have achieved we did ourselves. When we look round and see all the handouts people are getting from this Welfare State, we sometimes feel so sad that what should be a wonderful thing has really turned out to sap the goodness and initiative from so many of our people.

So let there be no mistake: economic choices have a moral dimension. A man is now enabled to choose between earning his living and depending on the bounty of the State, a choice which comes about because benefits rise and remain tax-free, while earnings rise more slowly, if at all, and tax is high at very low income levels.

A man must choose between spending and saving, between housing himself and depending on the State to house him at his fellow-citizen's expense, between paying for his children's education and accepting whatever the State provides, between working for a wage or salary and setting up on his own, between longer hours of work or study and spending more time in leisure with his family, even between spending more of his money on himself and more on his family, between joining a union and not joining, even if it means persecution by union and State.

The Socialists would take away most or all of these choices. A man would do what he was told by the State and his union, work where work was 'found' for him, at the rate fixed and degree of effort permitted. He would send his children to school where the education authority decided what the children are taught and the way they are taught. Irrespective of his views, he would live in the housing provided, take what he could get, give what he was obliged to give.

This does not produce a classless society; on the contrary, it produces the most stratified of all societies, divided into two classes: *the powerful and the powerless*; the party-bureaucratic élite and the manipulated masses.

And are these rulers better fitted to make choices on our behalf or to dispose of resources? Are they wiser, less selfish, more moral? What reason have we for supposing that they are? As the French economist and critic of Socialism, Claude Frédéric Bastiat, asked a century and a half ago, how can the Socialists, who have such a low opinion of the people's ability to choose, have such a high regard for their own? I quote his own words:

> Since the natural inclinations of mankind are so evil that its liberty must be taken away, how is it that the inclinations of the Socialists are good? Are not the legislators and their agents part of the human race? Do they believe themselves moulded from another clay than the rest of mankind? They say that society, left to itself, heads inevitably for destruction because its instincts are perverse. They demand the power to stop mankind from sliding down this fatal declivity and to impose a better direction on it. If, then, they have received from heaven intelligence and virtues that place them beyond and above mankind, let them show their credentials. They want to be *shepherds*, and they want us to be their *sheep*.

We know from experience that these self-appointed guardians

use their power to perpetuate it. We have seen how the economic considerations, which in a market economy are decisive, are increasingly subordinated in a controlled economy to the party political interests of politicians, to the group interest of State-employees, and to workers in some nationalized industries. We pay through the nose in prices and taxes and take what we are given. In that sense, we don't own those industries, they own us. And have we not seen at home, and particularly abroad, how some Socialist politicians soon come to adopt the very 'ruling life-styles' they rose to power by denouncing?

In the market economy, people are free to give of their money and their time for good causes. They exercise their altruism on their own initiative and at their own expense, whether they give directly and personally through institutions, charities, universities, churches or hospitals. When the State steps in, generosity is increasingly restricted from all sides.

From the one side, the idea is propagated that whatever needs doing is best done by the State. Since the State knows best, causes it does not support must be of questionable worth. On the other side, since the State takes more and more of people's earnings, they have less inclination to give what money they still have left for those needs which the Welfare State fails to meet.

When people give directly, personally or through an institution they respect, they feel that the sacrifices they may make in giving, and the effort in earning, is worth while. People have always accepted the responsibility to sustain the young and the old, the unfortunate and the needy. But when the money is taken away and spent by Government, the blessing goes out of giving and out of the effort of earning in order to give.

This contrast is borne out by historical experience. The Victorian age, which saw the burgeoning of free enterprise, also saw the greatest expansion of voluntary philanthropic activity of all kinds: the new hospitals, new schools, technical colleges, universities, new foundations for orphans, non-profit-making housing trusts, and missionary societies.

Dr Barnardo's Homes was founded in 1866. It cares today

for 2,251 children in residential accommodation. The Soldiers', Sailors' and Airmen's Families' Association was founded in 1885 and now, with 12,000 volunteer workers, helps countless families. The National Society for the Prevention of Cruelty to Children, which now handles some 80,000 cases annually, was founded in 1884. The St John Ambulance Association was founded in 1877 to provide a service still essential to every centre of population. The Church Army, now giving help to 14,800 people, started in 1890. The Royal National Lifeboat Institution was founded in 1824 and now maintains 250 lifeboats at a cost of about £3 million a year, almost entirely from voluntary subscriptions.

The Victorian age has been very badly treated in Socialist propaganda. It was an age of constant and constructive endeavour in which the desire to improve the lot of the ordinary person was a powerful factor. We who are largely living off the Victorians' moral and physical capital can hardly afford to denigrate them. You may remember Lord Acton's aphorism that while only a foolish Conservative would judge the present by the standards of the past, only a foolish Liberal would judge the past by the standards of the present. There are many foolish Liberals in the Socialist camp; we can do without them in ours.

Why then, you may ask, did Socialist thought make so much headway? It is not only a fair question but a vitally important one for us. There are many possible answers. But one obvious reason stands out. Socialists criticized imperfect human reality in the name of a theory. So long as Socialism was only a theory, it made criticism of other ways easy for them. They could claim that their way was best. But now we are beyond the days of theory. For decades Socialists have extended their power until they control almost half the world's population. How has the thing worked out in practice? Disastrously. Wherever they have imposed their heavy hand, people are worse off and less free.

A leading Labour Party ideologist, Baroness Wootton, recently said proudly that during her lifetime she was glad to see that one-third of the world's population had come to earn its daily bread under Socialism. True, she made a brief reference to the fact that they seem to practise tyranny and racism, but very much *en passant*. She neither stopped to ask whether this was not inherent in Socialist rule, nor what the quality and quantity of Socialism's daily bread was like. Not all Lady Wootton's fellow Socialists are as frank as she is in claiming the Socialist world as soul mates, and as encouragement for their efforts to clamp down Socialism here 'irrevocably and irreversibly', to use one of the present Government's favourite phrases.

True, not all of the Labour Party are happy to accept Communist-ruled regimes as fellow Socialists. But they are remarkably muted in their opposition to the 'fraternal relations' adopted by a majority of their party and trade union movement. In so far as some are embarrassed by the behaviour of their fellow Socialists in the Soviet Union, Cambodia and East Germany, they have yet failed to produce a coherent explanation of why they believe that a doctrine which has produced such visibly inhuman results in a third of the world or more would lead us to Utopia in Great Britain.

To say that the others are not 'true Socialists' – no connection with the firm next door with the same name – gets us no further. Socialism is what Socialists do, and Socialists do more or less the same, as the opportunity permits. Gulag was the consequence of Socialism. It was not the work of one man. It only happened because Socialism demoralized the whole nation, replaced the individual conscience by the party, right and wrong by what was good for the revolution.

But as I argued earlier, we shall not win simply by showing the dark side of Socialism. That is why I began with our vision, and put it in the centre of the stage. I stress vision, not blueprint; values and principles, not doctrines. We are generally in no better position to prophesy than preceding generations were, and they always got it wrong; the more scientific they thought they were, the further they strayed. For the unfolding of human history is richer and more complex than our minds can foresee.

Yet by understanding the present and the past and adducing possibilities and probabilities as best we can, so long as we leave some margin for error we can influence the shape of things to come. We have learned much from the over-optimism of the immediate post-war era, when we thought Government could do it all. We need healthy scepticism, but not pessimism. We are not bound to an irrevocable decline. We see nothing as inevitable. Men can still shape history.

Because the post-war Keynesian recipe of endless growth and full employment through high demand levels went sour, this does not mean we turn our backs on the aspirations which underlay the 1944 White Paper on employment policy. Because we see that welfare can be abused, we do not neglect our responsibility to help people back on to their feet and to look after the handicapped.

We know that we must assure a better balance between what people receive and what they can earn, and between the hardship we see and are moved to mitigate through the welfare system and the reaction we create when taxes fall too heavily on the taxpayer.

This is a turning-point in our party's history, no less than in our nation's, comparable to the situation when Iain Macleod came back into civilian life after the war. He and his generation had been formed under the combined influence of their heavy wartime responsibilities, the high hopes for post-war Britain generated during the war, and the shock of our electoral defeat in 1945.

Iain let none of these put him off balance. He set to work with others of his generation to pick up the pieces, to begin from where they were. He and the 'One Nation' group set the tone for much of post-war Conservative thought and action. They did not blame their stars, or the voters. They set to work to ask what had gone wrong, and how to put it right.

That was a generation back. We now stand before the new challenges: how to revive the economy, how to enlarge our liberties, how to restore the balance between trade unions and the community, how to further our European partnership while protecting legitimate British interests, how to simplify the welfare maze which often baffles those who most deserve help, how to regain an underlying sense of nationhood and purpose.

Circumstances in the late Seventies are different from those of thirty years ago. Once again we have faced electoral defeat, drawn the necessary conclusions and come back with renewed vigour.

Iain Macleod's approach then was, in essence: if it *must* be done it *can* be done; if it *can* be done it *must* be done. 'We shall prevail' – one of his great speeches ended. We did, and we shall.

St Lawrence Jewry

CITY OF LONDON, 30 MARCH 1978

Mrs Thatcher's speech at St Lawrence Jewry was on the theme of Christianity and politics. She described the manner in which her own strict Christian upbringing had influenced her outlook, while making it clear that religious doctrines had not determined her political actions. 'The truth of the matter is this: the Bible as well as the tradition of the Church tells us very little directly about political systems or social programmes.' The need for a high level of public spending, or a particular set of welfare arrangements, could not therefore be determined – as some churchmen appear to think – by reference to the Gospels. Indeed, Mrs Thatcher drew attention to the serious practical and moral dangers that can arise if the State is accorded too much responsibility in social and economic affairs. 'The role of the State in Christian society is to encourage virtue, not to usurp it.'

She rejected the view that free enterprise is inferior to Socialism: the essential difference between them, she argued, is that the former (correctly) does not promise Utopia in this life whereas the latter (misleadingly) does. But all those who want to live in freedom should recognize the importance of religion in providing the moral framework and spiritual heritage needed to sustain it. However, religion alone could not create the basis for a free society: in this crucial area there was a distinct role for a strong State to keep sinful man in check, and uphold the rule of law. That was the essence of the relationship between Christianity and politics as described in this speech.

Need I say that this is not a party political speech? To offer you such a speech would indeed be to abuse your rector's hospitality. What is more, it would be extremely imprudent, if not quite impossible.

It is a long time since it was said that the Church of England was the Tory Party at prayer. That famous dictum was never wholly true. Historically, it would be nearer the mark to say that the Tory Party in its origin was the Church of England in politics, for the old concept of a partnership between Church and State lies very near the heart of traditional Tory thinking, and in that partnership Tories always believed that the Church had primacy because it was concerned with those things which matter fundamentally to the destiny of mankind.

So how does my religion affect my work as a politician? I was brought up, let me remind you, in a religious environment which, by the standards of today, would seem very rigid. We often went to church twice on Sundays, as well as to morning and afternoon Sunday School. We attended a number of church activities during the week. We believed it was wrong to spend very much on personal pleasure. We were taught always to make up our own minds and never to take the easy way of following the crowd.

I suppose what this taught me above everything else was to see the temporal affairs of this world in perspective. What mattered fundamentally was man's relationship to God, and in the last resort this depended on the response of the individual soul to God's Grace.

Politics, when I began to think about them, seemed naturally important because they were one of the ways in which individuals could discharge that duty to their neighbours which God has enjoined on mankind. They were also important because, though good institutions and laws cannot make men good, bad ones can encourage them to be a lot worse.

I never thought that Christianity equipped me with a political philosophy, but I thought it did equip me with standards to which political actions must, in the end, be referred. It also taught me that, in the final analysis, politics is about personal relations, about establishing the conditions in which men and women can best use their fleeting lives in this world to prepare themselves for the next.

I was also brought up to believe that it was only through whole-hearted devotion to this preparation that true earthly happiness could be achieved. Experience gives me no reason to revise this view.

Now all this may sound rather pious; but in those days religion had not been stripped by certain sophisticated theologians of its supernatural elements. The language in which we express our religious ideas may have changed – that is to say, when we are not too embarrassed to express them at all. But I still believe that the majority of English parents want their children to be brought up in what is essentially the same religious heritage as was handed to me. To most ordinary people, heaven and hell, right and wrong, good and bad, matter.

Now if all this is true, it has one very important implication for politics. In the face of all difficulties and temptations we must keep, and not go on diluting, the specifically Christian content of teaching and corporate life in our schools. That was uppermost in my mind when I was at the Department of Education, and will still be there if I am called to another ministerial office.

Today, we live in what the academics call 'a pluralist society'. My party, like most others, is not only drawn from all Christian denominations and other religions, but also contains some who would hotly deny that religion has anything at all to do with politics, or even with morality.

There are, to my mind, some advantages in this variety. I think some of the bitterness of political strife is reduced when we remind ourselves that many of the people who share our deepest convictions about life are on the other side in political controversy.

For the truth of the matter is this: the Bible, as well as the tradition of the Church, tell us very little directly about political systems or social programmes. The nearest we get is Christ telling his disciples to render unto Caesar that which is Caesar's, and unto God that which is God's. No doubt many political judgements rest on moral assumptions, but many of the issues on which we are passionately divided are disputes about fact and expediency.

In politics, as Edmund Burke taught us, there are very few universal and permanent truths. So when I speak of my political ideals I am most of the time speaking as the heir to a particular body of beliefs, and I hope of insights; I am talking about what seems to me to be right for this country, at this particular time, bearing in mind our past.

I think it is important to avoid confusing moral and political judgements. There is always a temptation, not easily resisted, to identify our opponents with the Devil, to suggest that politics presents us with a series of clear and simple choices between good and evil, and to attribute base motives to all who disagree with us. These are dangerous and evil tendencies; they embitter politics, and they trivialize religion and morality.

Certainly Christianity offers us no easy solutions to political and economic issues. It teaches us that there is some evil in everyone and that it cannot be banished by sound policies and institutional reforms; that we cannot eliminate crime simply by making people rich, or achieve a compassionate society simply by passing new laws and appointing more staff to administer them. In politics there are few simplicities and certainties, and loads of dilemmas. Let me give one or two practical examples of what I mean.

Of course it is true that all men of good will must be concerned with the relief of poverty and suffering, and in most Christian countries this has come to be regarded as one of the primary concerns of politicians.

But it is one thing to say that the relief of poverty and suffering is a duty, and quite another to say that this duty can always be most efficiently and humanely performed by the State. Indeed, there are grave moral dangers and serious practical ones in letting people get away with the idea that they can delegate all their responsibilities to public officials and institutions.

We know the immense sacrifices which people will make for the care of their own near and dear – for elderly relatives, disabled children and so on, and the immense part which voluntary effort, even outside the confines of the family, has played in these fields.

Once you give people the idea that all this can be done by the State, and that it is somehow second-best or even degrading to leave it to private people (it is sometimes referred to as 'cold charity'), then you will begin to deprive human beings of one of the essential ingredients of humanity – personal moral responsibility. You will, in effect, dry up in them the milk of human kindness.

If you allow people to hand over to the State all their personal responsibility, the time will come – indeed it is close at hand – when what the taxpayer is willing to provide for the good of humanity will be seen to be far less than what the individual used to be willing to give from love of his neighbour.

So do not be tempted to identify virtue with collectivism. I wonder whether the State services would have done as much for the man who fell among thieves as the Good Samaritan did for him?

I am not saying, of course, that the State has no welfare functions. This would be wholly against the tradition of my party. We have always believed that there must be a level of well-being below which a citizen must not be allowed to fall. Moreover, people cannot realize their potential without educational opportunity. But the role of the State in Christian society is to encourage virtue, not to usurp it.

Let me give a second example. We all feel the need to assist the people of developing countries and recognize that it is our duty to help them. But how much of the Gross Domestic Product can be properly used in this way? Are direct State subsidies to Governments the best way of offering help? Is not a free and open trading system between countries more mutually beneficial than aid handouts by Government? These are questions which honest people can disagree about.

In post-war Britain we have seen a tendency, particularly in some places of learning and even in some churches, to claim or assume a moral superiority for Socialist and collectivist ideas. The argument is presented in a compelling way. It is suggested that a system run on a basis of self-interest, profit and competition is somehow immoral and even structurally wrong.

Those who take this view point to some of the bad things in Victorian times, and before that, citing as evidence selected works of contemporary artists and writers. Now no one would deny that in every age and in every society there are features of which we should be ashamed, but can we honestly say that the system built up on private enterprise and freedom of choice has not produced an immense change for the better in the lot of all our people?

Would a system dominated by the State have produced the wealth, well-being and freedom that we enjoy today? In this life we shall never achieve the perfect society, in spite of the optimism of much humanist writing, but at least a system based on personal choice allows us to have and pursue ideals and interests.

Today, it seems as if people are made to feel guilty about being well-off. But Christ did not condemn riches as such, only the way in which they were used and those who put their trust in them. It is one of the Church's tasks to guide us about our use of this world's wealth. But it seems strange to me that a man can be appealed to for substantial contributions to many church and charitable causes, and yet be half-criticized for having the means to give generously.

Let me be quite clear: I am certainly not saying that Socialist theory and Socialist practice as we know them are contrary to the New Testament, nor am I saying that you can't be a good and sincere Christian and a dedicated social democrat. What we think about the proper organization of society must depend on our own reading of history and on our own view of the circumstances of society today.

Nevertheless, there is one heresy which it seems to me that some political doctrines embrace. It is the belief that man is perfectible. This takes the form of supposing that if we get our social institutions right – if we provide properly for education, health and all other branches of social welfare – we shall have exorcized the Devil. This is bad theology and it also conflicts with our own experience. In my own lifetime, we have expended vast efforts and huge sums of money on policies designed to make people better and happier. Have we really brought about a fundamental improvement in man's moral condition?

The Devil is still with us, recording his successes in the crime figures and in all the other maladies of this society, in spite of its relative material comfort.

If I am critical of what I believe to be the fallacies that underly Socialist doctrine, let me add that there are warnings which need to be heeded by those of us who favour a free market economy. As a Christian, I am bound to shun Utopias on this earth and to recognize that there is no change in man's social arrangements which will make him perfectly good and perfectly happy. Therefore, I do not claim that the free enterprise system of itself is automatically going to have these effects. I believe that economic freedom is a necessary, but not a sufficient, condition of our own national recovery and prosperity.

There is another dimension – a moral one. For a nation to be noted for its industry, honesty and responsibility and justice, its people need a purpose and an ethic. The State cannot provide these – they can only come from the teachings of a Faith. And the Church must be the instrument of that work.

Alexis de Tocqueville, writing on democracy in America, pointed out that:

> Religion . . . is more needed in democratic countries than in any others. How is it possible that society should escape destruction, if the moral tie is not strengthened in proportion as the political tie is relaxed? And what can be done with a people who are their own masters if they are not submissive to the Deity?

Freedom will destroy itself if it is not exercised within some sort of moral framework, some body of shared beliefs, some spiritual heritage transmitted through the Church, the family and the school. It will also destroy itself if it has no purpose. There is a well-known prayer which refers to God's service as 'perfect freedom'. My wish for the people of this country is that we shall be 'free to serve'.

So we must have freedom and we must have a morality. But

even these are not enough: man is inherently sinful and in order to sustain a civilized and harmonious society we need laws backed by effective sanctions. Looking at this country today, I am bound to say that upholding the law is one area of life where I would wish the State to be stronger than it is. Freedom can only exist on a basis of law to be observed by governors and the governed, and to be rigorously and fairly enforced. So the State's role in a democracy is first and foremost to uphold the rule of law.

But sometimes in history we have been so impressed with this truth that we have forgotten that ultimately true harmony consists in the willing co-operation of free men, and is not served by an over-regulated society. What is more, even when freedom, as it sometimes does, seems to be working against social harmony, we must remember that it has its own intrinsic value, just because men and women were born to be free.

It appears to me that there are two very general and seemingly conflicting ideas about society which come down to us from the New Testament. There is that great Christian doctrine that we are all members one of another, expressed in the concept of the Church on Earth as the Body of Christ. From this we learn our interdependence, and the great truth that we do not achieve happiness or salvation in isolation from each other but as members of society.

That is one of the great Christian truths which has influenced our political thinking; but there is also another, that we are all responsible moral beings with a choice between good and evil, beings who are infinitely precious in the eyes of their Creator. You might almost say that the whole of political wisdom consists in getting these two ideas in the right relationship to each other.

Of course there are many sincere Christians who will disagree with my practical conclusions. Totalitarian Marxists will disagree with me in principle. They make no bones about rejecting all the assumptions from which I begin. I believe that their philosophy is utterly inconsistent with the Gospel and the teaching of the Church.

What I am working for is a free and responsible society. But

THE REVIVAL OF BRITAIN

freedom is not synonymous with an easy life. Indeed, my own faith in freedom does not rest in the last resort on utilitarian arguments at all. Perhaps it would be possible to achieve some low-grade form of happiness in a thoroughly regimented State; but in such a State men would not be treated as what they are and what Christianity wanted them to be – free and responsible human beings. There are many difficult things about freedom: it does not give you safety; it creates moral dilemmas for you; it requires self-discipline; it imposes great responsibilities; but such is the destiny of man and in such consists his glory and salvation.

In such too consists our national greatness. As the Book of Proverbs says: 'Righteousness exalteth a nation.'

The Bow Group

THE ROYAL COMMONWEALTH SOCIETY, LONDON, 6 MAY 1978

Doubts about the future of democracy were not uncommon in the late 1970s. In this speech Mrs Thatcher set out to answer those doubts. She argued that there was no reason whatsoever to believe that Communism had stolen a march on the West. She then reminded her audience of the beliefs which give democracy its unique power and strength – the ideals of an open society which Britain in particular should always strive to attain. One of those ideals – the rule of law – had been badly damaged by the Labour Government. Another – the concept of limited Government – needed to be firmly restated and properly defined in order to ensure that the State concentrated on fulfilling its proper roles, described here with some care. In this connection Mrs Thatcher once again spoke of the need to limit Government intervention in the economy. Above all, a limited State could lead to the growth of 'private associations which contribute so much to the stability and richness of a society' – a strong Tory sentiment first defined by Burke.

Sometimes Britain and the free democracies of the West seem to be suffering more from a failure of nerve than from anything else. 'After the fall of Athens, in 404 BC,' wrote C. M. Bowra in *The Greek Experience*, 'something was extinguished, not merely a zest for life and a boldness of enterprise and experiment but certain assumptions which had never been seriously questioned now lost their authority and their hold.'

The evidence of every kind proves that our free democratic system is superior in technology to the Communist one. We are infinitely quicker to take advantage of promising inventions than is the Communist system. Since 1945, our system has brought benefits to large numbers.

The population of Communist countries, on the other hand, has suffered horribly and unnecessarily from the deadening hand which the State has held over them. No Communist country, for example, has made a success of collectivized agriculture. Russia, before the revolution, used to be a great exporter of wheat. She has often recently had to import that staff of life from the USA.

The writings of Solzhenitsyn made obvious, even to the wilfully blind, that it was not simply Stalin who was an evil man, but that Communism, in practice, is an evil system, which gave birth to Stalin.

Prosperity in the West can also be measured in direct relation to the role which the State has played in the economy concerned. West Germany and Japan, for example, where the part of the State has been modest, are more successful, measured in terms of output, than are Britain and Italy, where the hand played by the State has been strong.

Even so, morale among the free democracies is low. Prominent people have publicly wondered whether democracy can survive. Very few people describe themselves willingly as 'capitalists'. By contrast, the Communist States seem to be entrenched, and Communists have a strong position in several Western European countries. The Left of the Labour Party is stronger within that organization than it used to be when the country's standard of living was less good. The Labour Left has also shown itself, astonishingly, more friendly to Russia even than some of the European Communist parties.

There are also many who, while rejecting Communism as it has worked in Russia, openly despise the old ideals of the West: anarchists, Trotskyists, revolutionaries of the most diverse aspirations have made an appearance in almost every university in the free world. If it is not always easy to know what these sects want, it is usually easy enough to understand that they do not want democracy.

The reasons for the disillusion or even despair in the West are various. *First*, many suffer from a certain historical short-sightedness. People forget that democracy in the sense of a universal franchise is new. Even in Britain, it is only fifty years old. Thus, our version of democracy is not an old, ramshackle building which, after many generations, is beginning to fall down. It is a system still with growing pains – an infinitely new system in comparison with absolute systems, such as practised by our enemies. A hankering for absolutism, like a hankering for a single leader, is a throwback to the past, not a foreshadowing of the future.

Second, spokesmen for democracy too often allow their opponents to choose the ground for debate. It is not enough to say that private enterprise gives a better material life, true though that usually is. We should look more to ideas and realize that people respond to them often more than they respond to appeals to their material interests. Communists know the power of ideas, despite their doctrine of historical materialism. We too should show we are aware of their importance, despite our material success.

Third, a generation of easy liberal education has accustomed many to suppose that Utopia was soon to be achieved. Such education left the belief that, with the Welfare State, all ills would soon vanish and, with the UN, all tyrannies would soon crumble. That has proved an illusion. Each generation has to fight for its own liberties, in whatever way is appropriate. The ideal solutions of one generation may even become, unless refurbished and brought up to date, the cause of bondage, or at least bureaucracy for the next.

Fourth, we may have underestimated the shocks given by the two World Wars, the loss of Empire, and the threat of nuclear weapons. The long series of setbacks suffered by the West in the Middle East, the Far East, Cuba and now, it seems, Africa must also be having an effect.

The loss of Empire did not mean the eclipse of everything for which this country stood in the past. On the contrary, if all the various achievements of Britain in history were totted up, our role in evolving a political democracy with a record of tolerance second to none would probably rank first. It would be followed by our role in initiating the industrial age. Then, what of the glories of English literature? The Empire, magnificent construction though it was, surely did not exceed the greatness of these achievements.

Fifth, the friends of the free society have also too often accepted the argument of their enemies that the dominant issue in politics is a matter of social class. Policies with that as a basis are both divisive and meaningless. Those who, in the nineteenth century, worked out a theory of history based on class did so at a time when there were comparatively few urban wage-earners dependent on a powerful employer. Neither Marx nor Engels could possibly have recognized *their* 'working class' in present-day England or indeed elsewhere.

Of course, many workers of the mid-nineteenth century did feel lost, if they were working twelve hours a day, with the protection neither of unions nor of social legislation. But modern workers in Detroit, Coventry, the Ruhr, even Moscow, are now primarily citizens of their country, like everyone else. They are not members of an underprivileged and internationally recognizable 'class'.

The moral of all this is simple: Marx was wrong about the working class when he wrote his books; and his prescriptions have as little use today as other mid-Victorian arguments have as to what should, or should not, be done.

Let us now try and express some of the foremost ideals of an open society. *First* in importance among the things for which we stand must be the rule of law. This phrase means much more than a pious hope that everyone will be law-abiding. In the eighteenth century foreign visitors, such as Voltaire, were particularly struck by the fact that England was governed, as was not then the case with any other European country, by the rule of law. They meant by that not that our laws were especially lenient, nor even especially logical. They meant that no one should be punished, nor could lawfully be made to suffer in body, or suffer loss of goods, save for a definite breach of the law, established in the courts of the land. Our tradition is that a man can only be punished for a breach of the law, nothing else.

The second characteristic of the rule of law in this country is that everyone, whatever their rank, should be subject to the ordinary law of the land. The law applies to the governors and the governed alike.

Now, in the last few years, these principles have begun to be ignored and eroded. I don't mean simply to refer here to the Labour Party's curious attitude to the councillors of Clay Cross, nor even to the Labour Left's astonishing attempt to make martyrs of the Shrewsbury pickets [see note on p. 28]. Nor even do I mean Mr Michael Foot's attack on the judges [the previous year] on the occasion when the Attorney General seemed to have been worsted in the course of their party's interventions in the affair of the Grunwick film-processing factory [over union recognition].

No, the fact to which I refer is that, as a result of the growth of trade unions, men and women can be punished, even to the extent of losing their livelihoods, by kangaroo courts set up under those same unions, or by other action undertaken by those unions. Some would freely admit that they have joined unions not out of conviction but out of self-protection. Others fear flying pickets and similar manifestations of the power of unions more than they fear the law.

It is essential to restore the traditional way of conducting these affairs. The Greeks, during the golden age, knew perfectly well that what distinguished them from the barbarians of that day was their respect, and the respect of their leaders, for the law. John Locke put the matter plainly when he said 'Where Law disappears, tyranny begins'. Unless we restore and guard it, the rule of law will generally fall into disrespect. If that were to happen, there is no certainty whatever about who would profit in the end. Time and again in history, a political system which surrenders on this sort of point has been overthrown, and has deserved to be, but not always by its most obvious enemies.

There is a fashionable theory, deriving from Marx, that law and law courts exist to protect the rich and powerful. Experience suggests, on the contrary, that the poor and weak need law more than anyone else. Our faith in the rule of law has a long ancestry. I have mentioned the ancient Athenians' understanding of the question. The desire to restore the rule of law was an important allied aim during the last war. We were not then insisting on the establishment of any particular law, but on re-establishing systems of Government in which the rule of law would prevail in place of the rule of force.

Our *second* main principle is our sense of the limit which we must impose on the power of the State. The State should not be allowed, and should not allow itself, to spill outwards, upwards and outwards, in every direction, in Ramsay MacDonald's famous formulation, as if it were the only institution to be relied upon. We should have far too great respect for the State to allow it to extend its tentacles too far.

The State has, it seems to me, three main roles. *First*, it must defend the population against its enemies within and without and act as the force behind the law: in this, the State should have a monopoly of power. *Second*, it must discharge its function in social services, where it can play a big part but should not have a monopoly. *Third*, it has a role in the economy, where not only should the State refrain from a monopoly, but its every activity should be scrutinized to be sure that it cannot be more effectively carried out by private enterprise. I wish to say a word about each of these three roles in turn.

First, defence, and law and order. If a potential enemy seems more formidable than we can reasonably be expected to cope with alone, it is the first business of the State to ensure alliances which will enable us to withstand any such menaces.

The forces concerned must also be adequate to ensure essential services if the worst comes to the worst, whether that derives from a breakdown of order which the ordinary police cannot cope with (as has been the case since 1969 in Ulster) or from a strike, say, in the fire services. The other role, in which the State should have a monopolist position, is to provide the sanction to ensure that rule of law which I earlier described as the first of our principles.

In both these departments, the part of the Government in the last four years has been inadequate. Our armed services are not properly provided for and our police are below strength. The

National Executive of the Labour Party scarcely bother to hide that they would prefer to run down our defence so much that an unbridled appeasement of Russia would be the only way out.

The second role of the State is in respect of the social services. Whether it be in cash benefits, health, or education, the State should not be the only agency concerned. Voluntary organizations, private pension and insurance funds, personal health provision, and above all family and friends, will always have a vital part to play.

Consider housing – an expensive area of Government initiative. It is also one where the effect of Government has been to create new problems without solving existing ones. Council housing provides low-rent accommodation at high cost to the public and does more than any other single factor to stress class divisions in the community. Anything which helps council tenants to become owners of their houses must be encouraged. We should surely wish to look forward in the long run to a nation in which only a small minority of the population live as municipal tenants. Yet we are in danger of moving in the other direction.

Much the same applies to education where, given the history of the last 100 years, the State's contribution will always be much larger than the private sector. There is cause for alarm at the extent to which greater State involvement, to the point of virtual monopoly in higher education, has coincided with a decline in educational standards.

In medicine, we are dealing in Britain with a myth, as well as an achievement. The achievement is the Health Service, and the myth is that its establishment necessarily creates a system of public health superior to that elsewhere, where a higher proportion is financed through private insurance, including occupational and trade union schemes.

The third role of the State is its involvement in the economy. Now some of its activities are so old (for example, in relation to the currency and tariffs) as to be a part of the history of the concept of Statehood. But most of the State's intervention in the economy is new. The habit of intervention derives as much as anything else from the taste acquired by Governments for regulation of private enterprise during the abnormal circumstances of the two World Wars. Indeed, it was during the wars that the Government – or rather its economic advisers – first began to believe that one of the State's duties was to 'manage' the economy; an idea which would not have occurred to any administration during the days of our economic greatness.

The role of private enterprise in ensuring a successful economy is something which can be proved from history time and again. In the nineteenth century, the German economist List (no friend of free trade) observed in his work *The National System of Political Economy*, 'The enormous producing capacity and the great wealth of England are not the effect solely of national power and individual love of gain. The people's innate love of liberty and justice, the energy and the religious and moral character of the people have a share in it.'

The fact that Britain was a free country was plainly one of the main reasons why she was able to be the initiator of industrialization at the end of the eighteenth century. In the essay *On Liberty*, J. S. Mill points out that if the main economic institutions of the country are run by the Government, 'not all the freedom of the press and popular constitution of the legislature would make this or any other country free otherwise than in name'.

Some of our economic problems now stem from nationalization. The motives for nationalization were variously explained in the 1940s as being to achieve better labour relations, to ensure greater efficiency and to prevent private shareholders from profiting from undertakings of national importance. All those arguments sound strange today, as indeed does George Brown's remark, in the 1960s, that his party would only then nationalize industries which were 'failing the nation'. But, as we now know, no provision was made for nationalized industries which might fail the nation.

The State's concern in economic affairs must be primarily to service the nation. Its task should be to ensure that as few obstacles as possible are placed in the way of our own pursuit of enterprise, not to try and organize how we should do that. Thus the State should be concerned with such matters as the enforcement of private contracts, the encouragement of competitive markets, the guarantee of fair trading, maintenance of incentives, regulation of health and safety standards. It must concern itself with the abuse of monopoly. The State may also feel constrained to mitigate the effects of industrial change.

Inevitably, arising out of a national emergency or a past commitment, the State may feel called on to do more than this. But in every such venture there may be some disadvantage to the community as a whole, though it may benefit a comparatively small number. The balance of advantage must be definite and considerable and be looked at in the long, as well as the short, term.

We are not anti-State. On the contrary, we seek a proper balance between State and society. The more the State's powers are extended, the less its authority is respected by the people. Only if the State's role in our society is kept to modest dimensions will respect for it be combined with respect for the large number of private associations which contribute so much to the stability and richness of a society, associations ranging from business to charity, and from voluntary organizations to the family.

The essence of a free society is that there are whole areas of life where the State has no business at all, no right to intervene. The spontaneous coming-together of people in a common interest leads to creative relations between people in a way with which authority's forced groupings cannot compete. Many of the best achievements of our history derive from this. De Tocqueville, writing over 100 years ago, thought that such associations would be essential in mass democracies above all, if tyranny were to be resisted.

Our third national ideal should be our respect for the sovereignty of Parliament. This respect for Parliament has a very long and dramatic history, marked by a continuity which differentiates this nation from all others in Europe. Like the ideal of the rule of law, the 'sovereignty of Parliament' is a deceptively simple phrase, often repeated without recognition of its real meaning. That meaning can best be grasped by recalling that, in the old struggles of Parliament against royal

79

power, our ancestors never tried to destroy the authority of the Crown. Their aim was to bind the Crown to recognized ways of procedure by recognized checks and balances which would ensure the supremacy of law and the sovereignty of Parliament.

We are, of course, proud of the parliamentary institutions which have resulted. They are also much admired abroad. But institutions are like all fortifications; they need to be well maintained. In the last few years, Governments have often treated Parliament in a very high-handed manner. The enormous mass of legislation, the sudden changes in parliamentary rules during the passage of bills, and the use of marginal majorities to force through highly contentious legislation, have sadly diminished Parliament's standing.

Two years ago, the then Minister for Employment, Mr Michael Foot, accepted the amendments which the unions wanted on the closed shop, while he rejected those that the House of Commons put forward, even the ones designed to safeguard the freedom of the press.

The difficulties of ensuring the accountability to Parliament of nationalized industries are now well known to all. There is also the Labour Party's attitude to the House of Lords. Many would not regard that chamber as being ideally constituted at the moment, but having helped to defeat every positive effort to reform that House, the Labour Left now desires to abolish it. That would mean single-chamber Government, despite the fact that there is general acceptance among constitutional lawyers and historians here, as in most countries of the old Commonwealth (based, of course, upon our experience here), that a second chamber is an essential part of the constitution.

It is an institution designed to give time for tempers to cool and to allow the revision, or at least the reconsideration, of legislation which may have been hastily passed in the Commons. There are, of course, instances in history (for example, the Convention in the French Revolution) where unicameral legislatures have imposed dictatorships.

In conclusion let me touch on the Christian basis of our national way of life. We cannot claim that our society is entirely

a Christian one. Nor indeed would we claim that Christian
societies are necessarily always good. But we are the heirs of a
society whose religion, and whose way of life, has been
Christian for century on century. Most of us, whether Christian
or not, are thus inspired directly or indirectly by the absolute
value which Christianity – deriving in part from the Old
Testament and Greek philosophy – gives to the individual soul,
and hence to man's innate responsibility for his own actions
and omissions, and his duty to treat other men as he would have
them treat him.

These teachings underlie the essential values in our society.
No effort is too great to preserve them and to ensure that new
generations understand their heritage. All these values and
their underlying ideas are old and well-tested. They were
relevant 2,000 years ago in the Athens of Pericles and the Holy
Land of the prophets. They will be as relevant in 100 years'
time as they are now.

Do you remember Socialists used to say that the Labour
Party was 'a crusade or it is nothing'? We, by contrast, believe
in a society whose solidarity and integration are provided by
individuals in free association, sharing common values. The
classical lines of our political philosophy may seem more harsh,
more demanding, in that they leave much to individual conscience, and they promise less. But I have no doubt whatever
that they will be more enduring.

Our generation has lived through the great illusion of Socialism, seeing its promises falter and turn sour, its human mask
fall away to show envy, hatred, destruction. You will begin
where we have left off. Your main task will be to rediscover,
restore, restate and reapply creatively traditional values based
on the full human spirit.

This clash of philosophies has come to be embodied more
closely in the party line-up than any of us foresaw or wished.
But battle is joined and we must win. For this reason the next
general election will be a watershed in our national history. We
are, as it were, today on a ridge from which streams flow down
to different seas. The ridge-path itself is narrow, so that the
springs of the streams are close together, as close, let us say, as

81

those whom it is customary to call the 'social democrats' seem to be on some important matters to the Conservatives. But actually the streams flow down in different directions: one stream flows to a dark cold sea of further collectivization, the other to the warm and bright sea of the Open Society.

The Swinton Lecture at the Conservative Political Centre Summer School

CAMBRIDGE UNIVERSITY, 6 JULY 1979

This lecture, entitled 'The Renewal of Britain', provided Mrs Thatcher with her first opportunity as Prime Minister to explain how the policies which she had carefully fashioned in Opposition would now at last become the practical means of rebuilding the country's economic and moral strength. The dominance of left-wing, collectivist thinking was over; a new balance of responsibility could now be struck between the individual and the State. This speech conveys extremely powerfully Mrs Thatcher's determination to ensure that her 1979 election victory would indeed mark the start of a new political era. In it the range of opportunities for individuals and their families would, of course, be greatly enlarged, and their activities would assume central importance in improving the fabric and moral well-being of the community – for 'there is no adequate substitute for genuine caring for one another on the part of families, friends and neighbours'.

But at the same time Mrs Thatcher stressed that the State would not neglect its obligations: 'It is certainly the duty of Government to do all it can to ensure that effective succour is given to those in need, and this is a Conservative principle as much as a Socialist one.' This strong conviction that individual responsibility should be encouraged alongside effective and carefully directed State provision for the needy was to become the main tenet of Thatcherite social policy.

THE REVIVAL OF BRITAIN

The tone of the speech was fiercely patriotic in the Churchillian tradition. It reflected the strength of Mrs Thatcher's belief that it had now fallen to the Conservative Party once again 'to renew the spirit and the solidarity of the nation'.

Britain is a great nation. The Conservative Party is proud of our national past. We still acclaim the scientific and technological innovations to which Britain gave birth and which ushered in the industrial and scientific age. We can look back at the history of our Empire in the confidence that it was not a scourge to other peoples, but contributed to the well-being of mankind. It brought peace, law and dramatic development to a quarter of the globe. We have given to the world the English language, which is now close to being to the modern world what Latin was to the ancient. We know that our literature is a general inspiration. We rejoice that Britain is still respected in all free countries as the 'Mother of Parliaments' and the custodian of the principle of the rule of law.

Unlike the Socialists, our policies have never been merely a local version of an international creed; they have always been, and remain, British policies, for application within the framework of British institutions, which have evolved slowly since Saxon days. That slow organic growth has endowed our political life with a special virtue, offering a moral, as well as a political, example to mankind. We in our party are certain that we belong to a 'happy breed', as Shakespeare put it in the mouth of John of Gaunt.

We can still echo, in our time, much else in John of Gaunt's great deathbed speech. We should, however, read it to the end. For Gaunt died regretting that this 'dear, dear land – dear for her reputation through the world' was:

> Leas'd out . . . bound in with shame,
> With inky blots, and rotten parchment . . .
> That [Britain], that was wont to conquer others,
> [Had] made a shameful conquest of itself.

Richard II, Act II, Scene 1

In the last few years British patriots have, once again, had

84

cause, as John of Gaunt did, to feel ashamed of the way that the nation was being directed. We know that Britain has been in dire straits before, and that she has recovered. She will recover again. But that recovery depends on a recognition of just how far we have fallen.

When we took over the Government on 4 May, we found a nation disillusioned and dispirited. That was, I believe, the inevitable outcome of the Labour Government's Socialist approach. Last winter, there can have been few in Britain who did not feel, with mounting alarm, that our society was sick – morally, socially and economically. Children were locked out of school; patients were prevented from having hospital treatment; the old were left unattended in their wheelchairs; the dead were not buried; and flying pickets patrolled the motorways. Mr Bill Dunn [a spokesman for COHSE] seemed to express the spirit of January 1979 when he said, of the ambulance men's pay demands, if 'lives must be lost, that is the way it must be'.

I do not wish to dwell unnecessarily on the human failings of individuals and of the last Government. Nevertheless, we should not allow ourselves to lose a vivid memory of what happened, and of the reversion towards barbarism that took place. We ought to look searchingly at the causes of those events, so as to be able to achieve a more authentic, a more humane and a more successful *British* way of life. If we take the long view of the antecedents of the events of last winter, we note the dominance in British intellectual and political life, over a generation and more, of collectivist theory.

Theorists of Socialism, like Laski, Tawney and their followers, motivated by a genuine desire for social justice, elevated the State as an instrument of social regeneration. Simultaneously, Keynes and later various schools of neo-Keynesian economists, exalted the role of Government and humbled the role of the individual in their pursuit of economic stability and prosperity. The events that we witnessed last winter mark, I believe, the failure of these collectivist approaches.

The desire to bring about a society which promotes greater

human fulfilment is not the monopoly of any one political party. I acknowledge, readily, the sincerity and generosity of some Socialists. However, I believe that the Socialist approach is based upon a moral confusion which in practice is profoundly damaging. The moral fallacy of Socialism is to suppose that conscience can be collectivized. One sees this fallacy most plainly in Marxist theory. Marxists are quite unable to say why a proletarian revolution, a hate-filled and violent act of expropriation, should be morally cleansing and lead to a better society. Their failure in theory has been heavily and tragically underlined by the reality of life in twentieth-century Marxist States.

But the gentler proponents of Socialism, who stop short of subscribing to the full Marxist view of history, are equally unconvincing in their view of human nature. Experience has shown the practical failure of two fundamental Socialist arguments: that nationalization is justified because it makes economic power accountable to the people whose lives it affects; and that State planning can point to better ways forward than can be charted by free enterprise. The Socialists had grossly expanded State intervention in the economy. They were going so far as to claim that the State should have monopoly rights in the provision of health and education.

It is certainly the duty of Government to do all it can to ensure that effective succour is given to those in need, and this is a Conservative principle as much as a Socialist one. Where Conservatives part company from Socialists is in the degree of confidence which we can place in the exclusive capacity of a Welfare State to relieve suffering and promote well-being. Charity is a personal quality – the supreme moral quality, according to St Paul – and public compassion, State philanthropy and institutionalized charity can never be enough. There is no adequate substitute for genuine caring for one another on the part of families, friends and neighbours.

I think that this proposition would be widely accepted. And yet the collectivist ethos has made individuals excessively prone to rely on the State to provide for the well-being of their neighbours and indeed of themselves. There cannot be a welfare system in any satisfactory sense which tends, in this way, to break down personal responsibility and the sense of responsibility to family, neighbourhood and community. The balance has moved too far towards collectivism. In recent years, it has been quite widely held to be morally wrong for the individual to choose to make his own provision for the education of his children or the health of his family

Yet if the State usurps or denies the right of the individual to make, where he is able to do so, the important decisions in his life and to provide the essentials for himself and his family, then he is demeaned and diminished as a moral being. We need, therefore, to achieve a better balance between the spheres of public and private activity. The imbalance that Socialism has brought about is, I believe, part of the explanation for the irresponsibility and the inhumanity displayed by too many people last winter.

The wanton expansion of the State's responsibilities had been accompanied by a great drop in public spirit. Excessive public spending had (as usual) bred great private discontent. In the meantime, it was widely assumed that no large enterprise could be managed successfully without the help of the State. Private philanthropy and voluntary organizations were undermined. Heavy taxation had lowered fiscal morality. The malignant tumour of the so-called black economy was growing. We seemed to be losing our moral standards as well as our competence.

Then, partly as a result of high taxation, the idea of work well done had almost been forgotten. 'Try to do any bit of work as well as it can be done for the work's sake,' wrote C.S. Lewis. But that injunction seemed, in the last few years, to have become little more than a memory. Foreigners visiting this country shook their heads sadly when they remembered a resolute, industrious and great-hearted Britain which once had seemed to be able to move both 'Earth and Heaven'. Our industrial life seemed marked by petty labour disputes which were often both self-destructive and humiliating. The time spent by works managers upon trade union matters of a non-productive nature might be half of their day's work. That was one reason for the

87

failure of Britain both to gain and to fulfil export orders. Yet the trade union movement was also rent by rivalries. When its leaders, during the period of the last Government, seemed at their most powerful, they were also least effective in representing the true interests of their members.

What did all this mean for our country? It meant that the 1960s and the early 1970s became the great age of the countries which suffered defeat in the 1939/45 War. The peoples of Germany and Japan, and also of France, worked together to restore their countries, and then to move ahead. They did not behave as if the world owed them a living. In Britain, we spent too much time dividing up the cake and pursuing petty sectional interests. So, although we had won the war, we let other countries win the peace.

For a long time, too, many leaders of the Labour Party refused to recognize the reality of British decline, to which they had contributed more than their fair share. They seemed blind to the evident truth that, all over the world, capitalism was achieving improvements in living standards and the quality of life, while Socialism was causing economic decay, bureaucracy and, when it took authoritarian or totalitarian forms, cruelty and repression. Before our eyes, we see the pathetic exodus from Vietnam, where mothers prefer their children to face the perils of wind and storm in open boats rather than the slavery imposed by Hanoi.

Our decline has not been only economic. Our defences have been allowed to fall below danger level. There has been a failure to mount, let alone to sustain, a real war against crime and against the criminal. For the first time in generations large numbers of people have come to be fearful for their personal safety.

We won the election on 3 May because we pointed out these tragic shortcomings to the electorate. We believed that we could inspire the renewal of our past faculties and ingenuity. We communicated that belief to the people. We talked of the need for renewal of our traditional craftsmanship and civic spirit; renewal at every level, and in every profession, of our old vigour and vitality.

The extent of our decline compared with other countries may show up most clearly in economic statistics. But that does not mean that the remedy lies only in economics. The economics will come right if the spirit and the determination is there. The mission of this Government is much more than the promotion of economic progress. It is to renew the spirit and the solidarity of the nation. To ensure that these assertions lead to action, we need to inspire a new national mood, as much as to carry through legislation.

At the heart of a new mood in the nation must be a recovery of our self-confidence and our self-respect. Nothing is beyond us. Decline is not inevitable. But nor is progress a law of nature. The ground gained by one generation may be lost by the next.

The foundation of this new confidence has to be individual responsibility. If people come to believe that the State, or their employer, or their union, owe them a living, and that, in turn, the world owes Britain a living, we shall have no confidence and no future. It must be quite clear that the responsibility is on each of us to make the full use of our talents and to care for our families. It must be clear, too, that we have a responsibility to our country to make Britain respected and successful in the world.

The economic counterpart of these personal and national responsibilities is the working of the market economy in a free society. I am sure that there is wide acceptance in Britain, going far beyond the supporters of our party, that production and distribution in our economy is best operated through free competition.

A basic function of Government is to ensure that this market remains in being. The Government must be responsible, too, for ensuring the maintenance of social cohesion through the support of established customs and traditions. Governments can animate industry but they should not seek indefinitely to sustain it. Governments can purify the stagnant and corrupt parts of an economy and correct irregularities in the market, but they should not seek to regulate the market itself. Governments may provide certain goods or services which cannot easily be supplied competitively, but they should accept that one of their essential tasks is to define their limitations and those of the State.

Conservatives must work to make the idea of society so defined and so inspired as attractive as once it used to be and as it still is in other more successful nations. We need, for example, to create a mood where it is everywhere thought morally right for as many people as possible to acquire capital; not only because of the beneficial economic consequences, but because the possession of even a little capital encourages the virtues of self-reliance and responsibility, as well as assisting a spirit of freedom and independence.

Some may suggest that Britain, though economically in decline, is leading the way to some kind of post-industrial life. Well, there were few signs last winter that Britain had any unique capacity for growing poor gracefully. 'Zero growth', too, would probably mean that those in the prime of their working lives would have to accept cuts in their living standards in order to maintain the present level of assistance to the old, the poor and the sick. Preoccupation with 'zero growth', it seems to us, is little more than a fashionable self-indulgence on the part of people who are already well-off, or who are still young enough to be without responsibilities.

The actions of Government have to sustain and foster the new mood of greater freedom with greater responsibility.

After two months in office, let me give you some examples of steps we have taken already to achieve this. We have begun to make it much easier for council tenants to buy their homes and thus change their status from dependence on the council to independent property-owning citizens. This will help to realize the wish of one of the most humane of nineteenth-century Conservatives, Lord Shaftesbury, who believed that ideally every citizen should own his own house. We have prevented a further slide in education standards, by halting the undesired destruction of grammar schools. We have begun the business of refurbishing the good name of Britain abroad. We are beginning to ensure that our nation makes a more worthy contribution to the defence of the West by increasing the pay of the Armed Forces and modernizing military equipment. And we are showing the European Community that we intend to fight Britain's corner as well as, or better than, any Government, while remaining constructive members of the Community.

Then, in Geoffrey Howe's first Budget, we took a major step towards restoring freedom of choice and a sense of responsibility.

We see it as a first duty of responsible Government to re-establish sound money and to squeeze inflation out of the system. So the Budget set a framework of firm monetary discipline and control of the money supply. That meant a limit on public borrowing and strict control over public expenditure. I am afraid it also meant high interest rates for a time, until the measures we have introduced take effect.

This framework of Government financial responsibility needs to be matched by private sector responsibility. Each helps and underpins the other. In particular, employers and trade unions need to understand that this Government will not print money to bail them out if they make irresponsible pay settlements. Higher pay needs to be matched by higher output. If it is not, it will lead only to higher unemployment and higher prices.

One of the great curses of inflation is that the whole nation spends more of its time wrestling with the changing value of money, and arguing about the distribution of incomes and wealth, than it devotes to productive effort and creative management. In industry, in commerce, in house-keeping, inflation means more and more uncertainty; uncertainty about investment, about saving, about incomes, about the timing of spending. In this climate, it is easy to have a grievance, and tempting to try to steal a march on others.

There is no sound foundation for steady expansion unless the country is winning the fight against inflation. That is why the Budget had to do two things. It cut public expenditure and it cut the slice the Government was taking from everyone's pay packet. Too much tax makes people feel poorer and tempts them to make bigger pay claims, especially at a time of low growth. High public expenditure tempts Governments to print money, rather than impose high tax. Both these things – high public .expenditure and high tax – can therefore lead to inflation.

That is why the Budget set out to restore meaning to money, to restore financial responsibility to Government and to give more freedom of choice to the individual.

The Budget cut income tax in three ways. First, we raised the thresholds so as to take 1.3 million people out of tax altogether. Second, we cut the basic rate of income tax from 33 pence to 30 pence in the pound. Together with the improved personal allowances, this gives benefit to millions of taxpayers, and it reduces tax on every extra pound earned. It is an encouragement to effort. And the Chancellor made it clear that our long-term aim was to reduce the basic rate to 25 per cent.

Third, by reducing the top rate of tax on earned income to 60 per cent, we began to restore to the industrious and to the inventive the encouragement they need to work and to create work for others. Nations depend for their health, economically, culturally and psychologically, upon the achievements of a comparatively small number of talented and determined people, as well as on the support of a skilled and devoted majority. It was not possible for many of these talented people to believe that we valued them, and what they could do for our nation, when we maintained penal tax rates, decade after decade, in order to please those who seemed to be motivated mainly by envy. We have given a new sign of appreciation to talent and brought our top tax rates into line with those of other major countries.

Meanwhile, the switch from direct to indirect taxation in the Budget increases freedom of choice. It is also consistent with our view of the importance of the market. We leave people with more of their own incomes and levy more tax on spending. And a smaller reliance on income tax means a smaller advantage to the tax-dodging black economy, and is therefore fairer to income taxpayers, who abide by the rules.

I must make it clear that this Budget provides no justification whatever for higher pay claims. On the contrary, taking account of the income tax reductions, as well as the indirect tax increases, a family on average earnings will be better off over the period between the Budget and the end of the financial year. They will be paying about £2.75 a week more for what they buy ($3\frac{3}{4}$ per cent on the RPI) because VAT has gone up. But they will have about £4 a week more to spend (equal to $5\frac{1}{2}$ per cent on the RPI) because of the income tax reductions. It would be quite wrong, therefore, to base pay claims on the full RPI increase without giving credit for the increased net take-home pay.

So in this Budget we have cut back the amount Government takes from the pay packet; enlarged freedom of choice and signalled encouragement to effort and talent; given incentives to raise living standards; and more than offset the increase in VAT by increased take-home pay. We have done this in spite of major inherited problems. These included inflation already increasing before the election; a sharply rising public deficit; several large post-dated cheques for public sector pay; output of goods actually 4 per cent below the level of 1973; and less than ten months of the financial year in which to correct the situation and to implement reductions in public expenditure.

Since the election we have been examining all other possible measures which we might take in order to accelerate our national revival. During the next year, we will introduce new measures designed, specifically, to encourage effort and enterprise. We will remove some of the regulations and red tape which have accumulated to such an extent that some, who might otherwise have been working to create wealth and employment, gave up in despair. But though leadership can inspire, no Government, by itself, can supply the vital spark which has been removed from this nation. The ideas which will make for better lives for everyone in ten years' time are now in the minds of countless individuals. Many such ideas are locked up there for the moment. If we can create the right national mood, those ideas will flourish.

I believe it is entirely in the interest of the trade union movement to play a major part in this national revival and to put all their great weight behind better national economic performance. Like all of us, their members stand to gain from a stronger, more efficient, more united Britain. We all stand to lose from tactics which make Britain weaker.

It is because part of the trade union movement seems to have lost sight of this that the movement has become unpopular with the electorate, and has lost much of its old moral authority. If some unions continue to act as an engine of inflation, and a drag on improvements in industrial efficiency, they will go on alienating themselves from the people, including those whom they represent. They will go on losing authority – and looking more and more old-fashioned to unions in other more successful countries.

We know that the trade unions as a whole do not want inflation. But sometimes the few set the pace, with claims which bear no relation to increased output. Then the many feel obliged to follow the few and the whole process leads to higher unemployment and inflation. It is a patent contradiction for any who take a leading part in this exercise to urge the Government to treat pensioners more generously, when it is the inflation which they have helped to create that diminishes the value of the pensioners' money. To claim a social conscience in these circumstances can fairly be described as humbug.

I do not believe that this is the approach of the majority of the trade union leaders, still less of their rank-and-file members. I believe they can respond to the opportunity of free but responsible pay bargaining which we offer and intend to pursue. It is greatly in Britain's, and in their, interest that they should do so.

In our actions to renew the vitality and strength of our nation, we are sustained by the knowledge that we ride on the crest of a philosophical tide, which we know to be flowing with us. The new generation of British patriots knows that in emphasizing anew the decisive importance of the rule of law, and in redefining the proper boundaries of the State, they are acting within a Western world where those ideas are, once more, becoming imperative.

Everywhere there is a crisis of Socialism. Everywhere a confirmation that capitalism produces freedom and prosperity. Everywhere there is a demand, we sense, for firm and traditional Government.

My theme here has, as it were, four heads. The first is

articulated by the word 'opportunity' – opportunity for individuals to develop all their talents to the full, and so benefit themselves and others.

The second is expressed by the word 'choice'. Individuals must be able to make up their own minds for themselves, as to the kind of lives which they wish to live. People must be free to choose, if they wish, between wisdom and folly. We are, after all, very different in our skills, temperament, capacity for decision and capacity for courage.

The third theme is summed up in the word 'strength'. We need to be strong enough to protect our people from wreckers at home and enemies abroad, and also to protect our citizens against crime. Weakness leads to ruin. We must be strong enough to insist that the institutions of our nation are refurbished so that we can pass to those who come after us the treasures which we have inherited from those who have gone before.

My fourth theme is expressed well by the word 'renewal'. Here we know that the restoration of the confidence of a great nation is a massive task. We do not shrink from it. It will not be given to this generation of our countrymen to create a great Empire. But it is given to us to demand an end to decline and to make a stand against what Churchill described as the 'long dismal drawling tides of drift and surrender, of wrong measurements and feeble impulses'. Though less powerful than once we were, we have friends in every quarter of the globe, who will rejoice at our recovery, welcome the revival of our influence, and benefit from the message and from the example of our renewal.

Our recovery will give to all the free world a new hope and a new optimism. It will be not only Conservatives, and not only British people, who will then feel able to say with Tennyson:

> *We sailed wherever ship could sail,*
> *We founded many a mighty state,*
> *Pray God our greatness may not fail,*
> *Through craven fears of being great.*

The Conservative Party Conference

BLACKPOOL, 12 OCTOBER 1979

'We have to think in terms of several Parliaments,' Mrs Thatcher told the Conservative Party Conference five months after her accession to power. It was clear from this speech that, while she knew exactly what she intended to accomplish and how her essential objectives were to be attained, the scale of the task inevitably meant that a substantial period of office would be needed to bring the far-reaching process of reform (defined here with considerable precision) to a successful conclusion. Economic change, crucial though it was, would mark but one stage: from 'strong wealth-creating industries' could spring 'a caring, compassionate society'.

Similarly, trade union reform, which was given considerable prominence in this speech, was needed not only to remove a large obstacle to economic progress but also to provide an essential foundation for greater harmony and justice in society as a whole. The chief impression conveyed by this speech was, therefore, that although Thatcherism on the home front was bound initially to be mainly concerned with economic issues, it was certainly not going to be confined to them.

On Thursday, 3 May, we won a great victory. Yes, it was a victory for realism and responsibility. It was also a victory for conviction and commitment – *your* conviction and *your* commitment. And it was a victory for loyalty and dedication – *your* loyalty, *your* dedication.

Through the long years of Opposition you kept faith; and you will, I know, keep faith through the far longer years of Conservative Government that are to come.

An election victory such as ours is impossible without teamwork. It's invidious to single out this or that person for praise. However, one or two special tributes are due.

We owe a tremendous debt to all our agents who did so magnificently.

And I must also thank Lord Thorneycroft. He has been one of the most outstanding Chairmen the Conservative Party has ever had. This year he added another chapter to his memorable record of service to our party and our country.

Finally, I wish to say a personal thank you to someone who was, and is always, there to give strength and authority to our cause, not least in time of trouble. No Leader of a party can ever have been given more sound or more loyal advice than I have had from my friend and deputy, Willie Whitelaw.

The victory to which all of you in this hall gave so much was five years coming, but when it came it was handsome. We won with the largest swing since the war and the largest majority in votes.

I was particularly pleased by the support we attracted: the largest trade union vote in our history; the young people, so many of whom saw no future under Labour and who turned to us; and all those who have voted Labour before and who, this time, voted Conservative.

Winning an election is a splendid thing, but it is only the prologue to the vital business of governing. The work that the new Conservative Government has begun is the most difficult, the most challenging that has faced any administration since the war.

We have not wasted time. Already we have raised the pay of our police and Armed Forces. We have set in hand the sale of council houses and flats. In June we introduced our first Budget. We brought down income tax throughout the scale. We took care to protect the pensioners against inflation: next month's increases will be the largest in cash terms ever paid. And war widows' pensions have been relieved of tax altogether. At last they have received justice.

But all this is only the beginning. For this Government, it's not the first hundred days that count; it's the first five years – and the next five after that. We have to think in terms of several Parliaments. We have to move this country in a new direction – to change the way we look at things, to create a wholly new attitude of mind. Can it be done?

Well, the people have taken the first step by electing us – some with passionate conviction; others, I don't doubt, more in hope than belief, their fingers tightly crossed. I understand their caution. So much has been promised in the past, so much has come to nothing, no wonder they are sceptical. And impatient. Already I can hear some of them saying, 'The Conservatives have been in five months. Things don't seem to be that much better. What's happening. Do you think the Conservatives can really do it?'

Yes, the Conservatives *can* do it. And we *will* do it. But it will take *time*. Time to tackle problems that have been neglected for years; time to change the approach to what Governments can do for people, and to what people should do for themselves; time to shake off the self-doubt induced by decades of dependence on the State as master, not as servant. It will take time – and it will not be easy.

The world has never offered us an easy living. There is no reason why it should. We have always had to go out and earn our living – the hard way. In the past we did not hesitate. We had great technical skill, quality, reliability. We built well, sold well. We delivered. The world bought British and British was best. Not German. Not Japanese. *British*. It was more than that. We knew that to keep ahead, we had to change. People looked to us as the front-runner for the future.

Our success wasn't based on Government handouts, on protecting yesterday's jobs and fighting off tomorrow's. It wasn't based on envy or truculence or on endless battles between management and men, or between worker and fellow-worker. We didn't become the workshop of the world by being the nation with the most strikes. I remember the words written on an old trade union banner: 'United to support, not combined to injure'. That is the way we were.

Today we still have great firms and industries. Today we still make much of value – but not enough. Industries that were once head and shoulders above their competitors have stumbled and fallen. It's said that we were exhausted by the war. Those who were utterly defeated can hardly have been less exhausted. Yet they have done infinitely better in the peace. It's said that Britain's time is up, that we have had our finest hour and the best we can look forward to is a future fit for Mr Benn to live in.

I don't accept these alibis. Of course we face great problems – problems that have fed on each other year after year, becoming harder and harder to solve. We all know them. They go to the root of the hopes and fears of ordinary people: high inflation, high unemployment, high taxation, appalling industrial relations, the lowest productivity in the Western world. People have been led to believe that they had to choose between a capitalist wealth-creating society on the one hand, and a caring compassionate society on the other.

But that is not the choice. The industrial countries that out-produce and out-sell us are precisely those countries with better social services and better pensions than we have. It is because they have strong wealth-creating industries that they have better benefits than we have. What our people seem to have lost is belief in the balance between production and welfare. This is the balance that we've got to find. To persuade our people that it's possible, through their own efforts, not only to halt our national decline, but to reverse it, requires new thinking, tenacity and a willingness to look at things in a completely different way.

Is the nation ready to face reality? I believe it is. People are tired of false dawns and facile promises. If this country's story is to change, then we, the Conservatives, must rekindle the spirit which the Socialist years have all but extinguished.

Do we have the authority? Last month, I was accused of 'waving a phoney mandate'. In a democracy the word 'mandate' does not imply that a voter has read and accepted his party's manifesto from end to end, and so not only knows, but is voting for, everything it contains. It would be absurd if it did.

THE REVIVAL OF BRITAIN

Not everyone who votes for a political party has read everything in its manifesto. Not everyone who votes for a political
party has read anything in its manifesto. But when a voter
makes his decision and slips his paper in the ballot box, he does
know, broadly speaking, what the party of his choice stands for.
In this age of mass communication he can hardly help knowing.

Those who voted Conservative know the principal policies
we stood for and that in voting for us they were voting for those
policies. That was, and is, our mandate. We have every right to
carry it out and we shall. Four economic issues were central to
our Conservative campaign: inflation; public spending; income
tax; and industrial relations.

Now these are not four separate and distinct issues. They are
very closely related. You can't cut tax unless you curb public
spending. For it is *your* tax which pays for public spending: the
Government has no money of its own. Of course, if we *had* the
money, we could all think of good ways to spend it: hospitals
which should have been modernized years ago, more help for
the elderly, the sick, the disabled. But Government in one form
or another already spends nearly half our entire national
income. If Labour's lavish spending solved all problems we
would have no problems left to solve.

And inflation is a major problem which cannot be cured
without curbing public spending. If the Government over-
spends, and borrows or prints money to meet the deficit, then
prices and interest rates will go on rising – that's inflation – and
the poor, and the pensioners, and the young home-buyers will
all suffer. But there are some who think they have a right to
contract out of the effects of inflation, if they are organized in a
powerful union with enough muscle to impose their will on a
suffering public.

What madness it is, that winter after winter we have the
great set-piece battles, in which the powerful unions do so
much damage to the industries on which their members' living
standards depend. The struggles for wage increases disregard
output, profit or any other measure of success. They ignore the
reality that there is an inescapable link between prosperity and
production. Since 1979 began, scarcely a week has passed

without some group calling for higher pay: listening to the chorus of pay demands, you might imagine that a 100 per cent pay rise for everyone in the country would solve all our economic problems. But we all know that the only result would mean doubled prices. No one would have more food, more clothing, more anything.

The key to prosperity lies not in higher pay but in higher output. In 1979 you have all heard endless discussions about pay. How often have you heard similar discussions about how to raise output?

The reason why Britain is today the third poorest nation in the European Community has little to do with pay but it has everything to do with production. We hanker after a West German standard of living. But we fail to recognize that you cannot have a West German standard of living with a British standard of output. The truth is very simple: West German pay plus British output per man equals inflation. And that is exactly what has been happening.

The unions win pay awards their members have not earned: the company pays out increases it can't afford: the prices to the customer go up: Government prints the money to make it all possible, and everyone congratulates it on its success as an honest broker, with or without beer and sandwiches at Number Ten. It has been happening for years. The result has been the most uncompetitive industry, the lowest economic growth rate and the highest rate of inflation in the industrialized world. And in the trade unions the lesson is drawn that militancy paid again, that the company did have the money. It didn't. The Government just printed its way out of trouble – until next time round. This Government wants the greatest possible co-operation with both sides of industry and we will go a long way to get it. But we will not – repeat not – print money to finance excessive pay settlements.

Conquering inflation, controlling public spending and cutting taxes are the first three stages of a long journey. The fourth is to make certain limited, but essential, changes in the law on industrial relations. We have to make these changes in the law because, as we saw last winter, it is out of keeping with the

101

needs of the time. When the trade union movement began, it set out to secure for its members a fair return for their work from employers. Today the conflict of interest is not so much between unions and employers as between unions and the nation, of which trade unionists and their families form a large part. It is the British people who have to bear the brunt of the suffering which strikes impose on society.

We have to bring about a fair and just balance between a man's right to withhold his labour and the determination of a small minority to impose its will upon the majority. As a Government we cannot and will not coerce people, but we can and we must protect people against coercion. And so, before the year is out, we shall introduce legislation concerning secret ballots, secondary picketing and the closed shop. The majority of the unions' own rank and file, so many of whom helped to elect this Government, welcomed our proposals. I hope that the union leaders, who have said that they will work with the elected Government of the day, will accept them too.

The days when only employers suffered from a strike are long since past. Today strikes affect trade union members and their families just like the rest of us. One union can deprive us all of coal, or food, or transport easily enough. What it cannot do is defend its members against similar action by other unions. If schools and hospital wards are closed, if there is no petrol at the pumps, no raw materials on the factory bench, the trade unions are as powerless as the rest of society, and when the bills come in for the stoppage they have to pay up too.

Recently there was a strike which prevented telephone bills from being sent out. The cost of that strike to the Post Office is £110 million. It will have to be paid for by everyone who uses the telephone. This £110 million loss was caused by a strike of only 150 people in a public service. The recent two-days-a-week strike by the Engineering Union lost the industry £2,000 million sales. We may never make up these sales and we shall lose some of the jobs which depended on them. And who will send up a cheer? The Germans, the Japanese, the Swiss, the Americans. So instead of exporting engineering goods, we shall have exported engineering jobs.

I think the nation recognizes – indeed has recognized for a long time – that trade union power is out of balance. That is why people are supporting us in legislating for trade union reform. We place special emphasis on the secret ballot. We believe that the great power wielded by unions calls for greater accountability to their members. And we are particularly concerned about the working of the closed shop. The closed shop, together with secondary picketing, makes it possible for small groups to close down whole industries with which they have no direct connection. Cross the picket line to do your job – and you risk losing both your union card *and* your job.

During the engineers' strike news reached London of a new resistance movement in East Anglia. Whole factories were actually working, but so afraid were the employees of the consequences that they daren't reveal their identity, or that of the company, to the media. Millions of British workers go in fear of union power. The demand for this Government to make changes is coming from the very people who experience this fear. It is coming from the trade unionists themselves. They want to escape from the rule of the militants. We heard it in the conference hall yesterday. They look to us to help them.

Today trade unions have more power over working people and their families than any boss has. Unions can only exist in a free society. Those who seek freedom for their own purposes should not deny that freedom to others.

I have been speaking of the deep and difficult problems of industry – most of it big industry. But the future of this country depends largely on the success of small businesses. I would like to read to you a letter which I have received from a small businessman in the West Midlands. I asked him whether I might read his letter and here it is:

> I thought I would write to you about the profound effect the change of Government has had upon one small businessman. In 1977, at the age of thirty-eight, I was so disillusioned with the Socialist regime and its policies that I could see no future for the small to medium business and sold my company to a large group and virtually retired.
>
> Financially, this was a satisfactory state of affairs, but I yearned

to get back into what I knew best. When your Government was elected, I hoped there would be a change of emphasis and indeed that is what has happened. The letter-head on which I write to you is of a new company which I have formed recently, and the biggest factor in its creation has been the steps which you have taken to restore incentive to work at all levels of the community. Not only can self-employed proprietors of small businesses keep more of the profits of those businesses but, more important, those good and productive employees who are patently worth a high level of wages are also feeling the benefit of more cash in the pocket and it is now worth their while to work that bit harder or longer as the case may be.

He went on:

Please stick to your policy. It is the only way that we shall eventually solve our problems. It may be hard to bear in the short term but I truly believe that the bulk of public opinion is now behind a return to the basic common-sense fact that the country as a whole cannot continue to be paid more and more money for less and less work.

It is small businessmen like this who, given the chance, will provide more jobs and more wealth, and the only Government from whom they will get the chance is this Conservative Government.

So far I have spoken of matters of vital concern to us here at home. But we have important responsibilities overseas as well, particularly Rhodesia. In his speech on Wednesday, Peter Carrington described the progress which has been made in our efforts to bring Rhodesia to independence with the widest possible international recognition. I understand and share your impatience to bring this about. There have been too many wasted opportunities.

It is Britain's responsibility, and Britain's alone, to bring Rhodesia to legal independence. But it is also in Rhodesia's interests that we should bring as many other countries as possible along with us in recognizing an independent Rhodesia.

We undertook to give to Rhodesia the kind of independence constitution which we had given to our other former colonies. Those constitutions had certain fundamental principles in common. Each also contained provisions designed to meet the country's own particular circumstances. The same is true of the constitution under which we are ready to give independence to Rhodesia. Bishop Muzorewa has already accepted that constitution.

It must also be in Rhodesia's interests, and it is an inescapable duty for the British Government, to do everything possible to bring an end to a war which has caused the most cruel suffering. What is the purpose of continuing this war? It cannot be to bring about majority rule; that has already been accomplished. If it is to win power, then those who wish to do so must be prepared to proceed democratically through the ballot box and not through the bullet. At Lusaka the Heads of Government called for free and fair elections, supervised under the British Government's authority. We stand ready to do this.

I think we have some reason to be proud of what has been achieved since Lusaka. I trust that no one will now put that achievement in jeopardy. In view of what has been accomplished on the independence constitution, the time for lifting sanctions cannot be far off. There is no longer any vestige of excuse for the conflict in Rhodesia to continue.

Nearer home in Europe we are part of a Community of some 250 million people. It's no use joining anything half-heartedly. Five months after taking office we have done much to restore the trust and confidence that the last Conservative Government enjoyed with our partners in Europe and the Labour Government did not.

We are a committed member of the Community. But that does not mean that we are content with the way all its policies work. If nothing is done, we are faced in 1980 with the appalling prospect of having to pay £1,000 million more to our European partners than we receive from them, even though we have almost the lowest income per head in the Community. The hard-pressed British taxpayer will not stand for paying still more in order to reduce the tax bills of our wealthier Community partners.

At the European Council in Strasbourg in June, we persuaded the other Heads of Government to agree to tackle this

105

problem. We shall expect to make very real progress at the next European Council at the end of November. I do not under-estimate the problems that face us on the Budget, in fisheries or in reforming the Common Agricultural Policy. But equally we must not underestimate our opportunities as members of the Community. The future of Western Europe is our future too.

What in the end are the objectives of the States which have come to make up the Community? The three most important are: international peace and justice; economic prosperity; freedom under the law.

We in Europe have unrivalled freedom. But we must never take it for granted. The dangers are greater now than they have ever been since 1945. The threat of the Soviet Union is ever-present. It is growing continually. Their military spending goes up by 5 per cent a year. A Russian nuclear submarine is launched every six weeks. Every year the Russians turn out over 3,000 tanks and 1,500 combat aircraft. Their military research and development is enormous. The Soviet forces are organized and trained for attack. The Russians do not tell us why they are making this tremendous and costly effort to increase their military power. But we cannot ignore the fact that this power is there.

So far the North Atlantic Alliance has preserved our freedom. But in recent years the Soviet Union's growing strength has allowed them to pull ahead of the Alliance in many fields. We and our allies are resolved to make the effort that will restore the balance. We must keep up all our defences, whether nuclear or conventional. It is no good having first-class nuclear forces if we can be overwhelmed by an enemy's conventional forces. Deterring aggression cannot be piecemeal. If it is, our effort is wasted.

Recently we and our allies have all become more and more alarmed at the number of modern Soviet nuclear weapons targeted on Western Europe. At the same time, NATO's own nuclear forces in Europe are out of date. We and our friends in NATO will soon have to decide whether to modernize our nuclear weapons. These will be difficult decisions for some of our allies, and we must expect to see the Soviet Union mount a powerful psychological campaign to prevent the Alliance from redressing the balance.

We shall be looking very closely at President Brezhnev's recent speech to see whether it is the opening shot in that campaign or whether it is a genuine attempt to reduce tension in Europe.

Nor will we neglect our conventional forces. Our most precious asset is the men and women who serve in our Forces. We faced a grave situation on taking office. Recruitment was poor, and many of our most skilled and experienced servicemen were leaving the Forces. We immediately restored the pay of the Services to its proper level. We will keep it there. We have also taken steps to encourage the rebuilding of our Territorial Army and other reserve forces. After so much neglect it will take time to put right the weaknesses. None the less we must see that it is done. We owe it to our servicemen and women who give our country such magnificent service.

Nowhere has that service been more magnificent than in Northern Ireland. More than 300 of our servicemen have given their lives there. Their bravery is matched by the courage of the Royal Ulster Constabulary and the prison service.

It is hard to speak of Northern Ireland without emotion. One thinks of Warrenpoint, of Lord Mountbatten, of Airey Neave. To any who seek to advance their cause by violence, and who claim to be soldiers of an army fighting for freedom, let me say, in the words of the Lord Chancellor, Lord Hailsham: 'Such men are not soldiers. They are not an army. They are not fighting for freedom. They are fighting for chaos.'

We who believe in the one true freedom – freedom under the law – far outnumber and outweigh, in the strength of our resolve, those who set out to murder and to maim. No end could justify such means. The British Government is doing everything possible to strengthen the security forces in the fight against the men of violence. Our goal is the same peace for which the Pope appealed so movingly during his visit to Ireland.

To all the people of the Province of Ulster I repeat this pledge: we do not forget you, we will not abandon you. We must, and we will, find a way of restoring to you more control over your own affairs. We must, and we will, find a way to peace for your deeply troubled part of our United Kingdom.

We come to the closing moments of our victory conference. It has been a conference to remember. It was a victory to remember. Throughout most of my life, the chief complaint made against politicians has been that they shrank from telling the truth when the truth was in the least unpleasant or controversial, that they were inclined to woo when it was their duty to warn, to please when it was their business to prophesy. Early in my career, I decided that was one mistake I would not make. My harshest critics will perhaps agree that I have succeeded in that modest ambition; for the complaint they have against me is the opposite one – that I am inclined to speak my mind, even occasionally to nag!

Today, I have again pointed to the dangers as I see them and I have said what I believe the source of those dangers to be. But let us remember that we are a nation, and that a nation is an extended family. Families go through their hard times; they have to postpone cherished ambitions until they have the means to satisfy them. At times like these, the strength of the family is truly tested. It is then that the temptation is greatest for its members to start blaming one another and dissipating their strength in bitterness and bickering. Let us do all in our power to see one another's point of view, to widen the common ground on which we stand.

As we close our conference, a compassionate and united party, I think of last week's events at Brighton. I think of those members of the Labour Party and trade unionists (including some leading ones) who see the movement *they* serve abandoning the ideals to which they have devoted their lives. They do not share our Conservative ideals – at least they think they don't – but they do want free and responsible trade unions to play an honourable part in the life of a free and responsible society. So do we.

I give them my pledge that my colleagues and I will continue to talk to them, to listen to their views, so long as it is understood that national policy is the sole responsibility of

Government and Parliament. In return I would ask every man and woman who is called on in the next few months to take part in disruptive industrial action to consider the consequences for themselves, their children and their fellow-countrymen. Our supreme loyalty is to the country and the things for which it stands.

Let us work together in hope and above all in friendship. On behalf of the Government to which you have given the task of leading this country out of the shadows, let me close with these words: you gave us your trust. Be patient. We shall not betray that trust.

The Conservative Party Conference

BRIGHTON, 10 OCTOBER 1980

*By 1980 there was a quite widespread feeling that Mrs Thatcher was
asking too much of the British people. The painful consequences of
economic change were all too obvious. When deep-seated problems are
allowed to fester (as they had in Britain), the process of reform inevitably
imposes greater strains. Unemployment was now rising sharply as
industries that had been overmanned for years shed their superfluous labour
in order to achieve the efficiency they needed to compete successfully for
markets. In addition, the world recession was taking its toll.*

*At this point Mrs Thatcher came under strong pressure to change the
most fundamental of her economic policies. She answered her critics with
characteristic vigour and force in this speech, underlying her determination
to see her economic strategy through to a successful conclusion. Her
resolution was summed up in a sentence which instantly became famous:
'You turn if you want to. The lady's not for turning.'*

Most of my Cabinet colleagues have started their speeches of
reply by paying very well-deserved tributes to their junior
Ministers. At Number 10 I have no junior Ministers. There is
just Denis and me, and I could not do without him. I am,
however, fortunate in having a marvellous deputy who is
wonderful at all times in all things – Willie Whitelaw.

At our Party Conference last year I said that the task in
which the Government was engaged – to change the national

attitude of mind – was the most challenging to face any British administration since the war. Challenge is exhilarating. This week we Conservatives have been taking stock, discussing the achievements, the setbacks and the work that lies ahead as we enter our second parliamentary year. Our debates have been stimulating and our debates have been constructive. This week has demonstrated that we are a party united in purpose, strategy and resolve. And we actually like one another.

When I am asked for a detailed forecast of what will happen in the coming months or years I remember Sam Goldwyn's advice: 'Never prophesy, especially about the future.'

This week at Brighton we have heard a good deal about last week at Blackpool. I will have a little more to say about that strange assembly later, but for the moment I want to say just this. Because of what happened at that conference, there has been, behind all our deliberations this week, a heightened awareness that now, more than ever, our Conservative Government must succeed. We just must, because now there is even more at stake than some had realized.

There are many things to be done to set this nation on the road to recovery, and I do not mean economic recovery alone, but a new independence of spirit and zest for achievement. It is sometimes said that because of our past we, as a people, expect too much and set our sights too high. That is not the way I see it. Rather it seems to me that throughout my life in politics our ambitions have steadily shrunk. Our response to disappointment has not been to lengthen our stride but to shorten the distance to be covered. But with confidence in ourselves and in our future what a nation we could be.

In its first seventeen months this Government has laid the foundations for recovery. We have undertaken a heavy load of legislation, a load we do not intend to repeat, because we do not share the Socialist fantasy that achievement is measured by the number of laws you pass. But there was a formidable barricade of obstacles that we had to sweep aside. For a start, in his first Budget, Geoffrey Howe began to restore incentives to stimulate the abilities and inventive genius of our people. Prosperity comes not from grand conferences of economists but from countless acts of personal self-confidence and self-reliance.

111

THE REVIVAL OF BRITAIN

Under Geoffrey's stewardship Britain has repaid $3,600 million of international debt, debt which had been run up by our predecessors. And we paid quite a lot of it before it was due. In the past twelve months Geoffrey has abolished exchange controls over which British Governments have dithered for decades. Our great enterprises are now free to seek opportunities overseas. This will help to secure our living standards long after North Sea oil has run out. This Government thinks about the future. We have made the first crucial changes in trade union law to remove the worst abuses of the closed shop, to restrict picketing to the place of work of the parties in dispute, and to encourage secret ballots.

Jim Prior [the Employment Secretary] has carried all these measures through with the support of the vast majority of trade union members. Keith Joseph, David Howell, John Nott and Norman Fowler [Ministers responsible for Industry, Energy, Trade and Transport respectively] have begun to break down the monopoly powers of nationalization. Thanks to them, British Aerospace will soon be open to private investment. The monopoly of the Post Office and British Telecommunications is being diminished. The barriers to private generation of electricity for sale have been lifted. For the first time nationalized industries and public utilities can be investigated by the Monopolies Commission – a long overdue reform.

Free competition in road passenger transport promises travellers a better deal. Michael Heseltine [Secretary of State for the Environment] has given to millions – yes, millions – of council tenants the right to buy their own homes. It was Anthony Eden who chose for us the goal of 'a property-owning democracy'. But for all the time that I have been in public affairs that has been beyond the reach of so many, who were denied the right to the most basic ownership of all – the homes in which they live.

They wanted to buy. Many could afford to buy. But they happened to live under the jurisdiction of a Socialist council, which would not sell and did not believe in the independence that comes with ownership. Now Michael Heseltine has given them the chance to turn a dream into reality. And all this and a lot more in seventeen months.

The Left continues to refer with relish to the death of capitalism. Well, if this is the death of capitalism, I must say that it is quite a way to go. But all this will avail us little unless we achieve our prime economic objective – the defeat of inflation. Inflation destroys nations and societies as surely as invading armies do. Inflation is the parent of unemployment. It is the unseen robber of those who have saved. No policy which puts at risk the defeat of inflation – however great its short-term attraction – can be right. Our policy for the defeat of inflation is, in fact, traditional. It existed long before Sterling M3 embellished the *Bank of England Quarterly Bulletin*, or 'monetarism' became a convenient term of political invective.

But some people talk as if control of the money supply was a revolutionary policy. Yet it was an essential condition for the recovery of much of continental Europe. Those countries knew what was required for economic stability. Previously, they had lived through rampant inflation; they knew that it led to suitcase money, massive unemployment and the breakdown of society itself. They determined never to go that way again.

Today, after many years of monetary self-discipline, they have stable, prosperous economies better able than ours to withstand the buffeting of world recession. So at international conferences to discuss economic affairs many of my fellow-Heads of Government find our policies not strange, unusual or revolutionary, but normal, sound and honest. And that is what they are. Their only question is: 'Has Britain the courage and resolve to sustain the discipline for long enough to break through to success?'

Yes, Mr Chairman, we have, and we shall. This Government is determined to stay with the policy and see it through to its conclusion. That is what marks this administration as one of the truly radical ministries of post-war Britain. Inflation is falling and should continue to fall.

Meanwhile, we are not heedless of the hardships and worries that accompany the conquest of inflation. Foremost among these is unemployment. Today our country has more than two million unemployed.

Now you can try to soften that figure in a dozen ways. You can point out – and it is quite legitimate to do so – that two million today does not mean what it meant in the 1930s; that the percentage of unemployment is much less now than it was then. You can add that today many more married women go out to work. You can stress that, because of the high birth rate in the early 1960s, there is an unusually large number of school leavers this year looking for work and that the same will be true for the next two years. You can emphasize that about a quarter of a million people find new jobs each month and therefore go off the unemployment register. And you can recall that there are nearly twenty-five million people in jobs compared with only about eighteen million in the 1930s. You can point out that the Labour Party conveniently overlooks the fact that of the two million unemployed, for which they blame us, nearly a million and a half were bequeathed by their Government. But when all that has been said, the fact remains that the level of unemployment in our country today is a human tragedy. Let me make it clear beyond doubt. I am profoundly concerned about unemployment. Human dignity and self-respect are undermined when men and women are condemned to idleness. The waste of a country's most precious assets – the talent and energy of its people – makes it the bounden duty of Government to seek a real and lasting cure.

If I could press a button and genuinely solve the unemployment problem, do you think that I would not press that button this instant? Does anyone imagine that there is the smallest political gain in letting this unemployment continue, or that there is some obscure economic religion which demands this unemployment as part of its ritual? This Government is pursuing the only policy which gives any hope of bringing our people back to real and lasting employment. It is no coincidence that those countries, of which I spoke earlier, which have had lower rates of inflation have also had lower levels of unemployment.

I know that there is another real worry affecting many of our people. Although they accept that our policies are right, they feel deeply that the burden of carrying them out is falling much more heavily on the private, than on the public, sector. They say that the public sector is enjoying advantages but the private sector is taking the knocks and at the same time maintaining those in the public sector with better pay and pensions than they enjoy.

I must tell you that I share this concern and understand the resentment. That is why I and my colleagues say that to add to public spending takes away the very money and resources that industry needs to stay in business, let alone to expand. Higher public spending, far from curing unemployment, can be the very vehicle that loses jobs and causes bankruptcies in trade and commerce. That is why we warned local authorities that since rates are frequently the biggest tax that industry now faces, increases in them can cripple local businesses. Councils must, therefore, learn to cut costs in the same way that companies have to.

That is why I stress that if those who work in public authorities take for themselves large pay increases, they leave less to be spent on equipment and new buildings. That in turn deprives the private sector of the orders it needs, especially some of those industries in the hard-pressed regions. Those in the public sector have a duty to those in the private sector not to take out so much in pay that they cause others unemployment. That is why we point out that every time high wage settlements in nationalized monopolies lead to higher charges for telephones, electricity, coal and water, they can drive companies out of business and cost other people their jobs.

If spending money like water was the answer to our country's problems, we would have no problems now. If ever a nation has spent, spent, spent and spent again, ours has. Today that dream is over. All of that money has got us nowhere, but it still has to come from somewhere. Those who urge us to relax the squeeze, to spend yet more money indiscriminately in the belief that it will help the unemployed and the small businessman are not being kind or compassionate or caring. They are not the friends of the unemployed or the small business. They are asking us to do again the very thing that causes the problems in the first place. We have made this point repeatedly.

I am accused of lecturing or preaching about this. I suppose

115

it is a critic's way of saying, 'Well, we know it is true, but we have to carp at something.' I do not care about that. But I do care about the future of free enterprise, the jobs and exports it provides and the independence it brings to our people. Independence? Yes, but let us be clear what we mean by that. Independence does not mean contracting out of all relationships with others. A nation can be free but it will not stay free for long if it has no friends and no alliances. Above all, it will not stay free if it cannot pay its own way in the world. By the same token, an individual needs to be part of a community and to feel that he is part of it. There is more to this than the chance to earn a living for himself and his family, essential though that is.

Of course, our vision and our aims go far beyond the complex arguments of economics, but unless we get the economy right we shall deny our people the opportunity to share that vision and to see beyond the narrow horizons of economic necessity. Without a healthy economy we cannot have a healthy society. Without a healthy society the economy will not stay healthy for long.

But it is not the State that creates a healthy society. When the State grows too powerful, people feel that they count for less and less. The State drains society, not only of its wealth but of initiative, of energy, the will to improve and innovate as well as to preserve what is best. Our aim is to let people feel that they count for more and more. If we cannot trust the deepest instincts of our people, we should not be in politics at all. Some aspects of our present society really do offend those instincts.

Decent people do want to do a proper job at work, not to be restrained or intimidated from giving value for money. They believe that honesty should be respected, not derided. They see crime and violence as a threat not just to society but to their own orderly way of life. They want to be allowed to bring up their children in these beliefs, without the fear that their efforts will be daily frustrated in the name of progress or free expression. Indeed, that is what family life is all about.

There is not a generation gap in a happy and united family. People yearn to be able to rely on some generally accepted standards. Without them you have not got a society at all, you have purposeless anarchy. A healthy society is not created by its institutions, either. Great schools and universities do not make a great nation any more than great armies do. Only a great nation can create and evolve great institutions – of learning, of healing, of scientific advance. And a great nation is the voluntary creation of its people – a people composed of men and women whose pride in themselves is founded on the knowledge of what they can give to a community of which they in turn can be proud.

If our people feel that they are part of a great nation and they are prepared to will the means to keep it great, a great nation we shall be, and shall remain. So, what can stop us from achieving this? What then stands in our way? The prospect of another winter of discontent? I suppose it might.

But I prefer to believe that certain lessons have been learnt from experience, that we are coming, slowly, painfully, to an autumn of understanding. And I hope that it will be followed by a winter of common sense. If it is not, we shall not be diverted from our course.

To those waiting with bated breath for that favourite media catchphrase, the 'U' turn, I have only one thing to say: 'You turn if you want to. The lady's not for turning.' I say that not only to you, but to our friends overseas and also to those who are not our friends.

In foreign affairs we have pursued our national interest robustly while remaining alive to the needs and interests of others. We have acted where our predecessors dithered and here I pay tribute to Lord Carrington. When I think of our much-travelled Foreign Secretary I am reminded of the advert, you know the one I mean, about 'The peer that reaches those foreign parts that other peers cannot reach.'

Long before we came into office, and therefore long before the invasion of Afghanistan, I was pointing to the threat from the East. I was accused of scare-mongering. But events have more than justified my words.

Soviet Marxism is ideologically, politically and morally bankrupt. But militarily the Soviet Union is a powerful and growing threat.

117

Yet it was Mr Kosygin who said, 'No peace-loving country, no person of integrity, should remain indifferent when an aggressor holds human life and world opinion in insolent contempt.' We agree. The British Government are not indifferent to the occupation of Afghanistan. We shall not allow it to be forgotten. Unless and until the Soviet troops are withdrawn, other nations are bound to wonder which of them may be next. Of course there are those who say that by speaking out we are complicating East–West relations, that we are endangering *détente*. But the real danger would lie in keeping silent. *Détente* is indivisible and it is a two-way process.

The Soviet Union cannot conduct wars by proxy in South-East Asia and Africa, foment trouble in the Middle East and Caribbean and invade neighbouring countries and still expect to conduct business as usual. Unless *détente* is pursued by both sides it can be pursued by neither, and it is a delusion to suppose otherwise. That is the message we shall be delivering loud and clear at the meeting of the European Security Conference in Madrid in the weeks immediately ahead.

But we shall also be reminding the other parties in Madrid that the Helsinki Accord was supposed to promote the freer movement of people and ideas. The Soviet Government's response so far has been a campaign of repression worse than any since Stalin's day. It had been hoped that Helsinki would open gates across Europe. In fact, the guards today are better armed and the walls are no lower. But behind those walls the human spirit is unvanquished.

The workers of Poland in their millions have signalled their determination to participate in the shaping of their destiny. We salute them. Marxists claim that the capitalist system is in crisis. But the Polish workers have shown that it is the Communist system that is in crisis. The Polish people should be left to work out their own future without external interference.

At every Party Conference, and every November in Parliament, we used to face difficult decisions over Rhodesia and over sanctions. But no longer. Since we last met the success at Lancaster House, and thereafter in Salisbury – a success won in the face of all the odds – has created new respect for Britain. It has given fresh hope to those grappling with the terrible problems of Southern Africa. It has given the Commonwealth new strength and unity. Now it is for the new nation, Zimbabwe, to build her own future with the support of all those who believe that democracy has a place in Africa, and we wish her well.

We showed over Rhodesia that the hallmarks of Tory policy are, as they have always been, realism and resolve. Not for us the disastrous fantasies of unilateral disarmament, of withdrawal from NATO, of abandoning Northern Ireland.

The irresponsibility of the Left on defence increases as the dangers which we face loom larger. We for our part, under Francis Pym's brilliant leadership [as Defence Secretary], have chosen a defence policy which potential foes will respect.

We are acquiring, with the co-operation of the United States Government, the Trident missile system. This will ensure the credibility of our strategic deterrent until the end of the century and beyond, and it is very important for the reputation of Britain abroad that we should keep our independent nuclear deterrent, as well as for our citizens here.

We have agreed to the stationing of Cruise missiles in this country. The unilateralists object, but the recent willingness of the Soviet Government to open a new round of arms control negotiations shows the wisdom of our firmness.

We intend to maintain and, where possible, to improve our conventional forces so as to pull our weight in the Alliance. We have no wish to seek a free ride at the expense of our allies. We will play our full part.

In Europe we have shown that it is possible to combine a vigorous defence of our own interests with a deep commitment to the idea and to the ideals of the Community. The last Government was well aware that Britain's budget contribution was grossly unfair. They failed to do anything about it. We negotiated a satisfactory arrangement which will give us and our partners time to tackle the underlying issues. We have resolved the difficulties of New Zealand's lamb trade with the Community in a way which protects the interests of the farmers in New Zealand while giving our own farmers and our own housewives an excellent deal, and Peter Walker [Minister of Agriculture] deserves to be congratulated on his success. Now he is two-thirds of his way to success in making important progress towards agreement on a common fisheries policy. That is very important to our people. There are many, many people whose livelihoods depend on it.

We face many other problems in the Community, but I am confident that they too will yield to the firm yet fair approach which has already proved so much more effective than the previous Government's five years of procrastination.

With each day it becomes clearer that in the wider world we face darkening horizons, and the war between Iran and Iraq is the latest symptom of a deeper malady. Europe and North America are centres of stability in an increasingly anxious world. The Community and the Alliance are the guarantee to other countries that democracy and freedom of choice are still possible. They stand for order and the rule of law in an age when disorder and lawlessness are ever more widespread.

The British Government intends to stand by both these great institutions, the Community and NATO. We will not betray them.

The restoration of Britain's place in the world, and of the West's confidence in its own destiny, are two aspects of the same process. No doubt there will be unexpected twists in the road, but with wisdom and resolution we can reach our goal. I believe we will show the wisdom, and you may be certain that we will show the resolution.

In his warm-hearted and generous speech, Peter Thorneycroft [the Party Chairman] said that when people are called upon to lead great nations they must look into the hearts and minds of the people whom they seek to govern. I would add that those who seek to govern must in turn be willing to allow their hearts and minds to lie open to the people.

This afternoon I have tried to set before you some of my most deeply held convictions and beliefs. This party, which I am privileged to serve, and this Government, which I am proud to lead, are engaged in the massive task of restoring confidence and stability to our people.

I have always known that that task was vital. Since last week it has become even more vital than ever. We close our conference in the aftermath of that sinister Utopia unveiled at Blackpool. Let Labour's Orwellian nightmare of the Left be the spur for us to dedicate with a new urgency our every ounce of energy and moral strength to rebuild the fortunes of this free nation.

If we were to fail, that freedom could be imperilled. So let us resist the blandishments of the faint hearts; let us ignore the howls and threats of the extremists; let us stand together and do our duty, and we shall not fail.

St Lawrence Jewry

CITY OF LONDON, 4 MARCH 1981

Mrs Thatcher confirmed her abiding interest in the relationship between politics and religion when she returned to St Lawrence Jewry to deliver a second speech on the subject. On this occasion she reflected on the values and beliefs which, in her view, had given Britain its distinctive national character. Because they were deeply rooted in the Christian religion, they had created a country in which great importance was attached both to individual personal responsibility and to the welfare of society as a whole. So in Britain 'we must never think of individual freedom and the social good as being opposed to each other'. Those who strove to make the nation richer ought not to be condemned, but praised. 'Creating wealth must be seen as a Christian obligation if we are to fulfil our role as stewards of the resources and talents the Creator has provided for us.' Outrage should be reserved for matters such as inflation which damaged the whole of society.

This speech contains a particularly full and clear statement of the underlying moral principles on which Thatcherism rests. By implementing policies derived from them, Mrs Thatcher argued, it would be possible 'to establish in the minds of young and old alike a national purpose which has real meaning for them'. In that task the Church could play a vital part by insisting on high ethical standards, but the functions of Government would always lie with the State alone.

Today is Ash Wednesday, the day when traditionally Christians begin a period of thoughtfulness about their re-

122

lationship with God and how they are trying to serve Him here on earth. It is therefore fitting that on this occasion we consider some of the things which have made our nation flourish in the past and some of the challenges we face today.

My theme will be that the virtue of a nation is only as great as the virtue of the individuals who compose it.

Two years ago, in this church, I spoke as both a Christian and a politician about how I found my religious convictions affecting the way I approached the responsibility of Government. Since then I have been, as it were, called to higher service! My approach to my present responsibilities remains the same as it was then, and I am indeed thankful that I was brought up in a Christian family and learnt the message of the Christian faith.

This afternoon, I want to consider some of the characteristics of our way of life which have stood our people in such good stead in times past.

John Newton preached a sermon exactly 200 years ago in a City church only a step away from this one. In the course of it he said: 'Though the occasion will require me to take some notice of our public affairs, I mean not to amuse you with what is usually called a political discourse.' I too, Rector, will endeavour to keep to this self-denying ordinance.

The concept of the nation is at the heart of Old Testament Judaism and one which those who wrote the New Testament accepted. But there is an even more fundamental idea which is also common to both – the idea of personal moral responsibility. It is to individuals that the Ten Commandments are addressed. In the statements, 'Honour thy father and thy mother', 'Thou shalt not steal', 'Thou shalt not bear false witness', and so on, the 'thou' to whom these resounding imperatives are addressed is you and me.

In the same way, the New Testament is preoccupied with the individual, with his need for forgiveness and for the Divine strength which comes to those who sincerely accept it. Of course, we can deduce from the teachings of the Bible principles of public, as well as private, morality; but, in the last resort, all these principles refer back to the individual in his relationships to others. We must always beware of supposing that somehow we can get rid of our own moral duties by handing them over to the community; that somehow we can get rid of our own guilt by talking about 'national' or 'social' guilt. We are called on to repent our own sins, not each other's sins.

Therefore each person is all-important in the Christian view of life and the universe. But human beings have social needs as well. So it is that, in the course of history, the family, the neighbourhood and the nation come into being. All these communities have certain things in common. However they grew up, they are held together by mutual dependence, by the experience which their members have in common, by common customs and belief.

They all need rules to enable them to live together harmoniously, and the rules must be backed by some kind of authority, however gently and subtly exercised. The nation is but an enlarged family. Because of its traditions, and the mutual love and loyalty which bind its members together, it should ideally need little enforcement to maintain its life. But alas, because of man's imperfection, evil is ever-present, and the innocent must be protected from its ravages.

So the first, and in a sense the most important, point I have to make to you is this. We must never think of individual freedom and the social good as being opposed to each other; we must never suppose that where personal liberty is strong, society will be weak and impoverished, or that where the nation is strong the individual will necessarily be in shackles. The wealth of nations, the defence of national freedom, and the well-being of society, all these depend on the faith and exertions of men and women. It is an old and simple truth, but it is sometimes forgotten in political debate.

But what of the common beliefs and habits which hold this British nation of ours together? There was, of course, a time when the Christian religion was the only permitted form of worship in our land. Today we live in what is called a 'plural society', one in which many different traditions of belief exist alongside each other and also alongside other more recent fashions – those of total disbelief or even nihilism. No doubt we have absorbed much from other systems of belief and contributed much to them. The change, however, has also brought its dilemmas, not least for the legislator.

We now have to concern ourselves not only with how Christians should behave towards each other within the framework of the nation, but with how they should seek to organize the nation's life in a way that is fair and tolerant towards those who do not accept the Christian message. What I am suggesting to you today, however, is that even though there are considerable religious minorities in Britain, most people would accept that we have a national way of life and that it is founded on biblical principles.

As we emerged from the twilight of medieval times, when for many life was characterized by tyranny, injustice and cruelty, so we became what one historian [J.R. Green] has described as 'the people of a book and that book was the Bible'. What he meant, I think, was that this nation adopted, albeit gradually, a system of Government and a way of living together which reflected the values implicit in that Book. We acknowledged as a nation that God was the source of our strength and that the teachings of Christ applied to our national, as well as our personal, life. There was, however, a considerable gap between the precept and the practice. Even when men had become free to speak for themselves, to invent, to experiment and to lay the foundations of what became known as the Industrial Revolution, considerable blotches remained on the canvas of our national life.

It took the vision and patience of men like Lord Shaftesbury, and William Wilberforce, to convince Parliament that it was inconsistent for a nation whose life was based on Christ's teachings to countenance slave labour, children and women working in the mines, and criminals locked up in degrading conditions. These leaders were motivated first and foremost by their Christian beliefs. It is also significant that most of the great philanthropists who set up schools and hospitals did so because they saw this as part of their Christian service for the people of the nation. Indeed, something of that same vision can be seen today. Wherever there are refugees, or suffering or poverty in the world, there you find Christians working to relieve pain, to provide comfort, hope and practical help.

The spirit of our nation also includes some clear convictions about such things as fair play, which we regard as almost a religion in itself, and bullying, which we loathe. Perhaps Kipling put it best in one of his poems called 'Norman and Saxon' set in AD 1100:

> 'My son,' said the Norman Baron. 'I am dying, and you will be heir
> To all the broad acres in England that William gave me for my share
> When we conquered the Saxon at Hastings, and a nice little handful it is.
> But before you go over to rule it I want you to understand this:—
> The Saxon is not like us Normans. His manners are not so polite.
> But he never means anything serious till he talks about justice and right.
> When he stands like an ox in the furrow with his sullen set eyes
> on your own,
> And grumbles, "This isn't fair dealing," my son, leave the Saxon alone.'

This sense of fair play is based on the acceptance by the majority in the nation of some moral absolutes which underpin our social and commercial relationships. In other words, we believe that just as there are physical laws which we break at our peril, so there are moral laws which, if we flout them, will lead to personal and national decline. If we as a nation had accepted, for instance, that violence, stealing and deception were plausible activities, then our moral fibre would soon have disintegrated.

There is one other characteristic of our nation which is, I think, worth mentioning: we have always had a sense that work is not only a necessity, it is a duty, and indeed a virtue. It is an expression of our dependence on each other. Work is not merely a way of receiving a pay packet but a means whereby everyone in the community benefits and society is enriched. Creating wealth must be seen as a Christian obligation if we are to fulfil our role as stewards of the resources and talents the Creator has provided for us.

These characteristics of our nation, the acknowledgement of the Almighty, a sense of tolerance, an acknowledgement of moral absolutes and a positive view of work have sustained us in the past. Today they are being challenged. Although we are still able to live on the spiritual capital passed down to us, it is self-deceiving to think we can do so for ever. Each generation must renew its spiritual assets if the integrity of the nation is to survive.

Today, in spite of the work of the churches, I suspect that only a minority acknowledge the authority of God in their lives. Perhaps that is why we have turned to the State to do so many things which in the past were the prerogative of the family; why crimes of violence are increasing, and a few people are even suggesting that murder can be justified on the grounds that it is political – a view which must be abhorrent to Christians. Furthermore, the respect for private and public property seems to be diminishing, and outside this City we can no longer assume that a man's word is always his bond.

In terms of ethics and national economics, I should like also to refer to what I believe is an evil, namely sustained inflation. For over thirty years the value of our currency has been eroding. It is an insidious evil because its effects are slow to be seen and relatively painless in the short run. Yet it has a morally debilitating influence on all aspects of our national life. It reduces the value of savings, it undermines financial agreements, it stimulates hostility between workers and employers over matters of pay, it encourages debt and it diminishes the prospects of jobs. This is why I put its demise at the top of my list of economic priorities. It is, in my view, a moral issue, not just an economic one.

The second and equally great human and economic problem is the level of unemployment, which has been rising for over two decades and is still rising. I cannot conceal that of all difficulties I face, unemployment concerns me most of all. Leaving aside world recession and the details of economic policies necessary to defeat inflation (which would be the subject of a political discourse) what can we as individuals do to help?

None of us can opt out of the community in which we live. Whether we do something or nothing, our actions will affect it. First, those who are in work must fully accept their duty to provide for those who cannot find work. Second, if we are employers we can try to take on as many young people as

127

possible, to give them experience of the world of work. There are a number of schemes available for this purpose, and I must say that employers are responding splendidly. They, too, know how depressing it must be for a young person to feel that he is not needed and cannot find a niche for himself.

Third, we could perhaps buy more British-made goods. Not *everything* British-made, because there are jobs in exports, too, and we expect others to buy *our* goods – but we could help our people by buying more 'home-made' products. Fourth, we can recognize that if at a time when output is not rising we ourselves demand more pay, it can only come from the pockets of others, and it will reduce the amount they can spend on other goods. That kind of pay claim can price your own job out of existence, or cause someone else to lose his job. And that responsibility cannot be shirked – it is a *personal* responsibility. It is a *moral* responsibility.

There is another factor which affects us at present. It is a sense of pessimism brought on because of the frustrations of not seeming to have a national purpose. When this happens to a nation, groups within it tend to work towards their more limited goals, often at the expense of others. This pessimism is expressed in two ways. There are those who want to destroy our society for their own purposes – the terrorists and other extremists that we all too frequently see in action these days. Then there are those who adopt a philosophy of 'eat, drink and be merry, for tomorrow we die'. That can result in a grasping of wealth for its own sake and the pursuit of selfish pleasure.

If I am right, we need to establish in the minds of young and old alike a national purpose which has real meaning for them. It must include the defence of the values which we believe to be of vital importance. Unless the spirit of the nation which has hitherto sustained us is renewed, our national way of life will perish. Who is to undertake this task? Throughout history it has always been the few who took the lead; a few who see visions and dream dreams: there were the prophets in the Old Testament, the Apostles in the New, and the reformers in both Church and State. I well remember hearing a sermon after the Battle of Britain in which this was said about the few pilots to whom so many owed so much. John Stuart Mill once said that 'one person with a belief is a social power equal to ninety-nine who have only interests'. If we as a nation fail to produce such people then I am afraid the spirit of the nation, which has hitherto sustained us, will slowly die.

What then are the institutional means by which these values can be revived – for ideas and sentiments need institutions if they are to survive and be effective? Because we are talking primarily of the values bequeathed to us by a predominantly Christian culture, we must think first of the role of the Church.

The Church, thought of as the bishops, clergy and laity organized for public worship, has clear duties of its own – to preach the Gospel of Christ, to celebrate the Sacraments and to give comfort and counsel to men and women struggling with the trials and dilemmas of life. Politicians must respect and accept its authority in these spheres. In our own country the State pays homage to the Church in many ways. The Queen is Supreme Governor of the Church of England and Protector of the Church of Scotland. These arrangements may seem to many to be antiquated, but they express the State's fundamental respect for the Christian religion. I hope we shall never see here what we have seen in other countries – temporal Governments trying to usurp the role of spiritual leadership which properly belongs to the Church. That is a recipe for State tyranny as well as the corruption of religion.

The Church, on the other hand, can never resign altogether from what are called temporal matters. It has always rightly claimed to set before us the moral standards by which our public affairs should be conducted. But I hope you will forgive me for stating what I think these days needs to be pointed out, namely the difference between defining standards and descending into the political arena to take sides on those practical issues over which many good and honest Christians sincerely disagree. This, surely, can only weaken the influence and independence of the Church whose members ideally should help shape the thinking of all political parties. Bernard Shaw, in his preface to *Androcles and the Lion*, makes the breathtaking statement 'Christ was a first-class political economist', but it was Christ himself who said of those who were too preoccupied with material things, 'Seek ye first the kingdom of God and his righteousness, and all these things shall be added unto you.' I wonder if some people are not demanding that 'things be added unto them' *before* they seek the kingdom of God, indeed regardless of whether they seek it or not.

As for the role of the State (what the Bible calls 'the things that are Caesar's'), I have never concealed my own philosophy. I believe it is a philosophy which rests on Christian assumptions, though I fully recognize that some Christians would have a different view. To me the wisdom of statesmanship consists of: knowing the limits within which Government can, and ought to, act for the good of the individuals who make up society; respecting those limits; ensuring that the laws to which the people are subject shall be just and consistent with the public conscience; making certain that those laws are firmly and fairly enforced; making the nation strong for the defence of its way of life against potential aggression; and maintaining an honest currency. Only Governments can carry out these functions, and in these spheres Government must be strong.

But (and here we come back to the point from which we started today) every one of these objects depends for its achievement on the faith and the work of individuals. The State cannot create wealth. That depends on the exertions of countless people motivated not only by the wholesome desire to provide for themselves and their families, but also by a passion for excellence and a genuine spirit of public service.

The State cannot generate compassion; it can and must provide a 'safety net' for those who, through no fault of their own, are unable to cope on their own. There is need for far more generosity in our national life, but generosity is born in the hearts of men and women; it cannot be manufactured by politicians, and assuredly it will not flourish if politicians foster the illusion that the exercise of compassion can be left to officials. And so, I repeat, it is on the individual that the health of both Church and State depends.

Perhaps we have lost the idea that is inherent in Christ's parable of the talents. The steward who simply did not use the resources entrusted to him was roundly condemned. The two who used them to produce more wealth were congratulated and given more. To put up with the mediocre, to flinch from the challenge, to mutter 'the Government ought to be doing something about it', is not the way to rekindle the spirit of the nation.

What should we conclude about the relationship between the individual and the nation? I make no secret of my wish that everyone should be proud of belonging to this country. We have a past which, by any standard, is impressive; much in our present life and culture, too, commands great respect. We have as a nation a sense of perspective and a sense of humour; our scholars win international acclaim, our Armed Forces are renowned for their bravery and restraint, and our industries, in spite of economic recession, continue to do well in the markets of the world.

I want us to be proud of our nation for another reason. In the comity of nations, only a minority have a system of Government which can be described as democratic. In these, economic and cultural life flourish because of the freedom their people enjoy. But a democratic system of Government cannot be transferred to other nations simply by setting up imitations of our institutions – we have realized this all too clearly in recent times. For democracy to work, it requires what Montesquieu described as a special quality in the people: virtue, and, I would add, understanding. I believe this quality of virtue to be that derived from the biblical principles on which this nation, and the United States, among others, are founded.

I want this nation to continue to be heard in the world and for the leaders of other countries to know that our strength comes from shared convictions as to what is right and wrong, and that we value these convictions enough to defend them.

Let me sum up. I believe the spirit of this nation is a Christian one. The values which sustain our way of life have by no means disappeared but they are in danger of being undermined. I believe we are able to generate the will and purpose to revive and maintain them. John Newton put it elegantly in the sermon to which I earlier referred. 'Though the Island of Great

THE REVIVAL OF BRITAIN

Britain exhibits but a small spot upon a map of the globe, it makes a splendid appearance in the history of mankind, and for a long space of time has been signally under the protection of God and a seat of peace, liberty and truth.' I pray we may continue to receive such blessing and retain such qualities.

TO

The Scottish
Conservative Party Conference

PERTH, 8 MAY 1981

As a strong Unionist, Mrs Thatcher has always been determined to ensure that Scotland's interests are properly safeguarded. That means, of course, that Thatcherism north of the border has to be adapted and refined to take account of the distinctive features of Scottish life. Nowhere has this been more evident than in economic policy, with which Mrs Thatcher was mainly concerned in this speech. At the same time, it was by pursuing the same basic approach in Scotland as she followed elsewhere, that Mrs Thatcher ensured that it benefited fully from the dramatic improvement in the economy which was then about to begin. By 1983 average earnings, for example, were higher in Scotland than in any other region except the South-East of England.

Scotland has always had close links with Northern Ireland. Mrs Thatcher devoted one section of this speech to the IRA's terrorist campaign which, at that time, was being pursued chiefly by means of a hunger strike at the Maze prison. One suicide had already occurred, and nine others were to follow before this particular phase of the IRA's activities came to an end the following October. Mrs Thatcher referred to this matter in the uncompromising terms she has always used when confronted by terrorism.

This great gathering in Perth, drawing together as it does men and women from every walk of life and every constituency across the length and breadth of Scotland, comes just two years after the first meeting of this Parliament. So today I want to

133

take stock with you; to chart our progress and our disappointments; and then to set our goals for the years that lie ahead. For my purpose this afternoon is to lay before you our strategy for the next election when it comes in two or three years' time.

Two years ago we inherited a nation wracked by domestic strife. Our predecessors' vaunted 'Social Contract' had collapsed in social discord. Essential public services to the old, the sick and the disabled were disrupted by the ruthless pursuit of narrow sectional self-interest. The nation's ability to defend itself in an increasingly dangerous world had been undermined by years of neglect. The morale of our police force, and its capacity to protect the citizen on the streets and in the home, had been sapped by the absence of support from Government. In the European Community, sulking had brought us nothing more tangible than contempt and isolation. Prices, steadied briefly by the intervention of our international creditors, were fast accelerating. Post-dated cheques to buy a temporary pre-election respite from industrial strife filled every departmental in-tray which awaited us. We could not go on that way, and we haven't.

We have lost less time through strikes than we have for a generation. We can now regain our markets. We have given the priority which we pledged to give to national defence, and we have acted swiftly to restore the morale of our police. Every police force in Scotland has been expanded, and all save one today are up to strength or better. Notwithstanding the vital need to curb our over-spending, we have increased resources for defence, and we are proud to give a lead to the whole Alliance. We have brought peace and international recognition to Rhodesia after fifteen years of frustrated effort. We have got a far fairer distribution of the European Budget – not by obstruction and hostility, but by combining a whole-hearted commitment to the European purpose with a stout defence of our national interest within it. We have restored rewards for effort and achievement by cutting those very high levels of taxation which destroyed incentive and offered little return to the Exchequer. They only gave satisfaction to those obsessed with envy.

134

We have attacked some of the worst abuses of trade union power by giving rights of appeal and compensation to the victims of vindictiveness and by restricting the right to picket. We have offered every union the chance to practise the democracy they too often only preach, by consulting the membership in secret ballot. In the Nationality Bill we are now engaged on a long-overdue redefinition of the privilege of British citizenship. For, as I have told our friends abroad, we, and we alone, must have the right to define our own nationality. Last – but in my book first, for without it all we seek to achieve for this nation would be at risk – we are making steady progress towards stability of prices and the restoration of sound money.

I do not seek to shroud our disappointments. In one part of the United Kingdom a challenge to the rule of law, to democracy itself, is being mounted. It is no comfort to us to know that a similar challenge is being mounted in other European countries. In Germany, France, Italy and Spain, groups whose only mandate is their fanaticism, backed by bullet and bomb, have been seeking to replace the ballot box as the means by which civilized communities resolve their differences.

In Northern Ireland, the Provisional IRA have, of late, extended their criminal violence from the streets of Belfast and Londonderry, and from the fields of Armagh, into the prison cell. One of their members has chosen to kill himself – a needless and futile waste of his life. I say 'futile', Mr President, because the political status sought by the hunger strikers will not be granted. The Government's position is clear. Crime is always crime, whatever the motive. Murder is never anything other than murder.

It is argued that the Government has been intransigent. It has not. In the months before the first hunger strike began, last autumn, we implemented a series of justified changes for all prisoners. The conditions in prisons such as the Maze are now as humane as those anywhere in the world. We have respected, and will continue to respect, the views of the European Commission for Human Rights. One is bound to wonder about the motives of those who choose to ignore all we have done.

135

It is argued that we should take political initiatives in Northern Ireland. We have. The Secretary of State for Northern Ireland has done everything in his power to try to build up political institutions acceptable to all sides of the community in the Province. But that community cannot be coerced into accepting such institutions if it does not want them. We are not in the business of replacing one form of instability by another. There can be no short cuts.

Our commitment to Ulster is clear. So long as the majority of the people of Northern Ireland wish to remain part of this Kingdom, that wish will be upheld and defended. However long and hard the road may be, the Government will not flinch from their duty. We recognize, of course, that our neighbours south of the Border, the Republic of Ireland, are concerned about the situation in the North. That is why over the last year and more we have joined in an effort to improve the relationship between London and Dublin. We both have much to gain from working more closely together.

Above all, we have an overriding and shared interest in securing peace and reconciliation in Northern Ireland. If that prize is to be won, the challenge of terrorism must be resisted and turned back. The challenge will be resisted patiently – for we shall not be provoked into over-reaction. It will be resisted with scrupulous legality – for any other way lies anarchy. It will be resisted effectively – for we shall commit whatever resources are necessary to ensure that violence does not succeed.

Let me, Mr President, pay tribute here to the work in Northern Ireland of the Royal Ulster Constabulary, the Ulster Defence Regiment, and the Army. Their performance in recent days, as always, has been beyond praise. Eventually the challenge from the terrorists will be defeated. For no one should doubt that the Government and people of this country have the resolve and stamina to make certain that in the United Kingdom the gun shall not prevail over the will of the people.

Another deep disappointment is the toll of unemployment. Enforced idleness is a personal tragedy. The Welfare State has taken the harsh edge of deprivation from redundancy, and all of us who are at work must, and do, accept the obligation to

136

contribute through our taxes to the help of those less fortunate than ourselves. But no amount of cushioning can take away the loss of a purpose to our lives which comes when businesses in which we work have closed, or been forced to make redundancies. It is hardest of all when businesses collapse through no fault of their own.

We are not going to rid Scotland or Great Britain of the scourge of unemployment by mouthing empty slogans. If full employment could be delivered on a conveyor-belt from the Cabinet we should never have had half a million out of work at one time in the 1950s, or a million out of work at one time in the 1960s, let alone a million and a half in idleness at the very moment in the 1970s when the present Leader of the Opposition was said to be in charge of full employment policy. A Government which genuinely cares about the frustration of the dole queues owes to the unemployed a proper diagnosis of the reasons why the jobs have gone; and how real ones can be created.

First, we have to recognize that what has happened here in Scotland has been happening right across the world. For twenty-five years after the Second World War the real costs of power to turn the wheels of industry were getting cheaper year by year. Thus was sustained one of the longest periods of expansion in our recent history. But the inevitable correction, when it came, was sharp. In 1973, and again in 1979, the oil price increase brought a massive shift of wealth from industrial countries which spend their income through trade to other countries that can't. The easy sellers' market of the 1950s and 1960s suddenly gave place to fierce competition for the shrunken custom which was all the world could offer, after paying for its oil.

But for us in Britain, the shock was doubly severe. For over the years we had sought to compensate for lost competitiveness by debasing the coinage. Many still lost their jobs: but many more remained on payrolls where they were not really needed. That was possible – albeit at increasing cost – so long as international trade was booming. When the boom was over, that option was no longer open to us.

And successive Governments had regularly deferred the painful decisions where they could. Take the steel industry, for example. It was quite obvious that by the time the last Government took office: 'There would have to be a rationalization of steel. If it had been done earlier, there would have been fewer closures and less unemployment. We have not done the Welsh valleys' – or the West of Scotland, I might add – 'any favours by holding back.' That's not my assessment – although I'm certain that it's true. That is the assessment of a senior Cabinet Minister in the last administration.

Redundancies that had been deferred have come upon us all at once. And the loss of jobs has been multiplied again because we've tried to pay ourselves to meet our expectations, and not what firms we worked in could afford. In five short years we doubled money wages – but we only added 2 per cent to the volume of the goods that we produced. The balance came in dearer prices – but it also came from cash that should have gone to new equipment and to servicing investment. That, in a nutshell, is why *our* unemployment has been so extra harsh. We saved our living standards – our jobs we could not save.

This is where so many jobs have gone. The world condition, our own past errors and short-sightedness, the rigidities of our labour market, all have played their part. We simply cannot buy those jobs back with extra public spending. That is what we have tried to do so often in the past, and with less and less success. As we know only too well, the printed money so created didn't increase output, but it did increase prices. As my predecessor once explained to *his* Party Conference a few years back, spending our way out of recession is not an option that any longer exists.

That is why we had, albeit reluctantly, to call on our people to bear some tax increases in Geoffrey Howe's latest Budget. Of course we would have had it otherwise. But partly because of the severity of the recession, and partly because of the poor performance of the nationalized industries and over-spending by local Government, there were extra bills to be met. By insisting that these extra bills were honestly accounted for from increased revenues, we were able to cut interest rates to the benefit of our industries and agriculture.

Productive industry *is* responding. We *are* winning orders at home and abroad in the face of all that international competition can throw at us. Let me remind you of just one or two of the orders won for Scotland in the last six months alone. N.E.I. Peebles: transformers worth £1½ million for Kuwait. Kelvin Diesels: marine engines worth £7 million for Burma. John Brown Engineering: gas turbines worth £13½ million for Brunei, £9½ million for Oman, and £35 million for Iraq. Babcock Power: boilers worth £60 million for Hong Kong. Caledonian Airmotive: a contract worth £2.3 million for the overhaul of aero-engines for West Germany. Anderson Strathclyde: machinery worth £8 million for Romania, and £2 million for the USA. Redpath de Groot Caledonian: an oil platform worth £35 million for Norway.

Did you know that last year, notwithstanding all the problems of an exchange rate riding high, and dear money at home, we increased our sales of drilling bits to the oilfields of the world by 6 per cent in volume? Of office machinery by 10 per cent? Of high-quality woollen and cashmere textiles by 28 per cent? And of electronic micro-circuitry by no less than 75 per cent in a single year? All of them products in which Scotland is proving its ability to beat the world.

Later this year I look forward to opening a new factory at Renfrew in which the Howden Group is investing £6 million to make gas circulators for the nuclear power stations at Torness and Heysham. Meanwhile down the Tay from here, Timex is tooling up with a £12 million investment to produce the world's first 3D camera for the retail market, while another 1,000 jobs are due at the same factory in Dundee with work upon another world-beater – the first genuinely pocket-sized TV. Further up the coast at Aberdeen, there is the John Wood Group. Ten years ago this was a small fishing and ship repair business earning less than £600,000 a year. Last autumn they won a £13 million order from Shell for North Sea work. Or Christian Salvesen of Edinburgh: £61 million ploughed back into the business over the past five years; 1,600 houses built and sold for private homes in Scotland.

I could go on. But every single one of these achievements – and many others that I have not mentioned – have one thing in common. They mean jobs for Scotland. Jobs which earn their keep. Jobs which make a real and a lasting contribution to the national balance sheet. Jobs which help to pay for better living standards, and better services for all our people, in the years to come. Jobs won not by Government purchase and therefore extra tax on successful Scottish businesses, but by the resource, the perseverance, and the aggressive salesmanship of Scottish firms and Scottish people. More power to their elbow!

Oh yes, I know, we have recently been told by no less than 364 academic economists that such things cannot be, that British enterprise is doomed. Their confidence in the accuracy of their own predictions leaves me breathless. But having myself been brought up over the shop, I sometimes wonder whether they back their forecasts with their money. For I can't help noticing that those who have to do just that – the investing institutions which have to show performance from their judgement – are giving us a very different message. Unless the stock markets have got it very wrong we are in for a dramatic recovery in the profitability of British industry in the months ahead.

Now I know that to our opponents this is just about irrelevant. The Leader of the Opposition apparently thinks we shall get more mileage out of marching. Not for him the microchip. Not even the wheel. He offers us the pedestrian revolution. Left Foot forward. Others have more sinister ambitions. They have no time for Parliamentary democracy. They look to the manipulators of the black vote: the tiny caucuses which plot and scheme to win power through apathy. Power in a party which is so desperately vulnerable because, unlike ours, it has no mass membership. Power over unions where the mass membership – voluntary and involuntary – has to battle to be heard against the barriers artificially erected to genuine participation. Power for one purpose: to impose upon this nation a tyranny which the peoples of Eastern Europe yearn to cast aside.

Some, in desperation, have departed to launch new formations of their own – formations which agree on anything, save what their actual policies ought to be. Others remain to fight again the battles with the Marxists that they have lost so many times before. But I doubt if we dare confide the defence of Parliamentary democracy to those who, not so long ago, did not hesitate to join hands to blockade the streets outside Grunwick to deny to others their democratic right to go to work. Or to those who prefer posturing in the streets before the television cameras to attendance at debates on employment in the Parliament to which they were elected.

We in the Conservative Party have better things to do: to help the nation build upon the recovery which is now upon us. There are those who say that the new spirit in British industry will fade and vanish as the order books improve: that we shall be back to the bad old ways of restrictive practices and irresponsible wage bargaining. I do not believe it. And I will tell you why. The evidence of our eyes and ears, as well as every survey taken over many years, has shown that the overwhelming majority of the working population longs to be released from the tyranny too often exercised by handfuls of the militants. The fear of reprisal held them back. But in recent months they have found it possible to defy the militants: and the earth has not opened up beneath their feet. They have cast aside their fetters. They are not going to submit tamely to that yoke again simply because the industrial prospect shows improvement.

This is crucial: for it is only by matching French or German productivity that Scotland will catch up once more with French and German living standards. We in Government are determined to build upon that progress, and we will use all the measures open to us to bring new profitable investment to Scotland from across the globe. During the last twelve months George Younger and his team helped create almost 50,000 new jobs by putting your taxes to work in partnership with private enterprise. In the last six months alone not far short of £30 million has been pumped into new plant and new machinery with the active support and involvement of your Scottish Ministers. And let me assure you that with George Younger beside us, none of us in Cabinet is allowed to forget for one moment the potential and priorities of Scotland.

But you, too, have your part to play. We need your help as local electors and ratepayers to insist on better housekeeping from the town halls and the regional headquarters. It can be done: and the figures prove it. This spring Tory-controlled Scottish district councils raised their rates by $14\frac{1}{2}$ per cent, and Tory-controlled regional councils raised their rates by 23 per cent. That is far too much. And you and we will expect them to do better in future. But look at Labour. Labour regions and districts raised their rates by 39 and 40 per cent respectively. Such extravagance is totally unnecessary: and we have got to bring it under better control. For rate increases of 30 or 40 per cent are nothing more than an attack on local jobs. Firms cannot pay them. They move elsewhere, or go under. They do not have a vote in local government elections. But their voice *must* be heard – before it is too late. You have a most important debate tomorrow on rating reform; and I have asked Malcolm Rifkind to report to me personally on your views on this subject, which I know will be expressed with your customary Scottish zeal.

We also need your help to alert people in Scotland to the new rights and opportunities opened up for them by this Government. We have given to every parent in Scotland, for the first time in our history, the *right* to a proper say in the schooling of his or her own children. We have given to every council tenant the *opportunity* to become the owner of the family home. Already since the last election 25,000 Scottish families have availed themselves of this opportunity or are in the process of so doing. And let me assure you that we shall not allow Socialist councils to flout the law and stand in their tenants' way. George Younger has the powers to enforce the law where there is wilful obstruction – and he will not hesitate to use them. But all of us in the Tory Party have a duty to ensure that our neighbours are fully aware of these new-found rights and opportunities, and of how to take advantage of them.

Building upon recovery also has an international dimension. When I travel abroad in your name it is no longer as a suitor or a supplicant. Instead I make a point of telling the leaders of the nations that I visit how British industry can, and will, perform. We seek no special favours: by the same token I am determined to see we get equal treatment. Where others resort to unfair trading practices, we have not hesitated to take action to prevent damage to British industry, and we shall take action in similar circumstances in the future. But that is light years removed from a retreat into blinkered protection. Do those who urge us to put up the shutters to international trade realize that a higher proportion of our jobs depend on exports than in almost all the other major trading nations – including West Germany, Japan and the United States? Free trade is a vital national interest to the British people, which we simply dare not put at risk.

Similarly, within the European Community we shall continue to insist on fair treatment. It is not acceptable to us, for example, that those of our partners who have drained their own coastal waters by over-fishing should now be free to lay waste the waters around our shores. In George Younger and Alick Buchanan-Smith, the fishermen of Scotland have tireless champions. They have the united backing of the whole Cabinet for their insistence that the fisheries policy of the Community must reflect in full the substantial contribution of our inshore fleet to the total European catch. And where national aids give artificial advantages to producers in one or other of the Member Countries, we must pursue our own national interests as we did last week with the subsidy on fuel for our glasshouse growers.

But it's precisely because the determination of this Government to make a success of the European Community is undoubted, that we are in a strong position to insist upon the recognition of our national interests within it. We cannot – we really cannot – put up to two-fifths of our trade in jeopardy by stalking out in feeble protest. Indeed, I don't believe our opponents, whatever they may be saying to try and save their seats and faces from the lunatic Left, would ever dare to do so. What I fear is that if the electorate were ever unwise enough to give them the opportunity, they would do what they did last time – exasperate our partners and achieve nothing for ourselves.

Nor is it only from the European Community that they say they would withdraw. They are even more impatient to deprive us of the ultimate means of national self-defence. Now I wholly understand the generosity of spirit which leads some of our young people in particular to campaign for nuclear disarmament. I share their aspirations. If I believed there was any serious chance of the old men of the Kremlin responding in a similar spirit of generosity, I would be the first to join them. Sadly, experience tells us otherwise. After years of patient, step-by-step negotiation of mutual arms reductions – negotiations in which the West has, time and again, gone to the limit of prudence in taking promises of Russian performance on trust – Russian tanks rolled into Afghanistan. Two years later a bitter and bloody battle between the Afghan resistance and the invaders still continues.

Of course, I would rather spend the nation's resources and its taxes on schools and hospitals than on nuclear armaments. But the best schools in the world would be of little value to our children if we were unable to shield them from the imposition of an alien and tyrannical system by the hand of foreign conquest. That's the reality which has led successive Governments, under every single one of my predecessors since the war, to conclude that until we can win comprehensive international agreement on nuclear disarmament, we must maintain the effectiveness of our own national nuclear shield. That is the reality which led that Socialist and patriot, Nye Bevan, to warn his party not to 'send him naked into the conference chamber'. I find it tragic that Mr Bevan's erstwhile comrades and disciples should now turn their backs upon that warning. Perhaps the only fitting comment came from one member of the Shadow Cabinet who warned the other day that the first act of another Labour Government would be to reimpose exchange controls. It would need to be.

I have dwelt this evening upon your Government's material priorities: to restore the value and stability of our coinage; to clear the road ahead for industrial recovery and progress; to defend our commercial interest; to shield our national security. I make no apology for that. With your encouragement, your loyalty, and your support – and nothing is possible without them – I look forward to leading you into the battle for the renewal of our mandate when the moment comes against a background of more stable prices than we have known for a generation, of industrial peace and rising output, of shrinking dole queues and more moderate taxation. I believe that we shall be able to tell the electorate with good reason that the performance which our continental neighbours have achieved in turn, but which has so often eluded us, is at long last in our grasp.

But I did not join the Tory Party nearly forty years ago merely because I thought it best equipped to mind the shop – although I certainly did think that, and have not changed my mind (looking at our opponents, who would?). I joined the Tory Party above all because I saw in it an overriding commitment to the tradition of service to the community and the family.

More than thirty years have passed since the post-war creation of the Welfare State. We all have a duty to help others. Our tragedy is that because our performance as a trading nation was poor for so long, we were unable to achieve the standard of provision which is now commonplace among our more successful continental partners. Yet there is also an insidious danger about the Welfare State, for all its merits. It is that we offload upon the State our obligations as good neighbours. That when we've paid our rates and taxes to provide suitable accommodation for the elderly, suitable treatment for the sick, and suitable schooling for the young, we have done our stuff. But we haven't.

The community in which the elderly are consigned to comfortable isolation, and forgotten; in which the sick are nursed and yet remain unvisited; and in which standards of performance and behaviour in the young are deemed too much trouble for their parents to attend to – such a community has no right to call itself caring or compassionate. For caring and compassion are, in the end, personal and not collective virtues.

The State can provide the X-rays, the blackboards and the underfloor heating. It can't provide an ever-present human ear to listen or a human voice to comfort and console.

Over the years the high ideals of personal service and private duty have been all too often sneered at in this country. The helping hand has been scorned as 'charity'; commitment to the family derided as 'old-fashioned'; respect for the police attacked as 'authoritarian'; even loyalty to the nation itself demeaned as 'out of date'. Yet in the hearts of our people these true sources of our nation's inner strength lived on, longing and waiting for their chance to be heard and respected once again. That chance has come: and this party, which has never wavered in its commitment to old virtues tried and true, is proud to set them out upon the high ground. Let us go to it together.

The Conservative Party Conference

BLACKPOOL, 16 OCTOBER 1981

1981 was a time of critical importance for Thatcherism. It was the year when 364 economists published a letter declaring that 'present policies will deepen the depression, erode the industrial base of our economy and threaten its social and political stability'. Quite simply they, like a whole host of other less well-informed commentators and politicians, wanted the Government – which had just cut its borrowing further in the April Budget – to start increasing its spending and borrowing in the hope of boosting output and employment. Mrs Thatcher knew it was a vain hope. As she said in this speech, when that method of tackling unemployment (which had been used time and again since the war) had last been tried by the Labour Government, 'all the extra money went into wages and prices and not into more jobs'.

Neither the clamour in the press and amongst politicians, nor the appearance of a new political challenge in the shape of the SDP/Liberal Alliance, would therefore lead her to change course. The policies from which she had consistently refused to depart had been explained and justified on a number of previous occasions, but never perhaps with more confidence and assurance than in this speech. Her tone reflected a clear conviction that her firmness would soon be vindicated. Indeed, the signs of success were already becoming apparent, as she told her audience: large orders were at last being won by British business, nationalized industries were being liberated from State control, and the property-owning democracy was on the march. It was, as Mrs Thatcher indicated, the

*beginning of a revival which would, by the end of the year, be well
established. By standing firm in 1981, Mrs Thatcher made it possible for
Britain to embark on a period of economic growth which has continued ever
since – creating the extra wealth that has enabled the Government to regain
respect for Britain abroad and to raise public spending on health and
social services at home to record levels. This speech, therefore, marked the
end of the first phase of Thatcherism. Without its success, other subsequent
achievements would have been impossible.*

This week in Blackpool we have had the grand assize of the
nation. Once more the Conservative Party has demonstrated
that it is the party of all the people. We are not here to
manipulate millions of block votes in some travesty of
democracy; nor were we drawn here by the tinsel glamour of a
marriage of convenience. We are here as representatives of a
myriad of different interests from every constituency in the
land. We are here because we share a deep and abiding concern
for the future of our country and our party.

There has been strenuous discussion and dissent. I welcome
it. For years as our conference has assembled I have grown used
to the charge that we are bland and anodyne, careful to avoid
differences. I do not think that that is a charge that can be
levelled at us this year. We have witnessed here this week a
party conscious of its awesome responsibilities as Government
at an immensely difficult time, difficult not only for us but for
many other countries in the world as well, for we are not alone
in our problems. The diversity of our party is not a source of
weakness; it is a part of our strength, for it is a reflection of the
personal commitment that each one of us brings to the task that
lies ahead. Let me say at once that I am glad that Ted Heath
addressed our conference and delighted that he will be helping
us in the Croydon by-election.

Our country is weathering stormy waters. We may have
different ideas on how best to navigate but we sail the same
ocean and in the same ship. This afternoon I want to draw
together what seem to me to be the main strands of your
wisdom and advice to the Government and to express some of
your worries. First among these is the deep and heartfelt

concern for the personal hardship and waste reflected in every factory closure and redundancy. I learnt from childhood the dignity which comes from work and, by contrast, the affront to self-esteem which comes from enforced idleness. For us, work was the only way of life we knew, and we were brought up to believe that it was not only a necessity but a virtue.

The concern of this conference is focused on the plight of the unemployed. But we seek not only to display and demonstrate that concern, but to find and pursue those policies which offer the best hope of more lasting jobs in future years. To do that we must learn the lessons of the past in order to avoid the mistakes that led to the increase of inflation and unemployment in the first place. Today's unemployment is partly due to the sharp increase in oil prices; it absorbed money that might otherwise have gone to increased investment or to buying the things which British factories produce. But that is not all. Too much of our present unemployment is due to enormous past wage increases unmatched by higher output, to union restrictive practices, to overmanning, to strikes, to indifferent management, and to the mistaken belief that, come what may, the Government would always step in to bail out companies in difficulty. No policy can succeed that shirks those basic issues.

We have to earn our living in a world which can choose between the goods we produce and those of other countries. The irony is that many of our people spend five days of the week making British goods and on Saturday go out and spend their earnings on goods produced abroad, goods made in countries which have embraced more modern technology and where management and workforce understand that they are on the same side.

Unemployment is the most emotional issue in our country, and however much we may explain what has led to it, we cannot alter the fact that many people who worked loyally and well for firms up and down the country feel bruised and resentful when, after long and devoted service, they suddenly find themselves without a job. I understand this – I would feel the same. But that would make it even more inexcusable if any Minister, let alone the Prime Minister, were to deceive them with false hopes or spurious remedies. We are dealing with one of the most complex and sensitive problems of our time and neither rhetoric nor compassion is enough, and demonstrating will not help either.

There have been many voices in the past few weeks calling on us to spend our way back towards a higher level of employment and to cut interest rates at the same time. It is a familiar treatment, and it has been tried by many different Governments these past thirty years.

In the early days it worked well enough. In the 1950s a few million pounds of what we learnt to call reflation earned a swift reward in jobs and output. But as time went on the dose required grew larger and the stimulus achieved grew less. By the 1960s it was needing hundreds of millions of extra spending to lift some hundreds of thousands of our people back into employment. By the 1970s we found that after thousands of extra millions had been spent we still had unemployment at levels which, ten or twenty years before, would have been unthinkable. The trick had been tried too often. The people, as earners and consumers, had rumbled what the Government was doing to their money. They knew the Government was creating inflation and they took that into account in their wage demands. So all the extra money went into wages and prices and not into more jobs.

So today, if we were to heed the calls to add another thousand million pounds to our plans for spending we might thereby create an extra 50,000 jobs in two years' time and even those would be all too swiftly cancelled out by the loss of other jobs in private industry as the result of what we had done.

The fact is that a good chunk of the higher taxes and the higher interest rates needed to find the money for the extra spending would come from the tills of every business in the land. 'Ah,' but we are told, 'don't put up the taxes or the interest rates – put them down instead.' In other words, 'print the money'. That way, I must tell you, lies a collapse of trust in sterling both at home and abroad; lies the destruction of the savings of every family. It would lead to suitcase money and penury as the sole reward for thrift. That is not what this Government was elected to do.

But these problems are not peculiar to Britain. Governments all over the world are seeking to borrow on a scale hitherto unknown, and that is why interest rates in every major financial centre have been rising steeply. Indeed, if we had been members of the European Monetary System we might very well have found our interest rates going up long before this September.

That is why it is not a question of choosing between the conquest of inflation and the conquest of unemployment. Indeed, as one of our speakers reminded us yesterday, we are fighting unemployment by fighting inflation. Of course there are those who promise success without tears. I wish they were right. Who more than the Prime Minister would benefit from an easy answer to our troubles? If there were a way of beating inflation and unemployment by displeasing no one in the meantime I should take it like a shot. I can tell you unhesitatingly that if I thought Britain could solve her problems more easily, if I found that world conditions opened up a less rugged road, I should not hesitate to take it. There would be no question of sticking doggedly to so-called dogma. I do not want to prove anything, except that Britain can once again succeed and that all of us can share in the fruits of that success.

But I cannot bow to the pressures to take a route which I know will lead us even further from that prospect. That is not obstinacy. It is sheer common sense. The tough measures that this Government have had to introduce are the very minimum needed for us to win through. I will not change just to court popularity. Indeed, if ever a Conservative Government starts to do what it knows to be wrong, because it is afraid to do what it is sure is right, then is the time for Tories to cry 'Stop'. But you will never need to do that while I am Prime Minister.

In the teeth of international competition British business is beginning to win the major orders that for too long went elsewhere. £1,000 million of British goods are sold abroad every week. In the last month alone Standard Telephones has won the £170 million contract for a telephone cable right across the Pacific from Australia to Canada – the longest contract that has ever been put out to tender. British Steel has gained contracts worth £70 million in the North Sea and across the world in Hong Kong. The Davy Corporation leads the international consortium to build the £1,250 million steelworks for India. Foster Wheeler has started work on a £140 million petrochemical plant in Greece. Great international companies like Texas Instruments, Hewlett Packard and Motorola are demonstrating their faith in Britain's future by choosing this country under a Conservative Government as the main location for their expansion.

This is the way to get extra jobs – thousands of extra jobs for Britain. That is the real recovery. And it is happening now. We are winning through.

These are the headline-catching stories, but every bit as important to this Government is the health of the many small and thrusting businesses. We have already taken some sixty measures of direct practical help for small businesses. Indeed, our business start-up scheme is one of the most radical and effective in the Western world. Ten thousand new businesses are starting every month. From them will come so much of the new and lasting employment of the future. I salute their work and their enterprise and we all wish them well.

But yes, I know. You have said it all week. Private business is still being held to ransom by the giant monopolist nationalized industries. And you are right. They do not price themselves on to the dole queues. They do that to other people. They do not have to match the competition. They have captive markets at their beck and call. While free enterprise prices are going up in single figures, prices in the nationalized industries are going up by 20 per cent.

The fact is that only when we introduce the spur of competition in the State-owned industries do they begin to respond to the needs of the customer. That is why, for example, Norman Fowler, when he was at the Ministry of Transport, stripped away the veto powers of British Rail on bus coach licences. If you can travel now from Manchester to London or from Edinburgh to Bristol by road or rail at fares lower than when we took office, that is thanks to Norman Fowler, just as it is thanks to Freddie Laker that you can cross the Atlantic for so much less than it would have cost you in the early 1970s. Competition works.

You heard Patrick Jenkin [Industry Secretary] speak of companies as different as Cable and Wireless and British Transport Hotels. I never thought that we should be able to make so much progress with denationalization in these first two and a half years. And I can assure you that there will be more of these measures in the next session of Parliament. If this is dogmatism, then it is the dogmatism of Mr Marks and Mr Spencer, and I'll plead guilty to that any day of the week.

But the thought does sometimes occur to me that if only we had never had all those nice Labour moderates – the sort that now join the SDP – we should never have had these problems in the first place. For it was the Labour moderates who nationalized those industries. They are the guilty men. And they have now shacked up with David Steel – although I do not think that Mr Gladstone would have put it in quite those words. The Liberal Leader seems to have quite a passion for pacts, associations, understandings and alliances – a sort of man for all fusions. But, of course there is nothing wrong with pacts, provided they are based on a broad identity of principle. But without any genuine common ground, parties that cannot advance on their own two feet tend to be trodden on by their partners.

The marriage is for one election only. After that either party can call it a day and go its separate way. Well, of course, nothing is for ever. But it is an odd couple that pencils in a date for divorce before they have even sat down to the wedding breakfast. Perhaps the caution is understandable. Little is known about the SDP, except that its four leaders were senior members of Labour Cabinets of the 1960s and 1970s. And if the country is in difficulty today, they played their part in bringing that difficulty about. And they have not repudiated their Socialism. Mr Jenkins may remark that, good Lord, he has not used the word 'Socialism' for years, but he has not disowned it. Nor have his former Cabinet colleagues, the other leaders of the new party, whom the Liberals are being asked to embrace.

153

THE REVIVAL OF BRITAIN

At a time of growing danger for all who cherish and believe in freedom, this party of the soft centre is no shield, no refuge and no answer. As Quintin Hailsham said so vividly a few days ago, 'In a confrontation with the politics of power, the soft Centre has always melted away.' And when the soft centre SDP has melted away, we are left with the hard shell of the Labour Party.

And make no mistake, the leadership of the Labour Party wants what it has always wanted, the full-blooded Socialism that has been the driving force and purpose of its political life and leadership. Mr Wedgwood Benn says that 'the forces of Socialism in Britain cannot be stopped'. They can be, and they will be. We shall stop them. We shall stop them democratically, and I use the word in the dictionary sense, not the Bennite sense. What they cannot be is half-stopped, least of all by those who for years helped to nurture and support them.

Some of the most important things in life are beyond economics. Last Sunday I visited the victims of the IRA bomb outrage in Chelsea, the kind of outrage that has occurred time and again in Northern Ireland. After seeing the injured children and young soldiers, the heartbreak of their parents and wives, one began to count one's blessings. For their world had been suddenly and cruelly shattered by the bombers and terrorists who are the enemies of civilized society everywhere.

We are all in it together, because a breakdown of law and order strikes at everyone. No one is exempt when the terrorists and the bully-boys take over. We look to the police and to the courts to protect the freedom of ordinary people, because without order none of us can go about our daily business in safety. Without order fear becomes master, and the strong and the violent become a power in the land. This was why the first action after the riots in Brixton and Toxteth was to restore order. Nothing, but nothing, could justify the violence that we saw that week.

I listened to every word of the debate on Tuesday. You made your views absolutely plain. Much as we are doing to support the police and uphold the rule of law, you urge us to do even more. I will give you this pledge. Above all other things this

Government is determined to maintain order and uphold the Queen's peace. Order depends upon discipline, overwhelmingly upon self-discipline. It is lamentable that the virtues of self-discipline and self-restraint that mark a mature democracy have lately been so little preached in some homes and schools that they have become so poorly practised in our society.

It is when self-discipline breaks down that society has to impose order. It is in this sense that we Conservatives insist that Government must be strong – strong to uphold the rule of law, strong to maintain order, strong to protect freedom. This was the truth which our ancestors know well, but which some of our generation have managed to unlearn. What is freedom if it does not include freedom from violence and freedom from intimidation?

One of the most revealing things about the rhetoric of the Left is the almost total absence of any reference to the family. Yet the family is the basic unit of our society and it is in the family that the next generation is nurtured. Our concern is to create a property-owning democracy and it is therefore a very human concern. It is a natural desire of Conservatives that every family should have a stake in society and that the privilege of a family home should not be restricted to the few.

The fact that over 55 per cent own their own homes is a tribute to successive Conservative Governments, each one of whom has helped to build the property-owning democracy. It is now our turn to take a major step towards extending home ownership to many who, until now, have been deliberately excluded. Councils, particularly Socialist councils, have clung to the role of landlord. They love it, because it gives them so much power. So, more than two million families have seen themselves paying rent for ever. Petty rules aid restrictions and bring enforced dependence. Those are the marks of this last vestige of feudalism in Britain. It is the arrogance of the Socialist creed to insist that they know best. For them, equality of opportunity means their opportunity to make sure that everyone else is equal.

Nowhere is this more true than in education. For every family the chance to give your children a better start than you

155

had is one of the greatest joys. Yet we have been so obsessed with the reorganization of education and with buildings and equipment that we have failed to concentrate on the quality and content of what is taught in our schools. This is precisely what is of greatest concern to parents, and that is why this Government has given them so much more say in the way schools are run, so much more choice in which school to pick for their children, so much more responsibility for the next generation.

But the best schools, and the best housing, and the best education will avail us nothing if we lack the means or the resolve to defend the way of life of our people. For abroad, this is a time of danger. We face in the Soviet Union a Power whose declared aim is to 'bury' Western civilization. Experience has taught us that threats such as we now face do not disappear unless they are met calmly and with ingenuity and strength. We cannot defend ourselves, either in this island or in Europe, without a close, effective and warm-hearted alliance with the United States. Our friendship with America rests not only on the memory of common dangers jointly faced and of common ancestors. It rests on respect for the same rule of law and representative democracy. Our purpose must be not just to confirm but to strengthen a friendship which has twice saved us this century.

Had it not been for the magnanimity of the United States, Europe would not be free today. Nor would the peace have been kept in Europe for what is now thirty-six years. Assuming we hold this peace for eight more years, we shall then have enjoyed a longer time free from European war than for two centuries. What a triumph for the Western Alliance.

One thrust of Soviet propaganda is concerned to persuade the world that the West, and the United States in particular, is the arms-monger, not the Soviet Union. Nothing could be further from the truth. But it is not surprising that the Russians have found a ready audience, for none of us has any illusions about the horror of nuclear war and we all shrink from it. However, that should force us to consider what is the most likely way of securing peace. It is precisely because I believe that the unilateralists make war more likely that I seek another way.

Should we more easily get the Soviet side to the table to negotiate disarmament if we ourselves had already renounced nuclear weapons? Why should they negotiate if we had already laid down our arms? Would they follow our example? There are no unilateralists in the Kremlin. Until we negotiate multilateral disarmament we have no choice but to retain sufficient nuclear weapons to make it clear to any would-be aggressor that the consequences of an attack on us would be disastrous for them.

To those who want us to close down the American nuclear bases in this country, let me say this. We in Britain cannot honourably shelter under the American nuclear umbrella and simultaneously say to our American friends, 'You may defend our homes with your home-based missiles, but you may not base those missiles anywhere near our homes.' The cost of keeping tyranny at bay is high but it must be paid, for the cost of war would be infinitely higher and we should lose everything that was worth while.

It is in this dangerous world that Britain must live. She cannot escape it or retreat into an island bunker. Yet that is precisely what the Labour Party proposes. It has become the 'get out' party – to get out of our defence obligations, get out of our Nato nuclear commitments, and get out of the European Community.

It is in European affairs that the contrast with the Conservatives is particularly marked. When in power Labour did nothing to improve the European Community. In two and a half years this Government has slashed our budget contribution and set the Community on the road to far-reaching reform.

It is vital that we get it right. Forty-three pounds out of every £100 we earn abroad comes from the Common Market. Over two million jobs depend on our trade with Europe, two million jobs which will be put at risk by Britain's withdrawal. And even if we kept two-thirds of our trade with the Common Market after we had flounced out – and that is pretty optimistic – there

157

would be a million more to join the dole queues. That is only the beginning.

American and Japanese firms are coming to this country to build factories and provide jobs for us, so that they can sell to the whole of Europe. If we came out, future investors would not come here. They would go to Germany, France or Greece. Even those who are already here would not be satisfied with a market of fifty million 'cabin'd, cribb'd and confined' by import controls, customs duties and tariffs. They would up sticks and away. They would take their investment, their expansion and their jobs into the rest of Europe.

For the unspoken assumption behind policies of withdrawal from the Community and unilateral disarmament is that others will continue to bear their burdens and pick up ours as well. Others would continue to accept our products, even though we refused to accept theirs, others would continue to ensure the defence of Europe and provide a shield behind which we would shelter.

What a contemptible policy for Britain. Nothing is beyond this nation. Decline is not inevitable. They say I'm an optimist. In this job you get called all sorts of things. An optimist is one of the nicer ones and I would not deny the label. I remember what our country used to be like and I know what we can become again. But first we must rid ourselves of the idea that the laws of economic gravity can somehow be suspended in our favour and that what applies to other nations does not apply to ours.

We must finally come to accept what in some ways we have not accepted since the war: that although then we, with superb defiance, helped the free world to survive, the world has not since then, and on that account, owed us a living.

We in the Conservative Party know that you cannot get anything for nothing. We hold to the firm foundation of principle, grounded in common sense, common belief and the common purpose of the British people; the common sense of a people who know that it takes effort to achieve success; the common belief in personal responsibility and the values of a free society; the common purpose that is determined to win through the difficult days to the victory that comes with unity.

This Government, this Government of principle, is seeking the common consent of the people of Britain to work together for the prosperity that has eluded us for so long. There are those who say our nation no longer has the stomach for the fight. I think I know our people and I know they do.

Conservative Rally

CHELTENHAM, 3 JULY 1982

The deep and lasting impression which the Falklands War made on Mrs Thatcher emerges clearly from the speech she delivered at Cheltenham when victory had been won. The note that she struck was nationalist in the best sense of the term. Her concern was not to glorify Britain's achievement, but (much more constructively) to try and incorporate permanently in British life the spirit of common purpose that had developed during the conflict. Like Churchill before her, she saw clearly how bonds forged during war could strengthen a society at peace – particularly by helping to diminish industrial unrest. Such sentiments spring directly from one-nation Toryism.

Today we meet in the aftermath of the Falklands Battle. Our country has won a great victory and we are entitled to be proud. This nation had the resolution to do what it knew had to be done – to do what it knew was right.

We fought to show that aggression does not pay, and that the robber cannot be allowed to get away with his swag. We fought with the support of so many throughout the world: the Security Council, the Commonwealth, the European Community, and the United States. Yet we also fought alone – for we fought for our own people and for our own sovereign territory.

Now that it is all over, things cannot be the same again, for we have learnt something about ourselves – a lesson which we desperately needed to learn. When we started out, there were the waverers and the faint-hearts: the people who thought that Britain could no longer seize the initiative for herself; the people who thought we could no longer do the great things which we once did; and those who believed that our decline was irreversible – that we could never again be what we were. There were those who would not admit it – even perhaps some here today – people who would have strenuously denied the suggestion but – in their heart of hearts – they too had their secret fears that it was true: that Britain was no longer the nation that had built an Empire and ruled a quarter of the world.

Well, they were wrong. The lesson of the Falklands is that Britain has not changed and that this nation still has those sterling qualities which shine through our history. This generation can match their fathers and grandfathers in ability, in courage, and in resolution. We have not changed. When the demands of war and the dangers to our own people call us to arms – then we British are as we have always been – competent, courageous and resolute.

When called to arms – ah, that's the problem. It took the battle in the South Atlantic for the shipyards to adapt ships way ahead of time; for dockyards to refit merchantmen and cruise liners, to fix helicopter platforms, to convert hospital ships – all faster than was thought possible; it took the demands of war for every stop to be pulled out and every man and woman to do their best.

British people had to be threatened by foreign soldiers and British territory invaded and then – why then – the response was incomparable. Yet why does it need a war to bring out our qualities and reassert our pride? Why do we have to be invaded before we throw aside our selfish aims and begin to work together as only we can work, and achieve as only we can achieve?

That really is the challenge we as a nation face today. We have to see that the spirit of the South Atlantic – the real spirit of Britain – is kindled not only by war but can now be fired by peace.

We have the first prerequisite. We know we can do it – we

haven't lost the ability. That is the Falklands Factor. We have proved ourselves to ourselves. It is a lesson we must not now forget. Indeed, it is a lesson which we must apply to peace just as we have learnt it in war. The faltering and the self-doubt has given way to achievement and pride. We have the confidence and we must use it.

Just look at the Task Force as an object lesson. Every man had his own task to do and did it superbly. Officers and men, senior NCO and newest recruit – every one realized that his contribution was essential for the success of the whole. All were equally valuable – each was differently qualified. By working together, each was able to do more than his best. As a team they raised the average to the level of the best and by each doing his utmost together they achieved the impossible. That's an accurate picture of Britain at war – not yet of Britain at peace. But the spirit has stirred and the nation has begun to assert itself. Things are not going to be the same again.

All over Britain, men and women are asking – why can't we achieve in peace what we can do so well in war? And they have good reason to ask. Look what British Aerospace workers did when their Nimrod aeroplane needed major modifications. They knew that only by mid-air refuelling could the Task Force be properly protected. They managed those complicated changes from drawing-board to airworthy planes in sixteen days – one year faster than would normally have been the case. Achievements like that, if made in peacetime, could establish us as aeroplane makers to the world.

That record performance was attained not only by superb teamwork, but by brilliant leadership in our factories at home, which mirrored our forces overseas. It is one of the abiding elements of our success in the South Atlantic that our troops were superbly led. No praise is too high for the quality and expertise of our commanders in the field.

Their example, too, must be taken to heart. Now is the time for management to lift its sights and to lead with the professionalism and effectiveness it knows is possible. If the lessons of the South Atlantic are to be learnt, then they have to be learnt by us all. No one can afford to be left out. Success depends upon all of us – different in qualities, but equally valuable.

During this past week, I have read again a little-known speech of Winston Churchill, made just after the last war. This is what he said: 'We must find the means and the method of working together not only in times of war, and mortal anguish, but in times of peace, with all its bewilderments and clamour and clatter of tongues.'

Thirty-six years on, perhaps we are beginning to relearn the truth which Churchill so clearly taught us.

We saw the signs when, this week, the NUR came to understand that its strike on the railways and on the Underground just didn't fit – didn't match the spirit of these times. And yet on Tuesday eight men, the leaders of ASLEF, misunderstanding the new mood of the nation, set out to bring the railways to a halt. Ignoring the example of the NUR, the travelling public whom they are supposed to serve, and the jobs and future of their own members, this tiny group decided to use its undoubted power – for what? – to delay Britain's recovery, which all our people long to see.

Yet we can remember that on Monday nearly a quarter of the members of the NUR turned up for work. Today, we appeal to every train driver to put his family, his comrades, and his country first, by continuing to work tomorrow. That is the true solidarity which can save jobs and which stands in the proud tradition of British railwaymen.

But it is not just on the railways that we need to find the means and the method of working together. It is just as true in the NHS. All who work there are caring, in one way or another, for the sick. To meet their needs we have already offered to the ancillary workers almost exactly what we have given to our Armed Forces and to our teachers, and more than our Civil Servants have accepted. All of us know that there is a limit to what every employer can afford to pay out in wages. The increases proposed for nurses and ancillary workers in the Health Service are the maximum which the Government can afford to pay.

We can't avoid one unchallengeable truth. The Government has no money of its own. All that it has it takes in taxes or borrows at interest. It's all of you – everyone here – that pays. Of course, there is another way. Instead of taking money from our people openly, in taxation or loans, we can take it surreptitiously, by subterfuge. We can print money in order to pay out of higher inflation what we dare not tax and cannot borrow.

But that disreputable method is no longer open to us. Rightly this Government has abjured it. Increasingly this nation won't have it. Our people are now confident enough to face the facts of life. There is a new mood of realism in Britain. That too is part of the Falklands Factor. The battle of the South Atlantic was not won by ignoring the dangers or denying the risks. It was achieved by men and woman who had no illusions about the difficulties. They faced them squarely and were determined to overcome. That is increasingly the mood of Britain. And that's why the rail strike won't do. We are no longer prepared to jeopardize our future just to defend manning practices agreed in 1919 when steam engines plied the tracks of the Grand Central Railway and the motor car had not yet taken over from the horse.

What has indeed happened is that now, once again, Britain is not prepared to be pushed around. We have ceased to be a nation in retreat. We have instead a new-found confidence – born in the economic battles at home and tested and found true 8,000 miles away. That confidence comes from the rediscovery of ourselves, and grows with the recovery of our self-respect.

And so today we can rejoice at our success in the Falklands and take pride in the achievement of the men and women of our Task Force. But we do so not as at some last flickering of a flame which must soon be dead. No – we rejoice that Britain has rekindled that spirit which has fired her for generations past and which today has begun to burn as brightly as before. Britain found herself again in the South Atlantic and will not look back from the victory she has won.

The Conservative Party Conference

BLACKPOOL, 14 OCTOBER 1983

Speaking at the Conservative Party Conference four months after her second election victory, Mrs Thatcher reviewed the progress which her Government had made so far, and dealt with some of the major issues that were to dominate the next phase of Thatcherism. Nothing would be done which might jeopardize the economic achievements which underpinned Conservative success. In particular, public spending would continue to be managed prudently and sensibly. 'We have a duty to make sure that every penny-piece we raise in taxation is spent wisely and well.' That certainly did not mean, however, that the Government would fail to provide increased resources for key elements of the public sector, such as the National Health Service. On the contrary, as Mrs Thatcher pointed out, spending on the NHS was rising by very significant amounts year after year.

At the same time her Government was following the example set by its Tory predecessors in devising and paying for far-reaching measures to help those who had been affected by inevitable economic change. This speech provided a full account of the action that was being taken – and the often difficult choices that were being made – both at home and abroad to safeguard the interests of the entire nation.

We meet in the aftermath of a general election. I think we can say that the result was not exactly a photo-finish.

We are grateful for victory. We are grateful to you and the thousands of people in every part of the country who worked so hard to ensure success. And we do not forget today the man who so brilliantly organized the campaign [Cecil Parkinson].

Last June we again won the honour to serve the British people. How best shall we do it? Not by being complacent about our majority, not by assuming that our past achievements will automatically bring us future success. Our first four years were the preparation for further action. Further action there will be.

When we were first elected in May 1979, it was to tackle the real problems which others had shirked. We did tackle them. Anyone who understood those problems never expected them to be solved in the space of one Parliament. But we have made a start. And we shall see it through. We were elected to bring inflation down; we brought it down. It was, and still is, a series of continuing battles which commands our unremitting effort. The pessimists told us it could not be done. They underestimated three things: this Government, you, Mr President [Sir Geoffrey Howe], and the British people.

We were elected to reform the trade unions. With the support of millions of trade unionists we have passed two major Acts of Parliament. And what a lot we owe to Norman Tebbit [as Employment Secretary]. But there is a lot more to do – a great deal more, and you can rely on us to do it.

We were elected to extend home ownership and we gave council tenants the right to buy their own homes. And never let it be forgotten that Labour fought it tooth and nail, in their local councils, in Parliament and through the courts. It was not part of their philosophy that council tenants should acquire the rights and dignity of freeholders. It is because of Conservative conviction and persistence that nearly three-quarters of a million more council tenants have either bought, or are buying, their homes. And with Ian Gow as Minister of Housing there will be many, many more.

We were elected to reduce direct taxation. We have reduced the rates of income tax and we have raised the thresholds. But there are still too many people paying income tax and the burden is still too great. The fight for lower taxes will go on and no one will fight harder to bring them down than our new

Chancellor of the Exchequer, Nigel Lawson.

We were elected to strengthen the forces of law and order. Thanks to Willie Whitelaw [the former Home Secretary] there are now more policemen, better paid, better equipped than ever before – and more of them back on the beat. But, as you heard from Leon Brittan [the new Home Secretary], this Government is reinforcing its efforts. But it is not just a case of 'Leave it to Leon'. Law and order is not just his problem. It involves every citizen in the land. None of us can opt out.

We were elected with a clear commitment to the European Community and to fight tenaciously for British interests within it. We have honoured that commitment. We have both fought for our interests and extended our influence. But we are not half-hearted members of the Community. We are in. And we are in to stay. And I look forward to another famous victory in the European elections next June.

We were elected to secure the defence of the realm. We have made clear, through word and deed, to friend and foe alike, our resolve to keep Britain strong and free. No one doubts now that this country under this Government stands shoulder to shoulder with her allies to defend the cause of justice and freedom, and to work together for peace. Under Michael Heseltine's vigorous leadership [as Defence Secretary], we won the argument against one-sided nuclear disarmament.

That is the record we put before the British people at the general election. They are the ultimate jury and they found in our favour.

These things were achieved by strong Government – strong to do what only Governments can do. But a strong Government knows where to draw the line. It has confidence to trust the people. And a free people know that the power of Government must be limited. That trust and that confidence are the hall-mark of the Government which was re-elected on 9 June.

At that election, Socialism offered yesterday's policies for today's problems. Socialism was routed. The other day at Brighton they were given a re-spray, polished and offered once again to the people. But they are still yesterday's policies – and even yesterday they did not work. Our people will never 'Keep the red flag flying here'. There is only one banner that Britain flies – the one that has kept flying for centuries – the red, white and blue.

One of the great debates of our time is about how much of your money should be spent by the State and how much you should keep to spend on your family. Let us never forget this fundamental truth: the State has no source of money other than money which people earn themselves. If the State wishes to spend more, it can do so only by borrowing your savings, or by taxing you more. It is no good thinking that someone else will pay. That 'someone else' is you. There is no such thing as public money. There is only taxpayers' money.

Prosperity will not come by inventing more and more lavish public expenditure programmes. You do not grow richer by ordering another cheque book from the bank. No nation ever grew more prosperous by taxing its citizens beyond their capacity to pay. We have a duty to make sure that every penny-piece we raise in taxation is spent wisely and well. For it is our party which is dedicated to good housekeeping. Indeed, I would not mind betting that if Mr Gladstone were alive today, he would apply to join the Conservative Party.

Protecting the taxpayer's purse; protecting the public services; these are our two great tasks and their demands have to be reconciled. How very pleasant it would be, how very popular it would be, to say, 'Spend more on this, expand more on that.' We all have our favourite causes – I know I do. But someone has to add up the figures. Every business has to do it. Every housewife has to do it. Every Government should do it. And this one will.

But throughout history, clever men – some of them economists, not all of them rascals, but few of them businessmen – have tried to show that the principles of prudent finance do not really apply to this Government, this budget, that institution. Not so. They always do. And every sensible person knows it, no one better than you, Mr President, who had to deal with countries which flouted those principles and are now up to their eyes in debt. Who do they turn to? Those who follow prudent principles like us.

When there is only so much money to spend, you have to make choices. And the same is true of Government. It is sometimes suggested that Governments can opt out of these choices. They cannot. Let me for a moment take the subject which we have so much debated, the Health Service. People talk about a free service. It is not free. You have to pay for it.

Five years ago, just before I came into Number Ten, a family of four was having to pay, on average, through various taxes, some £560 a year for the Health Service. This year, that same family will have to pay £1,140 a year – more than double. Let me put it another way. This year the Health Service is costing over £15,000 million – half the total yield of income tax.

The Health Service has one million employees. It is the largest employer in Europe. It really is our job to see that it is managed properly. I pay tribute, as we all do, to those doctors, nurses and others who work so hard to keep up the standards of care. We are all thankful for the great advances in public health since the war – the continuing decline in child mortality, the virtual eradication of diseases like diphtheria and TB, the miraculous new techniques of surgery. But every human institution can be improved. I reject totally the Socialist view that the most efficient organization is the one that employs the largest number.

Now let me get one or two things through about that budget. Let me put the facts on record just a little bit more. The Health Service budget is very large. We are not cutting it. We are keeping to the plans we announced before the election. And which I repeated as a pledge during the campaign. I will say it again. We are spending £700 million more on health this year alone, another £800 million next year, and a further £700 million the year after that. That is the pledge I made and that is the pledge that will be kept. And we have to keep within that huge budget. That is what good management means and that is what we are doing – as Norman Fowler [the Social Services Secretary] explained in his outstanding speech yesterday morning.

Of course, our opponents, who could never begin to match our record, are once again trying to pin on us all the adjectives

169

in the dictionary of denigration – harsh, uncaring, uncompassionate and the rest. I am told that the new Leader of Her Majesty's Opposition – and long may he hold that office – went so far as to say at Brighton last week that I was engaged in 'terminating the Health Service'. Let me tell you how you really terminate the Health Service. You do it by pretending there are no hard choices; you do it by behaving as though Britain has a bottomless purse; you do it by promising what you cannot deliver; by assuming that all you need to do is to snap your fingers, cry 'abracadabra' and, lo! and behold, the sky's the limit. But the sky is not the limit, for this or any other Government, or indeed for any other country, and to imply that it is, or ever can be, is sheer humbug and a fraud on the people.

Our opponents would spend, spend and spend before they had even filled in the coupon, let alone won the pools. At this conference last year, you may remember that I said, 'The NHS is safe with us.' I will go further. The NHS is safe only with us, because only this Government will see that it is prudently managed and financed, and that care is concentrated on the patient, rather than on the bureaucrat. That is the true and the genuine caring.

When our opponents start demanding more spending on hospitals, schools, roads, or for the old folk, I do not hear them at the same time calling for more income tax, or an extra 5 per cent on VAT, or even more on local authority rates.

In facing up to this problem of controlling public expenditure, we in Britain are far from alone. Let me give you one or two examples of what is happening in other countries. In Socialist France, they have introduced boarding charges for hospital patients. The French and the West Germans have delayed pension increases and are cutting unemployment benefit. In Holland they are cutting social security benefits and the pay of the public service by $3\frac{1}{2}$ per cent. In Belgium and Denmark they have de-indexed social security benefits. Think what people would say in this country had we done some of those things. I do not say that those measures are the ones we should follow but I do say that no Government, whatever its political complexion, can suspend the laws of arithmetic or run away from reality.

There is something else we share with other nations. The world recession has brought high unemployment to almost every country. In such times, people understandably ask: where will the new jobs come from? There is always a temptation to believe that the dynamism of the past will be exhausted and that the best we can hope for is to share out the work we have already got. Nothing could be more mistaken: that is not how our fathers and grandfathers transformed the standard of living in the Western world. They did not wait for the boost, or scan the horizon for the upturn. They were the upturn and they provided the boost themselves.

If Britain had stayed as it was in 1900, millions of people in this country would still be working in agriculture and domestic service would still be at 1900 levels. If people had known then that by 1983 less than 3 per cent of the population would be in agriculture and only a tiny fraction in domestic service, they would surely have asked, 'Where will the other millions find jobs?' Who could have foretold then what people would want today, and what they would buy today? Who could have foretold then what inventiveness would produce decades hence? While some machines that were invented replaced unskilled work, others created new goods undreamed of – motor cars, kitchen equipment, new fabrics, films – and they created, those new machines, thousands of jobs.

But as new industries sprang into being, the old ones declined, causing unhappiness and hardship. We did not then have the means or the organization to temper the winds of change – the cash benefits, the re-training schemes, the redundancy benefits, that we have now. Tories have long been prominent in creating those schemes and benefits. Again and again, Tory governments took the lead: in extending unemployment insurance, in providing compensation for past industrial injury and disease, and in bringing in training schemes for the future. In the declining industries, we have made available compensation on a uniquely generous scale for those who have had to lose their jobs. Let no one accuse this party or this Government of failing to care about the unemployed. This Government has also taken two very far-reaching steps to see that Britain is never again left unprepared for technological change. Our Youth Training Scheme is the most imaginative in the Western world. And when it is well under way, every sixteen-year-old will have the choice either to stay on at school, or to find a job, or to receive training. At that age, unemployment should not be an option. That is our objective. We are responding to the needs of industry by reintroducing technical training into our schools. And not a moment too soon. This Government is building for the future.

We all want a higher standard of living – as individuals and as a community. The same is true in other countries. The challenge we face is not one of sharing out the limited amount of work, like spreading butter thinly on a slice of bread. It is how to translate our wants and aspirations into work to be done by our people. It is by producing what people want to buy that unemployment will be solved. The same drive and inventiveness that created the great industries of the past and brought prosperity to our people are still at work today. New industries are still being born. New products are still coming on to the market. New services are still developing. Only last month, I opened the largest oil production platform in the North Sea. Fifteen years ago, the oil and gas industry, the offshore industry, employed only a handful of people. Today, it employs more than 100,000.

Who, ten or twenty years ago, could have foretold that so many homes would have video recorders – which we are just beginning to produce here – music centres, home computers and pocket calculators? Who would have foreseen the revolution in office equipment and information technology? These may be called light industries, but they produce tens of thousands of solid new jobs.

In service industries too, the past ten years have seen some of the most rapid increases in jobs. Let me give you a few examples, because I know you are still wondering where the new jobs are going to come from, and I am trying to show you they have come from new machinery and new technology in the past and that is still happening today. Let us have a look at the new service industries and see what has happened recently. Over 300,000 more jobs have been created in insurance, banking and finance than there were ten years ago. There are over 600,000 more jobs in the scientific and professional services, over 200,000 more jobs in hotels and catering and nearly 60,000 more jobs in sport and other recreations. All of those are service jobs for skilled and unskilled workers alike. So, as we have redundancies in the declining industries, we are getting new jobs in the new industries, new jobs in some of the older industries that are modernizing themselves, and new jobs in some of the service industries. They are being created by our dynamic economy of today.

Let us not belittle our achievements. There must be quite a lot right about a country that can sell 30 per cent of its output in the teeth of fierce competition. And this is a country that can still export £1,000 million worth of goods every week without counting oil. Which is the second biggest exporter of services in the world – second to the United States? It is Britain. So let us send our warm thanks and congratulations to all of those whose splendid achievements are bearing such fruit.

But, although it is a marvellous record, we have to remember something else. Our competitors are improving all the time. And some of them started well ahead of us. So we must improve even faster than they do if we are to catch up. It is no good just beating our previous best; we have to beat our competitors. That means that our Government must not put a heavier burden on our industry than other Governments place on theirs. What does that mean? I will tell you. It means we must stick to the policies that get inflation and interest rates down, which keep business taxes down, and local rates down, policies that cut through the thicket of restrictions and policies that will reduce the time taken for planning permission. It is important that we continue with each and every one. If Atlas carries the world on his shoulders, we need a good strong Atlas – and not too heavy a world.

Our job in Government is to provide the right framework in which enterprise can flourish. And we are doing it. But, of course, it rests with the people themselves to pick up the challenge. And it is in the people that we Conservatives place our trust. The great surges of progress and prosperity in this country did not come directly from Government action. They were not based on national plans. They came from free men, working in a free society, where they could deploy their talents to their best advantage, for themselves, for their countries and for the future. That is our policy. It has worked in the past and it will work again. It is to achieve a new prosperity and the new jobs for our people in the future.

The first duty of Government is to make our future and our way of life secure. In the election campaign, it became clear that the overwhelming majority of our people were determined to see that our country was properly defended. They recognized that Britain's possession of nuclear weapons has helped to prevent not only nuclear war but conventional war too. Those of our opponents who said the opposite hastily had to pretend that they did not really mean what they said. Those of our friends overseas who might have doubted the resolve of the British people were reassured by our victory.

To retain peace with freedom and justice we must maintain the unity of NATO. Most of our people would never vote for a party that undermines NATO and snipes at our allies. The so-called peace movement may claim to be campaigning for peace, but it is NATO and the Western Alliance which have been delivering peace in Europe for more than thirty years. Peace does not come by chanting the word like some mystical incantation. It comes from that ceaseless vigilance which the Western allies have sustained for nearly two generations. Peace is hard work, and we must not allow people to forget it.

The Soviet challenge remains. To say that is not to welcome the fact and still less to take pleasure in it. But if we are properly to defend ourselves, we must first make a realistic assessment of the threat we face. No one can wish away the post-war history of the Soviet use of force, nor wipe out the grim calendar of Soviet suppression of freedom. You know the calendar almost as well as I do: 1953, East Germany; 1956, Hungary; 1961, the Berlin Wall; 1968, Czechoslovakia; 1979, Afghanistan; 1981, Poland; 1983, the South Korean civil airliner.

The Soviet Union is unlikely to change much, or quickly. Internal difficulties will not necessarily soften its attitudes. Nor should we overestimate the influence of the West on that vast suspicious country. Its leaders are likely to remain distrustful and hostile to the West and ruthless in their international deeds.

Economically, of course, you may say we have nothing to fear. Whatever the difficulties, economies that flourish do so under the banner of the market and not of Marx. In the battle of ideas, the Soviet Union is in retreat as more and more peoples in Africa and Asia discover what Europe has already discovered – the cruel emptiness of Marxism. And, you know, the Russian leaders know this. Why else do they prevent their people from travelling freely? Why else do they jam Western broadcasts? Why else do they lock away those of their fellow-citizens who have the temerity to ask that the Soviet Union should abide by its undertakings at Helsinki?

But whatever we think of the Soviet Union, Soviet Communism cannot be disinvented. We have to live together on the same planet and that is why, when the circumstances are right, we must be ready to talk to the Soviet leadership; that is why we should grasp every genuine opportunity for dialogue and keep that dialogue going in the interests of East and West alike. But such exchanges must be hard-headed. We do not want the word 'dialogue' to become suspect in the way the word '*détente*' now is.

A major element in that dialogue must be arms control – indeed, we in the Western world would like to have arms reduction, provided always that the balance is kept and the undertakings to reduce or destroy weapons can be verified. Arms reduction in those circumstances, on those grounds. That is our aim.

I think it is important that we understand exactly what kind of negotiations are going on in Geneva. We are negotiating about two classes of nuclear weapons, the intermediate weapons and also the long-range strategic missiles. Two sets of negotiations. Let me talk about the intermediate weapons first.

Some six years ago the Soviet Union began to replace theirs

by the more accurate SS20s which have three times as many warheads. We had nothing comparable, so NATO in 1979 decided to modernize our intermediate weapons with Cruise and Pershing II missiles in order to restore the balance. But at the same time we tried to persuade the Soviet Union to reduce the number of SS20s. There was no response.

Then we offered to eliminate our missiles if they would eliminate theirs. If they agreed, no Cruise or Pershing II missiles would be deployed. That is President Reagan's zero-option. Still there has been no positive response from the Soviet Union. And all the signs are that there will not be. In that case, the first Cruise and Pershing II missiles will be deployed at the end of this year. Nevertheless, in Geneva we shall persist in our efforts for an agreement to keep the numbers as low as possible on both sides. No weapons would be better than some. But few would be better than more.

Meanwhile the whole situation has been deliberately clouded and confused by the Soviet propaganda attempt to suggest that our strategic weapon, Polaris, should be included in the intermediate weapon talks. Now Polaris is our last-resort deterrent. We had it long before the SS20s and then, and now, we need it, in case we should ever be threatened by Russia's great arsenal of strategic weapons. And however you measure it, our strategic force amounts to only $2\frac{1}{2}$ per cent of theirs; forty of theirs to every one of ours.

There are separate talks in Geneva concerning strategic weapons. The Soviet Union and the United States have some 9,000 warheads each. In 1981, President Reagan suggested that as a first step the missile warheads should be cut on both sides by one-third. Once again there has been no positive response from the Soviet Union. But if ever this enormous strategic armoury were drastically reduced, then of course we should wish to consider how we in Britain could contribute to the arms control process.

The West has made proposal after proposal for arms reduction. And the day the leaders of the Soviet Union genuinely decide that they want, through arms control agreements, to make this a safer world, they will be pushing at an open door.

Until then our threefold policy will be the same – realistically to assess the potential aggressor, firmly to maintain our capacity to defend and deter, and always to stand ready to talk.

As I am sure you will understand, there is no one more anxious for genuine disarmament than the person who bears the ultimate responsibility for the nuclear deterrent in our own country. I wanted to say that to you. You will understand how important it is to me that we try to make those arms reduction talks succeed.

We won a great election victory on 9 June, and there is no reason on earth why we should not take pleasure in that alone, but I really believe that we have done more than that. The election showed that something remarkable has happened in this country. And our opponents were just as aware of it as those millions of people who supported us. What I think we discovered and expressed, both in our four years of Government and in the programme which grew out of those four years, was where the heart of the British people lies. We are a mature nation which through centuries of trial, sorrow and achievement has developed a common view of life.

There are things for which we, as a people, have stood for centuries: the will and capacity to defend our way of life; the rule of law; the belief in private property and home ownership; the protection of the elderly and the sick; the limitation of Government; and the freedom of the individual. And, by giving voice to these convictions in 1979, by holding fast to them for four years, by having them reaffirmed in 1983, I believe we have altered the whole course of British politics for at least a generation.

We have created the new common ground and that is why our opponents have been forced to shift their ground. Both the policy and direction of State Socialism on which they have been fighting for years have been utterly rejected by our people. State Socialism is not in the character of the British people. It has no place in our traditions. It has no hold on our hearts. A Socialist Party can only hope to survive in Britain by pretending that it is something else. We are told the Labour Party is reassessing its attitude to home ownership and is thinking

177

again about Europe. We are told the Social Democrats now sing the virtues of capitalism, competition and the customer. We have entered a new era. The Conservative Party has staked out the common ground and the other parties are tiptoeing on to it.

The Conservative Party has a greater responsibility than ever before. Now, more than ever, we draw our support from all sections of the nation. It is our pride and our purpose to strive always to be a national party – a party which speaks for, and to, the whole nation.

In 1975, standing where I am standing today, I said that I had a vision for Britain: a Britain strong in the defence of peace and justice; a Britain strong in support of personal freedom; a Government strong enough to protect the weak; but a Government with the strength to allow people to lead their own lives.

Visions do not become a reality overnight – or even in four years. They have to be worked for, consistently, unswervingly. We have set a true course – a course that is right for the character of Britain, right for the people of Britain and right for the future of Britain. To that course we shall hold fast. We shall see it through – to success.

The Conservative Party Conference

BRIGHTON, 12 OCTOBER 1984

The IRA bomb, which devastated the Grand Hotel at Brighton and killed five members of the Conservative Party, exploded at 2.54 a.m. on 12 October 1984 just after Mrs Thatcher had put the finishing touches to her conference speech. She herself only narrowly escaped death. When she came to deliver the speech (after amending the text) later the same day, her main purpose was to contrast the closed, evil world of terrorism with the open, democratic procedures of a political party. This she did very effectively, not by denouncing terrorism at length, but by reviewing in measured and dignified terms the constructive work being done in all the main spheres of national life by the political party that had been elected to power in Britain.

It was no mere catalogue of success stories: an important section of the speech was devoted to the unresolved issue of unemployment. This contained a full explanation of how the problem had arisen, which amply discharged the obligation that is accepted only by democratically elected politicians to keep the electorate properly informed. She also analyzed in some detail the issues at stake in the protracted miners' strike – Britain's most violent, politically motivated dispute. In Brighton that day the achievements of democracy were placed beside the wreckage created by terrorism – and they towered above it.

The bomb attack on the Grand Hotel early this morning was first and foremost an inhuman, undiscriminating attempt to

179

massacre innocent, unsuspecting men and women staying in Brighton for our Conservative conference. Our first thoughts must at once be for those who died and for those who are now in hospital recovering from their injuries.

But the bomb attack clearly signified more than this. It was an attempt not only to disrupt and terminate our conference; it was an attempt to cripple Her Majesty's democratically elected Government. That is the scale of the outrage in which we have all shared, and the fact that we are gathered here now, shocked but composed and determined, is a sign not only that this attack has failed but that all attempts to destroy democracy by terrorism will fail.

I should like to express our deep gratitude to the police, firemen, ambulancemen, nurses and doctors, to all the emergency services, and to the staff of the hotel, to our ministerial staff and the Conservative Party staff who stood with us and shared the danger. As Prime Minister and Leader of the Party, I thank them all and send our heartfelt sympathy to all those who have suffered.

Now it must be business as usual. We must go on to discuss the things we have talked about during this conference, one or two matters of foreign affairs and after that two subjects I have selected for special consideration, unemployment and the miners' strike.

This conference has been superbly chaired – and our Chairman came on this morning with very little sleep and carried on marvellously. The conference, with excellent contributions from our members, has been an outstanding example of orderly assembly and free speech. We have debated the great national and international issues, as well as those which affect the daily lives of our people. We have seen at the rostrum miner and pensioner, nurse and manager, clergyman and student.

In Government we have been fulfilling the promises contained in our election manifesto, which was put to the people in a national ballot. This Government is reasserting Parliament's ultimate responsibility for controlling the total burden of taxation on our citizens, whether levied by central or local Government. And in the coming session of Parliament we shall introduce legislation which will abolish the GLC and the metropolitan county councils.

In the quest for sound local Government we rely on the help of Conservative councillors. Their task should never be underestimated and their virtues should not go unsung. They work hard and conscientiously with a true spirit of service. I pay special tribute to the splendid efforts of Conservative councils up and down the country in getting better value for money through greater efficiency and putting out work to competitive tender. This is privatization at the local level and we need more of it.

At national level, since the general election just over a year ago, the Government has denationalized five major enterprises, making a total of thirteen since 1979. Yesterday, you gave Norman Tebbit a standing ovation. Today our thoughts are with him and his family.

Again and again denationalization has brought greater motivation to managers and workforce, higher profits and rising investment. What is more, many in industry now have a share of the firm for which they work. We Conservatives want every owner to be an earner and every earner to be an owner. Soon we shall have the biggest ever act of denationalization with British Telecom, and British Airways will follow. And we have not finished yet. There will be more to come in this Parliament.

Just as we have stood by our pledge on denationalization, it is our pride that despite the recession we have kept faith with nine million pensioners. Moreover, by keeping inflation down we have protected the value of their savings. This Government has not only put more into pensions but has increased resources for the National Health Service. Our record for last year, to be published shortly, will show that the Health Service today is providing more care, more services, and more help for the patient than at any stage in its history. That is Conservative care in practice. I think that it is further proof of the statement I made in Brighton in this hall two years ago. Perhaps some of you remember it. 'The National Health Service is safe with us.'

This performance in the social services could never have

been achieved without an efficient and competitive industry to create the wealth we need. Efficiency is not the enemy but the ally of compassion.

In our discussions here we have spoken of the need for enterprise, profits, and a wider distribution of property among all the people. In the Conservative Party we have no truck with outmoded Marxist doctrine about class warfare. For us, it is not who you are, who your family is, or where you come from that matters. It is what you are and what you can do for our country that counts. That is our vision. It is a vision worth defending and we shall defend it. Indeed, this Government will never put the defence of our country at risk.

No one in their senses wants nuclear weapons for their own sake. But equally no responsible Prime Minister could take the colossal gamble of giving up our nuclear defences while our greatest potential enemy kept theirs. Policies which would throw out all American nuclear bases – bases which have been here since the time of Mr Attlee, President Truman and Sir Winston Churchill – would wreck NATO and leave us totally isolated from our friends in the United States – and friends they are. No nation in history has ever shouldered a greater burden, or shouldered it more willingly or more generously, than the United States. This party is pro-American.

We must constantly remind people what the defence policy of the Opposition party would mean. Their idea that by giving up our nuclear deterrent we could somehow escape the result of a nuclear war elsewhere is nonsense. And it is a delusion to assume that conventional weapons are a sufficient defence against nuclear attack. And do not let anyone slip into the habit of thinking that conventional war in Europe is some kind of comfortable option. With the huge array of modern weapons held by the Soviet Union, including chemical weapons in large quantities, it would be a cruel and terrible conflict. The truth is that possession of the nuclear deterrent has prevented not only nuclear war but also conventional war. And to us, peace is precious beyond price. We are the true peace party.

The nuclear deterrent has not only kept the peace but it will continue to preserve our independence. Winston Churchill's warning is just as true now as when he made it many, many years ago. He said, 'Once you take the position of not being able in any circumstances to defend your rights against . . . aggression . . . there is no end to the demands that will be made or the humiliations that must be accepted.'

He knew, and we must heed his warning. Yet Labour's defence policy remains: no Polaris, no Cruise missiles in Britain, no United States nuclear bases in Britain, no Trident, no independent nuclear deterrent. There is, I think, just one answer the nation will give – no defence, no Labour Government.

In foreign affairs, this year has seen two major diplomatic successes. We have reached a detailed and binding agreement with China on the future of Hong Kong. It is an agreement designed to preserve Hong Kong's flourishing economy and unique way of life. We believe that it meets the needs and wishes of the people of Hong Kong themselves.

A few weeks ago the unofficial members of the Executive Council of Hong Kong came to see me. We kept in touch with them the whole time and they have frequently made journeys to Number Ten Downing Street as the negotiations with China have proceeded. We were just about to initial the agreement, and we consulted them of course about its content. Their spokesman said that while the agreement did not contain everything he would have liked, he and his colleagues could nevertheless recommend it to the people of Hong Kong in good conscience. In good conscience. That means a lot to us. If that is what the leaders of Hong Kong's own community believe, then we have truly fulfilled the heavy responsibility we feel for their long-term future.

That agreement required imagination, skill, hard work and perseverence – in other words, it required Geoffrey Howe.

In Europe, too, through firmness and determination, we have achieved a long-term settlement of Britain's Budget contributions, a fair deal for Britain and for Europe too. If we had listened to the advice of other party leaders, Britain would not have done half as well. But patient diplomacy and occasionally, I confess, a little impatient diplomacy, did the trick.

183

We have at last begun to curb surplus food production in the Community. We know that for some farmers this has meant a painful adjustment and we are very much aware of their difficulties. Their work and their success are the great strength to our country. Michael Jopling [Minister of Agriculture] and his colleagues will continue to fight to achieve a fair deal for them.

We have also won agreement on the need to keep the Community's spending under proper control. The Community can now enter on a new chapter and use its energies and influence to play a greater part in world affairs, as an example of what democracies can accomplish, as a very powerful trading group and as a strong force for freedom.

We had one of the most interesting debates of this conference on employment, which we all agree is the scourge of our times. To have over 3 million people unemployed in this country is bad enough, even though we share this tragic problem with other nations. But to suggest, as some of our opponents have, that we do not care about it is as deeply wounding as it is utterly false.

Do they really think that we do not understand what it means for the family man who cannot find a job, who has to sit at home with a sense of failure and despair? Or that we do not understand how hopeless the world must seem to a young person who has not yet succeeded in getting his first job? Of course we know; of course we see; and of course we care. However could they say that we welcome unemployment as a political weapon?

What better news could there be for any Government than the news that unemployment is falling? The day cannot come too soon for me. Others, while not questioning our sincerity, argue that our policies will not achieve our objectives. They look back forty years, to the post-war period, when we were poised to launch a brave new world, a time when we all thought we had the cure to unemployment.

In that confident dawn it seemed that, having won the war, we knew how to win the peace. Keynes had provided the diagnosis. It was all set out in the 1944 White Paper on employment. I bought it then, I have it still. My name is on the top of it: 'Margaret H. Roberts'. One of my staff took one look at it and said, 'Good heavens, I didn't know it was as old as that.' We all read that White Paper very carefully, but the truth was that some politicians took some part of the formula in it and conveniently ignored the rest. I re-read it frequently.

Those politicians overlooked the warning in that paper that Government action must not weaken personal enterprise or exonerate the citizen from the duty of fending for himself. They disregarded the advice that wages must be related to productivity, and above all they neglected the warning that without a rising standard of industrial efficiency you cannot achieve a high level of employment combined with a rising standard of living.

Having ignored so much of that, and having ignored other parts of the formula for so much of the time, the result was that we ended up with high inflation and high unemployment. Now, this Government is heeding the warnings. It has acted on the basic truths that were set out all those years ago in that famous White Paper.

If I had come out with all this today some people would call it Thatcherite, but in fact it was vintage Maynard Keynes. He had a horror of inflation, a fear of too much State control and a belief in the market. We are heeding those warnings. We are taking the policy as a whole and not only in selected parts. We have already brought inflation down below 5 per cent. Output has been rising steadily since 1981 and investment is up substantially.

But if things are improving, why, you will ask, does unemployment not fall? That was the question one could feel throughout that debate, even though people know that there is always a time lag between getting the other things right and having a fall in unemployment. Why does unemployment not fall?

May I try to answer that question? First, more jobs are being created. Over the last year more than quarter of a million extra jobs have been created, but the population of working age is also rising very fast, as the baby boom of the 1960s become the school leavers of the 1980s. So although the number of jobs is rising, the population of working age is also rising. And among the population of working age a larger proportion of married women are seeking work.

So you will see why we need more jobs just to stop unemployment rising and even more jobs to get it falling. On top of that, new technology has caused redundancy in many factories. But it has also created whole new industries, providing products and jobs that only a few years ago were undreamed of. So it has two effects. The first one is redundancies; the second, and slightly later, new jobs as new products become possible. This has happened in history before. A few days ago I visited York, where I saw the first railway engine, Stephenson's *Rocket*. I thought of the jobs, the prospects and the hope that the new steam engines and the railways then brought to many people.

Communities queued up to be on a railway line, to have their own station. Those communities welcomed change and it brought them more jobs. I confess, I am very glad we have got the railways. If we were trying to build those same railways today I wonder whether we would ever get planning permission, it sometimes takes so long. That is one thing that can sometimes delay the coming into existence of jobs.

That was one example from history, but let us go through the changes during my lifetime, as we had this same phenomenon – redundancies from new technology, more jobs from new technology. In the 1940s, when I took a science degree, the new emerging industries were plastics, man-made fibres and television. Later it would be satellites, computers and tele-communications. Now it is biotechnology and information technology. Today our universities and science parks are identifying the needs of tomorrow. So, there are new industries and new jobs in the pipeline.

I remember an industrialist telling me when I first went into business, and I have always remembered it, 'Our job is to discover what the customer will buy and to produce it.' And in Wrexham the other day, at a youth training centre, I was delighted to see a poster saying 'It is the customer that makes pay days possible.' So these young people were not only learning new technology, they were learning the facts of business life and how we create new jobs.

It is the spirit of enterprise that provides new jobs; it is being prepared to venture and build a business. And the role of Government in helping to do that? It is in cutting taxes, cutting inflation, keeping costs down, cutting through regulations and removing obstacles to the growth of small businesses, for that is where many of the new jobs will come from – small businesses.

It is also the role of Government to provide better education and training. The youth training scheme, now in its second year, was set up to give young people the necessary skills for the new technologies and the necessary approach to industry. A majority of the first year's graduates are getting jobs. A much bigger proportion of those leaving the youth training scheme are getting jobs, compared with those leaving the youth opportunities scheme. And so they should, because it is a much better training scheme and it will improve again this year.

I was very interested in it. David Young [as head of the Manpower Services Commission] started it, and I offered to take a trainee for our office, Number Ten Downing Street. We would love to have one. He or she might not have made it to be Prime Minister in one year, but the work at Number Ten, because we have a staff of about 100 to run the office, is varied and interesting and we really wanted to take on a trainee. We also said that we would take some trainees into the other parts of the Civil Service. At first the unions said yes; then they said no. And the result is that young people have been denied training places. The same problem arose at Jaguar. First the unions said yes; then they said no. So 130 unemployed teenagers have been denied training. That means young people were denied jobs. We cannot create jobs without the willing co-operation not only of employers but of trade unions and all the work force in industry and commerce.

Yesterday, in the debate, we were urged to spend more money on capital investment. It looks a very attractive idea, but to spend more in one area means spending less in another, or it means putting up taxes. In Government we are constantly faced with these difficult choices. If we want more for investment I have to ask my colleagues in Cabinet, 'What are you

THE REVIVAL OF BRITAIN

going to give up? Or you? Or you? Or you? Or you?' Or should I perhaps ask them, 'Whose pay claim are you going to cut? The doctors'? The police's? The nurses'?' I do not find many takers, because we have honoured the reviews of pay for doctors, nurses and the police, and others, in full.

You would not have cheered me if we had not done so, and quite right too. I am bringing this to you because although people can say that the way to solve unemployment is to give a higher capital allocation, I have to ask, 'What are we going to give up?' Or I have to turn to Nigel Lawson and ask him which taxes would he put up. Would it be income tax? Personal income tax is already too high. Value added tax? I should get a pretty frosty reception from Nigel and I should get a pretty frosty reception from you. But I would be loath to ask him, anyway. But, you see, Governments have to make these difficult choices, because, as you know, whether you are running households or your own businesses, there is a certain amount of income and you are soon in trouble if you do not live within it.

What I want to say to you is that we do consider these difficult choices in the public expenditure annual round, and we are just coming up to it. And we have managed to allocate a very considerable sum to capital investment. Indeed, we have found the money for the best investment projects on offer. It has been because of very good management in each and every department; it has been because waste has been cut so that we could make room for these things and be certain that we could say to you that we were getting value for money.

Let me give you a few examples of some of the investment projects for which we have found money by careful budgeting. There is the M25 road, for example. It has been completed. British Railways has been given the green light to go ahead with electrification if it can make it pay. We have started or built forty-nine new hospitals since 1979. Capital investment in the nationalized industries as a whole is going up. Of course, we look at various things like new power stations, and in a year after drought we look at things like more investment in the water supply industry. So we are going ahead with major capital investment.

So what is the conclusion that we are coming to? It is that it is the spirit of enterprise that creates new jobs. And it is the Government's task to create the right framework, the right financial framework in which that can flourish, and to cut the obstacles which sometimes handicap the birth of enterprise. And also to manage our own resources carefully and well.

That is more or less what that employment policy White Paper in 1944 said. Let me just return to it. On page one it states, 'For employment cannot be created by Act of Parliament or by Government action alone . . . the success of the policy outlined in this paper will ultimately depend on the understanding and support of the community as a whole – and especially on the efforts of employers and workers in industry.' It was true then. It is true now. And those are the policies that we are following and shall continue to follow, because those are the policies that we believe will ultimately create the genuine jobs for the future. In the meantime it is our job to try to mitigate the painful effects of change, and that we do, as you know, by generous redundancy payments and also by a community enterprise scheme, which not only finds jobs for the long-term unemployed, but finds them in a way which brings great benefits to the communities. And then, of course, where there are redundancy schemes in steel, and now in coal, the industries themselves set up enterprise agencies, both to give help to those who are made redundant and to provide new training. All of this is a highly constructive policy both for the creation of jobs and a policy to cushion the effects of change.

May I turn now to the coal industry. For a little over seven months we have been living through an agonizing strike. Let me make it absolutely clear. The miners' strike was not of this Government's seeking, nor of its making. We have heard in debates at this conference some of the aspects that have made this dispute so repugnant to so many people. We were reminded by a colliery manager that the NUM always used to accept that a pit should close when the losses were too great to keep it open; and that the miners set great store by investment in new pits and new seams. Under this Government that new investment is happening in abundance. You can almost repeat the figures with me – £2 million in capital investment in the mines for every day this Government has been in power. So no shortage of capital investment.

We heard moving accounts from two working miners about just what they have to face as they try to make their way to work. The sheer bravery of those men and thousands like them who have kept the mining industry alive is beyond praise. 'Scabs' their former workmates call them. Scabs? They are lions. What a tragedy it is when striking miners attack their workmates. Not only are they members of the same union, but the working miner is saving both their futures because it is the working miners, whether in Nottinghamshire, Derbyshire, Lancashire, Leicestershire, Staffordshire, Warwickshire, North Wales or Scotland, it is the working miners who have kept faith with those who buy our coal, and without whose custom thousands of jobs in the mining industry would be already lost.

Then we heard, unforgettably, from the incomparable Mrs Irene McGibbon who told us what it is like to be the wife of a working miner during this strike. She told us of the threats and intimidation suffered by herself and her family and even her eleven-year-old son. But what she endured only stiffened her resolve. To face the picket line day after day must take a very special kind of courage, but it takes as much, perhaps even more, for the housewife who has to stay at home alone. Men and women like that are what we are proud to call the best of British. And our police, who uphold the law with an independence and a restraint perhaps only to be found in this country, are the admiration of the world.

To be sure, the miners had a good deal. To try to prevent a strike the National Coal Board gave the miners the best ever pay offer, the highest ever investment and, for the first time, the promise that no miner would lose his job against his will. This we did despite the fact that the bill for losses in the coal industry last year was bigger than the annual bill for all the doctors and dentists in all the National Health Service hospitals in the United Kingdom. Let me repeat it: the annual losses in the coal industry are enormous – £1.3 billion last year. You have to find that money as taxpayers. It is equal to the sum we pay in salaries to all the doctors and dentists in the National Health Service.

This is a dispute about the right to go to work of those who have been denied the right to go to vote. And we must never forget that the overwhelming majority of trade unionists, including many striking miners, deeply regret what has been done in the name of trade unionism. When this strike is over, and one day it will be, we must do everything we can to encourage moderate and responsible trade unionism so that it can once again take its respected and valuable place in our industrial life.

Meanwhile, we are faced with the present executive of the National Union of Mineworkers. They know that what they are demanding has never been granted either to miners or to workers in any other industry. Why, then, demand it? Why ask for what they know cannot be conceded? There can be only one explanation. They did not want a settlement. They wanted a strike. Otherwise they would have balloted on the Coal Board's offer. Indeed, one-third of the miners did have a ballot and voted overwhelmingly to accept the offer.

What we have seen in this country is the emergence of an organized revolutionary minority who are prepared to exploit industrial disputes but whose real aim is the breakdown of law and order and the destruction of democratic parliamentary Government. We have seen the same sort of thugs and bullies at Grunwick, more recently against Eddy Shah in Stockport, and now organized into flying squads around the country. If their tactics were to be allowed to succeed, if they are not brought under the control of the law, we shall see them again at every industrial dispute organized by militant union leaders anywhere in the country.

One of the speakers earlier in the conference realized this fact, realized that what they are saying is 'Give us what we want or we are prepared to go on with violence.' He referred to Danegeld. May I add to what that speaker said? 'We never pay anyone Danegeld, no matter how trifling the cost; for the end of that game is oppression and shame, and the nation that plays it is lost.' Yes, Rudyard Kipling. Who could have put it better?

Democratic change there has always been in this, the home of democracy, but the sanction for change is the ballot box. It seems that there are some who are out to destroy any properly elected Government. They are out to bring down the framework of law. That is what we have seen in this strike. And what is the law they seek to defy? It is the common law created by fearless judges and passed down across the centuries. It is legislation scrutinized and enacted by the Parliament of a free people. It is legislation passed through a House of Commons, a Commons elected once every five years by secret ballot of one citizen, one vote. This is the way our law was fashioned, and that is why British justice is renowned across the world.

No Government owns the law. It is the law of the land, the heritage of the people. 'No man is above the law, and no man is below it; nor do we ask any man's permission when we require him to obey it. Obedience to the law is demanded as a right – not asked as a favour.' So said Theodore Roosevelt.

The battle to uphold the rule of law calls for the resolve and commitment of the British people. Our institutions of justice, the courts and the police require the unswerving support of every law-abiding citizen, and I believe that they will receive it.

The nation faces what is probably the most testing crisis of our time – the battle between the extremists and the rest. We are fighting, as we have always fought, for the weak as well as for the strong. We are fighting for great and good causes. We are fighting to defend them against the power and might of those who rise up to challenge them. This Government will not weaken. This nation will meet that challenge. Democracy will prevail.

The Carlton Lecture

LONDON, 26 NOVEMBER 1984

Shortly after the Brighton bombing, Mrs Thatcher delivered the second Carlton Lecture; her title was 'Why democracy will last'. The background against which she spoke gave the lecture added poignancy and significance. She argued that terrorism was only one manifestation of an alarming problem created by the pretensions of certain minority groups who believed they could dictate to the majority. 'There has come into existence a fashionable view, convenient to many special interest groups, that there is no need to accept the verdict of the majority: that the minority should be quite free to bully, even coerce, to get the verdict reversed.'

Though Mrs Thatcher did not mention them by name, that description clearly fitted the leaders of the miners' union who had not even sought the support of a majority of their own members through a ballot (as the rules of their union required) before launching a strike earlier that year designed to cripple the British economy. Such actions presented a direct challenge to the British democratic tradition which existed, first and foremost, to protect the most basic human rights 'which have been evolved and upheld across the centuries by our rule of law'. But those minorities which sought to subvert democracy had underestimated its strength. They would be defeated; it would last.

Just over two years ago, Mr Harold Macmillan delivered the first Carlton Lecture. All of us who were present to hear it, or who have since read it, hoped that this would be the first of a distinguished series. You do me a great honour in inviting me to deliver the second.

When he was Prime Minister, Mr Macmillan gave me my first ministerial job in 1961. Some twenty years later, as Prime Minister myself, it gave me the greatest pleasure to recommend Mr Macmillan for his highly deserved and widely acclaimed earldom on the occasion of his ninetieth birthday. Today, the Earl of Stockton may have a distinguished title; he may sit in a different chamber; but he speaks with the brilliance, wit, and understanding with which he has always spoken.

His lecture was entitled 'Civilization under threat' because he thought – and I quote his own words – something 'vague and meaningless and a little pompous would be about right'. Needless to say, the lecture was everything but that.

The title I first toyed with, for my lecture, was 'Democracy under threat' – because there are, as we know, enemies of democracy both within and without. But that would have been too pessimistic a title, because the defenders of democracy are far the more numerous. The overwhelming majority of the British people are democrats. Britain's democratic institutions are resilient. And the heart of our country is strong. I have confidence and faith in our people and have therefore called my lecture 'Why democracy will last'.

We meet here as practitioners in the craft of democracy. Indeed, this great club is a workshop of that craft. The families of some of those in this room have been practising this skill for several generations. Others have become master-craftsmen in one generation. Still more are serving their apprenticeships for the future.

Democracy has always been, and remains, one of the rarer forms of Government. The United Nations now numbers 159 countries, but no more than about sixty could be described as democracies. So steady and inevitable was our own progress towards democracy – so familiar are the landmarks of Magna Carta in 1215, Simon de Montfort's Parliament in 1265, Habeas Corpus in 1679, the Glorious Revolution of 1688, the Reform Bills from 1832 leading to universal suffrage – that it is easy to forget how unusual is our history. If we look wider, in the past or the present, we see not only how rare, but how vulnerable, democracy is: the brief flowering of Athens in the ancient world; the instant destruction of the fledgeling Russian democracy in 1917 by Lenin's *coup d'état*; and the infancy of most real democracies outside Europe now.

And even if we look at the kind of representative democracy which we practise in Britain today, we realize how long has been the road from Runnymede.

> *At Runnymede, at Runnymede!*
> *Your rights were won at Runnymede:*
> *No freeman shall be fined or bound,*
> *Or dispossessed of freehold ground,*
> *Except by lawful judgement found*
> *And passed upon him by his peers.*
> *Forget not, after all these years,*
> *The Charter signed at Runnymede.*
>
> *And still when Mob or Monarch lays*
> *Too rude a hand on English ways,*
> *The whisper wakes, the shudder plays*
> *Across the reeds at Runnymede.*
> *And Thames, that knows the moods of kings,*
> *And crowds and priests and suchlike things,*
> *Rolls deep and dreadful as he brings*
> *Their warning down from Runnymede!*

> Rudyard Kipling, 'The Reeds of Runnymede'

The first of the great parliamentary Reform Bills actually occurred in the lifetime of the father of one member of our present House of Lords, Lady Elliot of Harwood. Her father, Sir Charles Tennant, was born in 1823. Votes for women, albeit for those aged thirty or over, were one of the few beneficial consequences of the First World War. That was the only time when the age of thirty, in the life of women, has been of statutory significance. Votes for women under thirty, on the same terms as men, came during my own lifetime. It was as late as 1950 – by which time the university seats had been abolished – that the first general election was held, based on the principle of 'one person, one vote'.

But freedom depends on more than just a voting system. Long before democracy was valued, long before we had this form of representative Government, long before universal suffrage, we prided ourselves on being a free people. We'd freed ourselves from fear of foreign domination. We'd freed ourselves from absolute monarchy. Above all, we'd developed the common law which established protection for the common man against the overmighty and powerful. The debt we owe to the judges over many centuries has been incalculable.

There is no more eloquent statement of eighteenth-century England's reverence for freedom than that attributed to the Chief Justice, Lord Mansfield, in the case of James Somerset, the slave: 'The air of England has long been too pure for a slave, and every man is free who breathes it. Every man who comes into England is entitled to the protection of English law, whatever oppression he may heretofore have suffered, and whatever may be the colour of his skin.'

By the nineteenth century, Tennyson – the great poet of my native Lincolnshire – was able to call this nation 'A land of settled Government, a land of just renown'. But if we are to preserve and indeed strengthen democracy, we must encourage those forces which sustain it, which are friendly to it, and identify and isolate those elements which subvert it, which are its enemies. And the democracy of which we speak is not the counterfeit model of Communism but genuine democracy.

Economists and politicians have not always been the friends of freedom. Indeed, one of them would have led us into serfdom from the middle-class comfort of a house in Highgate and from the publicly provided reading rooms of the British Museum. But others knew more of human nature and had more respect for the importance of the individual. Great political economists, the greatest of them Adam Smith, have shown how a market economy, by devolving the power of consumer choice to customers, runs with the grain of democracy which disperses the power of political choice to voters.

The economic enemies of democracy are those who would impose on people systems of production and distribution based on compulsion, not on people's choice. Many live under systems whose rulers know only too well the connection between economic and political freedom, for they suppress economic freedoms precisely to prevent that political freedom which would ultimately follow.

But are there not closer to home some trends and fashions of thought which contain, in more respectable guise, the seed of the same danger? If some powerful group of producers says to us, 'You've got to buy our product, whether or not you want it, we'll force you to do so by the use of monopoly power or political muscle', then those producers are taking away from their fellow-citizens an economic freedom – and that is true, even if we were feeble enough to vote to allow it because we thought, 'Anything for a quiet life'. And if they are prepared to rob us of our economic freedoms, what is to stop them taking away other freedoms as well?

Let us never forget: democracies can vote, and in the past have voted, for measures which lead to their own destruction. The job of democratic leaders is to warn that measures which may seem easy or even popular, which may end some immediate conflict, must be resisted if in the end they risk destroying democracy itself. Doubtless consensus politicians mocked Demosthenes when he warned that the blandishments of King Philip of Macedon had only one object – the extinction of freedom in the Greek cities. But he was right. They certainly mocked Churchill in a comparable case. And he was right too.

Doubtless we could settle back into allowing industries, which we know should modernize, to levy on us all the compulsory costs of their own inefficiency, of their own protection. But that way lies, in the end, the erosion of the economic freedoms on which democracy rests, just as surely as Greek weakness in the face of the Macedonian king led to the extinction of political freedoms.

Technology too has profound implications for political life. Huge concentrations of people in great buildings simply repeating mechanical routines will be a thing of the past – and thank goodness for that. We can look forward to more and varied work being dispersed amongst smaller groups; less mass organization of people for mechanical purposes; more dispersal of economic power. All these bode well for a diverse and democratic society.

Other technical developments are more sombre. In the last century the Swiss cantons, secure in their mountains; Britain, secure behind her Navy; the New England cities, far from European dynastic wars; all could live in confident independence because, with reasonable vigilance, there was not much danger of destruction from outside. Powerful modern weapons and nuclear technology will never again allow us to live in so secure a world. Even if every nuclear weapon were destroyed, the knowledge of how to make them cannot be disinvented. Now only a ceaseless vigilance can keep us safe.

Having said all of this, let us never forget that the case for democracy rests ultimately on morality. Somebody once said that when politicians start to talk about morality, you had better count the spoons. But there is no way round the word if we are to discuss what is the greatest internal threat to democracy.

In the old days, political writers used to argue about something called 'the protection of minorities'. How could minority groups in a democracy be protected against the majority? Surely the 51 per cent might claim legitimacy for persecution of the 49 per cent? But democracy is about more than majorities. It is about the right of every individual to freedom and justice: a right founded upon the Old and New Testaments, which remind us of the dignity of each individual, his right to choose and his duty to serve. These rights are God-given, not State-given. They are rights which have been evolved and upheld across the centuries by our rule of law: a rule of law which safeguards individuals and minorities; a rule of law which is the cement of a free society.

But what I think we are now seeing is the reverse problem, and we haven't properly faced up to it yet – the problem of the protection of the majority. There has come into existence a fashionable view, convenient to many special interest groups, that there is no need to accept the verdict of the majority: that the minority should be quite free to bully, even coerce, to get the verdict reversed.

Marxists, of course, always had an excuse when they were outvoted: their opponents must have 'false consciousness': their views didn't really count. But the Marxists, as usual, only provide a bogus intellectual top-dressing for groups who seek only their own self-interest.

Plenty of groups operate more simply. They don't care whether they have persuaded their fellow-citizens or not, or whether constitutionally elected Governments undertake properly approved policies. These minorities will coerce the system to meet their own objectives, if we let them get away with it.

Many of the new 'campaigning' pressure groups, run by professionals who move from campaign to campaign – some in the trade unions; some even in parts of the system of Government itself – have seen how our democracy has evolved rules to temper the power of the majority and provide safeguards and rights for the minority. They have spotted that, if minorities bend the rules or simply ignore them, they may succeed in manipulating the whole system. The minority indeed may, in the end, effectively coerce the majority. You may recall that Burke had a phrase for it, as always: 'All that is needed for evil men to triumph is for good men to do nothing.'

Now I hope I won't be thought too provocative if I complain again about the sloppy use of the word 'consensus' in such cases. If there is a national debate and a constitutional vote about some matter, and if a recalcitrant minority says 'the vote be damned, we are going to do our level best to stop the majority having its way', then it's no good saying, 'we must seek consensus, we must negotiate'. Such a group will never consent, whatever the majority thinks, until it gets what it wants. That is when we have to stand up and be counted, that is when we have to do what we believe to be right.

We must never give in to the oldest and least democratic trick of all – the coercion of the many by the ruthless, manipulating few. As soon as we surrender the basic rule which says we must persuade our fellow-citizens, not coerce them, then we have joined the ranks of the enemies of democracy.

Now that democracy has been won, it is not heroic to flout

the law of the land as if we still struggled in a quagmire where civilization had yet to be built. The concept of fair play – a British way of saying 'respect for the rules' – must not be used to allow the minority to overbear the tolerant majority.

Yet these are the very dangers which we face in Britain today. At one end of the spectrum are the terrorist gangs within our borders, and the terrorist States which finance and arm them. At the other is the hard Left operating inside our system, conspiring to use union power and the apparatus of local Government to break, defy and subvert the laws. Their course of action is characterized by a calculated hostility towards our courts of justice.

Our courts have long been distinguished for their impartiality. Our judges are famous for their fair-mindedness, their objectivity and their learning. But it is precisely because the courts uphold the principles of reasoned justice and equality before the law that the Fascist Left is contemptuous of them.

Who is there to speak for the majority? The Labour Party cannot – it is itself the victim of a takeover of the passive majority by a ruthless minority. We see moderate Labour politicians having to eat their words or take their leave. And the Alliance? – it is a house divided: divided on principle, divided on policy, divided not once but many times over.

A unique responsibility is therefore placed on today's Conservative Party. And speaking to you in this building, it is right that I should dwell for a moment on the role of our party.

There are in the free world a number of powerful and distinguished parties in the Conservative tradition. But I think it is fair to say that none can rival our own Conservative Party for the length of its service to the nation, the durability of its philosophy, its tenacity of tradition, combined with its willingness to embrace and refine necessary change and, above all, for the sheer centrality of its role in the political life of our society. It can reasonably claim to be the leading democratic party in the world.

In our long history, the Conservative Party – as our name implies – has sought, successfully, to conserve many things: the

Established Church, the Monarchy, the House of Lords, the constitutional integrity of the United Kingdom. But now the mantle has fallen on us to conserve the very principle of parliamentary democracy and the rule of law itself – to conserve them for all people, of all parties and of none.

Each generation has to stand up for democracy. It can't take anything for granted and may have to fight fundamental battles anew.

My predecessor, in the first Carlton Lecture, dealt eloquently with the whole of civilization; the culture of the cities of Guatemala, the Oxford of 1914, Bretton Woods, even the cumbersome diplodocus roaming in the valley of the Thames who didn't get as far as Oxford – a vast array of lost worlds surveyed with inimitable style. I have concentrated on one strand of his argument – the uniqueness and vulnerability of our freedoms and our democracy – because I am still in the business of building defences for those freedoms, and standing up for that democracy and justice in the immediate hurly-burly of political life.

That is why I have pointed both to the dangers and to the opportunities. If we don't guard against the dangers and rise to the opportunities, Lord Stockton's heirs may, in some distant lecture, add us to his lost worlds.

But I am confident. Britons will never lack brave hearts nor sound laws to defend their freedoms. When injustice threatens we can mobilize the common sense and common law of Britain; and look to our parliamentary democracy to signal dangers and shape the laws. This year, as before in our history, we have seen men and women with stout hearts defying violence, scorning intimidation, defending their rights to uphold our laws. We have seen a new birth of leadership.

Individuals do count. Truth will prevail. Democracy does work and will endure. And we will defend it with our political lives. Let that be the message of this, the second Carlton Lecture.

TO

The Conservative Central Council

FELIXSTOWE, 15 MARCH 1986

Mrs Thatcher summed up her fundamental aims and objectives in clear, confident terms in this speech to the Conservative Central Council, which brings together representatives from all sections of the Party (though on a much smaller scale than the annual Party Conference). She defined her Conservatism as 'a crusade to put power in the hands of ordinary people. And a very popular crusade it is proving.' But, great as the achievements were, Mrs Thatcher stressed that they should never be taken for granted – given the extent of the threats to which they were exposed, principally from an extreme Labour Party. Furthermore, it was always necessary to be on guard against misrepresentation, particularly in relation to the Health Service where, despite the increases, 'people still talk of cuts'. This speech underlined Mrs Thatcher's determination to ensure that her Government's work and record were accurately understood.

Mr Chairman, we come to this conference confident in your support, confident in our policies, confident in the future of our country.

Of course, there are the professional grumblers who will always complain whatever we do. And if they ever got to the pearly gates, they'd grumble there. Because the gates squeaked; or they weren't pearly enough. And St Peter didn't bow low enough after all they'd done – or should I say, after all they had left undone. If we let the grumblers have their way, we

202

would be bending and turning with every twist in the opinion polls. That is not this Government's style, nor this Prime Minister's.

Our style is to decide what is right for the country, not what is temporarily convenient. Applause dies with the day. Belief lives on. We look to the future, for we are more than a one-generation society.

Soon we will enter our eighth year of Government. We are a free people: free to choose our way of life; free because of the rule of law. But that freedom can never be taken for granted. From one age to another, threats to its precious qualities come stealthily by different paths.

Seven years ago, that freedom was challenged by the Winter of Discontent. And the will of a Labour Government bowed to the might of the trade unions. More recently, it was challenged again by the miners' strike. But a Conservative Government stood firm. This Government has, step by step, diminished the industrial and political power of centralized trade unionism and restored strength to the hands of their own members. That battle for freedom wasn't won by the faint hearts but by the stout hearts. There are some things on which you can never give way.

Today there is a whole new atmosphere in industrial relations. There can be no better example than here in the port of Felixstowe, where we see trade unionists and employers equally committed to their enterprise. They know that if you work together, then the team can achieve great things. Pull apart and you perish. Pull together and you succeed.

A nation will not long remain free if its currency is debased. Money does not buy freedom; but misuse of money, the filching of its value by the State, can swiftly diminish freedom. We have restored honest money. And by so doing we have given more confidence to men and women that what they give to their work, they will harvest.

And we have recovered much of the freedom of the individual from the Socialist concept of the corporate State. Not only in home-ownership, where the most remarkable increase has been among manual workers and among young people in their twenties. We have also dismantled State industries and spread their ownership. In Jaguar, Cable and Wireless, Amersham, British Telecom, and many more such as National Freight. And I always like to see, on the National Freight vehicles, the slogan 'Now *we're* in the driving seat'. Not the Government. Not the bureaucrats. Not the bosses. Not the militant unions. But the workers and management working together.

Seven years ago, who would have dared forecast such a transformation of Britain? This didn't come about because of consensus. It happened because we said, 'This we believe, this we will do.' It's called leadership.

Conservative policies are winning the day; and even the grudging support of a few politicians elsewhere. Yet, at the time, they fought us tooth and nail. Today, they can see our success, and they want to claim it as their own.

But does anyone seriously think that Conservative achievements would be safe in their hands? So I warn you: don't take it for granted that inflation will stay low. If it weren't for the Tories, pensioners would have to watch out. Inflation destroys your savings. Don't take it for granted that mortgage interest relief will continue. If it weren't for the Tories, many young people wouldn't be able to buy their own home. Don't take it for granted that trade unionists will continue to have a vote in their union. If it weren't for the Tories, they wouldn't have one today. Don't take it for granted that you'll be allowed to keep all your shares. Nationalization lies right at the heart of Labour's policy. And don't take it for granted that this country will always have the defences we need. If it weren't for the Tories, far from being defended, Britain would be defenceless against any nuclear power in the world. Conservative achievements are safe only in Conservative hands.

Now let's look ahead a little. There has been the odd report recently that Thatcherism has run its course, and is on its way out. As an informed source close to Downing Street, I have to report that those reports are eyewash.

We're only just beginning. We've barely got past the stage of excavation, let alone of topping out! You may feel that the first seven years of Conservative Government have produced some benefits for Britain. And so they have.

But the next seven are going to produce more – many more. And the next seven after that, more still. Let me tell you why. Conservatism is not some abstract theory. It's a crusade to put power in the hands of ordinary people. And a very popular crusade it is proving. Tenants are jumping at the opportunity to buy their own council houses. Workers are jumping at the opportunity to buy shares in their own privatized companies. Trade unionists are jumping at the opportunity, which the ballot box now gives them, to decide 'who rules' in their union. And the rest of Britain is looking on with approval. For popular capitalism is biting deep.

It used to be Socialists who talked of crusades. Well, let them launch a new one on the old Socialist lines. What about a Socialist crusade to rehabilitate that old favourite, the municipal landlord, and to lure home-owners back into becoming council tenants? Or a Socialist crusade to renationalize Vickers, and take back the workers' shares. Or a Socialist crusade to abolish bothersome union ballots and get back to the good old days of Big Brother. After all, these aims are the very heartbeat of Socialism.

But you may have noticed how muted nowadays are the trumpets for such Socialist crusades. For popular capitalism, which is the economic expression of liberty, is proving a much more attractive means for diffusing power in our society. Socialists cry, 'Power to the People', and raise the clenched fist as they say it. We all know what they really mean – power over people, power to the State. To us Conservatives, popular capitalism means what it says: power through ownership to the man and woman in the street, given confidently with an open hand.

Today the climate for British industry is better than it has been for thirty years. Last year, investment was at an all-time record of £60 billion – new roads, modern factories, the latest equipment. That augurs well for the future. Industry is more profitable than it has been for twenty-five years. Since 1980 productivity in manufacturing industry has risen faster than in France, faster than in Germany. And, for the last six years,

THE REVIVAL OF BRITAIN

Britain has had a balance of payments surplus.

This economic success story does not always get the credit it deserves. Some people carry British understatement and self-criticism too far. The renaissance of enterprise and the renewal of our national fabric often go unsung. Maybe we feel about our industry as we feel about our weather: it is never quite right, the prospects are too often cloudy or overcast. Yet it is our weather, about which we always complain, which gives us our green and pleasant land.

What is it that now gives us such optimism for the future? First, oil. Only a year ago a single barrel of oil cost around $25 to buy. Today it costs about $13. To read some reports you'd think we all ought to go into mourning to mark the death of expensive oil. Yes, of course it will lose us some revenue and some exports. But all those who thought the oil price explosion of the 1970s did harm to our industry and slowed our growth rate were right. Falling oil prices are, on the whole, good news. There's more money to spend on other things. The spending power in the nation's pockets and purses is rising. Industry's costs are being cut. All this is a bit like a tax cut, but one for which, alas, the Government cannot take credit.

Second, interest rates. In the last few weeks the cost of borrowing money in several major countries has fallen. That too is good for the world economy and helps our own companies trading overseas. We are living at a time which calls for more partnership and co-operation, both between countries and between companies. We have to work together. Moreover, Britain receives a tidy income from our overseas investments – and will continue to do so long after North Sea oil is a thing of the past.

Third, exchange rates. Every industrialist I speak to has a different view of the exchange rate he wants. Markets, not Governments, set exchange rates; and it's just not possible to satisfy everyone all of the time. But the agreement reached last year between the five major industrial nations has contributed to a welcome change in the pattern of exchange rates. And that benefits all of us – and brings great opportunities.

But I must repeat my constant message to all industrialists.

Exchange rates go up and down. Success comes from your own efforts and your own efficiency. Never rely on the exchange rate to beat your rivals.

I have already mentioned the reform of trade union law, privatization, employee shareholdings, and lower inflation. And there have been a number of tax reforms. In this favourable climate new jobs are coming – 700,000 in under three years – more than in any other country in Europe. We need jobs in both manufacturing and services. What's the point of making a television set if there are no programmes to show on it? Who would want to buy a car if there were no garages to sell petrol and service it? What's the use of making radiators if there are no plumbers to install central heating? We need a well-serviced economy, which buys British – because British is best.

I recently held a meeting of businessmen at Number Ten, called 'Better made in Britain'. The purpose was to see how British-made goods could win a bigger share of the home market and so create more jobs. It's humbug to complain about unemployment if you drink French mineral water and drive an imported car.

This Government is backing business with a dynamic policy for enterprise. We're training people in the skills they need – high technology, design, marketing and engineering. We're strengthening competition and small business. We're battling for Britain in the export markets of the world. And we're going for more privatization, less regulation and wider share ownership.

And it's not only happening in Britain. Privatization is on the agenda in Turkey, Malaysia, Japan, Mexico and Canada. And China too is striving to create free enterprise. People are no longer worried about catching the British disease. They're queueing up to obtain the new British cure.

We've done better for the Health Service than any previous Government. I could reel off facts and figures to prove it. I do so regularly in the House of Commons, although the Opposition tries to stop me. That's because they don't like the truth, they do everything they can to drown it. But there's something you must often have asked yourselves. Why aren't we better at getting our excellent message across?

This Government hasn't cut investment in health – we've increased it. Over forty major hospital schemes have already been completed. A further 150 of varying sizes are under way. There are 11,500 new hospital beds; over 100 new X-ray departments; and nearly 200 new operating theatres. There are more doctors, dentists and nurses – and we can now treat more patients.

These are not just achievements of Government. We owe a debt to all those in the Health and Social Services who look after others with such commitment and dedication. Yet, despite all these increases in the Health Service, people still talk of cuts. Why?

We live in a television age – and television is selective. One camera shot of a pretty nurse helping an elderly patient out of an empty hospital ward speaks louder than all the statistics in Whitehall and Westminster. Never mind that the hospital is being closed because it's out of date. Never mind that, a few miles away, a spanking new hospital is being opened – with brighter wards, better operating theatres and the very latest equipment. In today's world, selective seeing is believing. And in today's world, television comes over as truth. I remember myself opening a beautiful new hospital. Virtually the only publicity was a demonstration outside – about cuts.

And there's something else. Medical science is advancing so fast that now there's almost no limit to how much we could spend. Indeed the Royal Commission on the National Health Service which reported in 1979 said, 'We had no difficulty in believing . . . that we can easily spend the whole of the Gross National Product' on the National Health Service.

The opportunities for spending money on health may not be limited, but taxpayers' money is. There are other deserving causes: the police, education, pensions and defence. Yet we have ploughed more money into the Health Service, precisely to bring these medical advances within reach of more and more people. And that is also the reason why we have prescription and health charges. Together they bring in £500 million. That £500 million can pay the salaries of some 60,000 nurses or buy half a million operations.

There are always difficult choices to be made. We choose to give priority to the Health Service, as you can see from one final statistic. When we came into office, spending on the National Health Service was £7¾ billion a year. This year it will be £18¾ billion – an increase which goes way above inflation.

The Opposition can keep on turning out its propaganda. But it can't alter facts. And it can't dislodge all the new doctors and dentists or destroy all the new hospitals.

I spoke earlier of freedom. In the eyes of many of our people, the freedom most at risk today is freedom to walk in the street without fear; freedom to answer the door without fear; freedom to be safe and secure in your own home.

The recent crime figures for England and Wales have appalled us all, with their record of brutality, violence and rape. The Lord Chief Justice has described rape as 'a violation which obliterates the personality of victims'. I'm sure you applaud the lead he has given in proposing sentences up to life imprisonment for this, one of the most savage of crimes.

Central and local Government carry, as they have for years, a duty to protect the citizen; to provide and equip police forces; to make by statute laws which will deter and punish the criminal; and to support, and if necessary augment, the numbers of those who administer justice. More police – we've seen to that. Better equipment – they have it. Another Criminal Justice Bill – it's in preparation.

But when crime is rife and people are troubled, they must not be passive. A free people must share the burden of law and order, not remit it all to the State.

There are many tasks to be shared: to check wrongdoing in home and school; to take practical measures of crime prevention; not to shrug shoulders when crime is committed under our nose; not to shield the offender; not to resist being a witness; and never to turn away, but to help the victims of crime to come through their traumatic experience.

Glancing back along the road we have come, and despite all the problems we have yet to face, I believe there are solid grounds for encouragement, to lift the spirit. We are no longer seen by our friends abroad as Europe's poor relation. Indeed, when I read what is written about us in other lands, I am tempted to think we are sometimes seen in higher regard than we see ourselves. In seven short years we have changed the face of this country of ours. But I am only too well aware that there is always another hill to climb, another battle to be won.

In a nation of our history, in a party of our traditions, it is the lamp at the top of the hill, to which the leader must always be drawn, must never lose sight of, must strive with might and main to keep alight. Amid all the tasks before us, and the obstacles – and the distractions, which we shall surmount – for this party, this Government, this nation, the lamp on the hill shines like a beacon. From that lamp our eye must not, and shall not, waver.

The Conservative Women's Conference

LONDON, 4 JUNE 1986

Mrs Thatcher has often spoken of the contrast between life in the Eastern Bloc and that in the Western democracies. It provided a major theme of this speech, in which she referred movingly to the unfulfilled hopes of those such as Mrs Yelena Bonner, the wife of the leading Soviet dissident, Andrei Sakharov, who were simply striving for things which were taken for granted in the West. Indeed, in Britain the crucial ingredients of civilized existence were more widely available than ever before – thanks to the success of Thatcherism.

Last Friday I had the privilege of seeing Mrs Yelena Bonner, the wife of the Soviet scientist and courageous human rights campaigner, Andrei Sakharov. Mrs Bonner, as you know, has been allowed out of the Soviet Union, where her husband is more or less under house arrest, to visit her daughter and two granddaughters in the United States and to receive medical treatment there.

What she had to say was fascinating. You may have read in the papers how her impression of life in America contrasted with life in Soviet Russia. What struck her most forcibly was the possibility of actually owning a home of her own, as her children do, and what this meant for human and family life. 'I'm sixty-three,' she wrote, 'and I've never had a house; not only that, I've never had a corner I could call my own.' She

211

went on, 'My dream, my own house, is unattainable for my husband and myself, as unattainable as Heaven on Earth.'

Yelena Bonner is a beacon of the human spirit. We have no right to take for granted what for her is a dream of Heaven on Earth, but for us in Britain is an everyday, attainable reality. We should take stock of what we have been able to achieve for family living standards here at home, with pride and gratitude, but without complacency. So, next time you go canvassing, think of Mrs Bonner. When you call on your first owner-occupied home, think of Mrs Bonner. In Britain, there are fourteen million homes like that.

Don't be surprised if the householder who answers your knock on the door is young. In the last seven years, a lot more young people have been able to buy their own homes. That's good news. And you may well see a child in the sitting room using a home computer pretty expertly – probably far better at it than mother or father.

In that same house, the chances are there will be a video and a deep freeze. Moreover, nearly seven out of every ten households now have central heating, an increase of one-fifth since 1979. Since then, many more homes have telephones – so important to the elderly, especially if they live alone. And incidentally, the family may well have bought some shares in British Telecom when it was privatized.

Of course, some commentators think that it is crudely materialistic to describe the everyday things that families want in the way I am doing. And then they go on to contradict themselves by complaining that not everyone enjoys them! Well, *our* aim is to spread these good things, and others, more widely – by leaving people with enough of their own money to afford them. Remarks about our society being debilitated by 'consumerism', so-called, is simply Socialist sour grapes. Look at Eastern Europe: Socialist economies have produced hardly anything worth consuming! Adam Smith, the canniest of economists, pointed out that the object of production is consumption. There's no earthly point in making goods unless someone's going to buy them.

I have deliberately spoken first about life in the family home.

212

For in a free society, it is not Government which is the centre of people's lives, but the family. The desire to do better for your family is the strongest driving force in human nature. And a secure and loving home life is the best start any child can have. Of course, a good standard *of* living is not enough. You also need to be taught good standards *for* living.

So our policy starts with the family, its freedom, and its well-being. The great Health and Social Services are meant, not to supplant, but to strengthen the family. This Government has consistently demonstrated its commitment to these services. Perhaps the rest of us don't proclaim our achievements enough. I was interested to see what somebody wrote the other day to the Minister of Health. This is what it said:

> I cannot speak too highly of the treatment and conditions obtained in this hospital . . . all in all, the care and facilities could not have been improved upon . . . Indeed, several of my fellow-patients from all walks of life urged me to write to you to place this on record . . . It is time that someone did something to put the other side of the picture.

Indeed, I see from a recent poll that the great majority of people who have received treatment under the National Health Service are well satisfied. We have built up the Health Service so it has more resources and more medical staff to treat more patients than ever before. Those are the facts. No wonder the Opposition tries to drown them in a flood of hostile propaganda against the Health Service. We must see they do not succeed.

And consider the pensioners of Britain. What are their concerns? They want the security of stable prices in the shops; and of savings that grow and are not destroyed by rampant inflation. Only our party offers them that security. They want to feel safe in their homes and on the streets. We are backing the police with more men than ever in the fight against violent crime. And having seen her on television, who can forget Lady Tucker, that marvellously plucky eighty-seven-year-old British lady in New York, who gave the mugger the fright of his life by beating him off with that indispensable item of equipment, the British umbrella. I bet that's the last time he'll have a go at a lady from Britain. No one should ever talk about elderly people as a problem. Many of them are an example to us all. We are seeing more and more of them actively involved in the life of their communities. And that's right. We need their experience and ideas.

Half of all social security spending goes to help the elderly. Some manage well by themselves with that support alone. But many look to other services as well. It matters that district nurses should visit them. Today we have more district nurses than ever, providing more treatment. Whether on pensions, help for the disabled, or the Health Service in general; this Government's record is better than that of any previous Government in Britain. So it should be under a Conservative Government. So it is.

In all these different ways, life in Britain is better. Yes, of course we still face problems. But we can tackle them with confidence, because of the problems we have already overcome.

How was it done? First, by sound financial management. Whether you're running a home, or a business or the Government, you've got to budget to live within your means. Anyone who tries to convince you that you can spend as if there were no tomorrow is leading you up the garden path. It's the easiest thing in the world to say, 'Go on, spend more, borrow more.' But the question any good housekeeper has to ask is, 'If the unexpected happens, have I left myself enough in reserve to cope?' Under so many previous Governments, the answer has been 'No'. Under this Government, the answer has been 'Yes'. The Falklands; a year-long coal strike; the collapse of oil prices and oil revenues: we withstood them all. There has been no economic crisis with this Government. That's *good* management.

Second, we had to decide on priorities within the total Budget – where we needed to spend more and where we could make savings. Your Government has spent more: on defence of the realm, because that is the first duty of Government. Nothing is more important than defending Britain and our way of life. It has spent more on the police because, when we took office, there was an urgent need to increase police numbers and

214

raise police morale. We have done both. It has spent more too on pensions; and, as you know, this Government has kept faith with the pensioners. In fact, the pension buys more than it ever did under Labour. And of course there has been more for health, where we have increased spending from £7¾ billion to £18¾ billion.

At the same time – and here's one of many crucial differences between us and Labour – we've made genuine savings, especially in the nationalized industries, where our aim has been to turn losses into profits. Take British Steel, which was running at a huge loss: over £600 million a year. You, the taxpayer, had to find it. Today, British Steel is in profit and ranks with the most efficient steel industries in Europe. Let's congratulate the management and workforce in nationalized industries who have worked together to bring about success.

We also set to work on making the machinery of Government more efficient and cutting bureaucracy and red-tape. This efficiency drive has brought forward savings worth over £750 million a year. And I want to pay tribute to all those Civil Servants who work with the Government, loyally and with dedication, in the pursuit of greater efficiency. They deserve our thanks.

Thirdly, we have looked to see whether the money is used effectively. It's not just how much you spend, but how you spend it. Whether we're talking about raising standards in education, improving health care, or creating a better environment and a cleaner Britain, of course, money matters. But other things matter too: how wisely the money is spent; the quality of the management; and the morale and dedication of each individual. So let us measure public services not just by how much taxpayers' money they take, but more by the standards of service they provide.

Today our principal opponents pretend – and, until the votes are counted, will go on pretending – *not* to be Socialists, in order to win power for Socialism. It won't work. And if Labour believes it will, they labour under a delusion. A party does not become a Government by slapping grey paint on the Red Flag and pretending to be what it patently is *not*. And you don't get rid of thousands of left-wing extremists firmly entrenched in the Labour Party by expelling a handful of councillors in Liverpool – and, to date, they haven't even managed that!

Labour has allies. The Liberals, when they're not being studiously vague, are quietly enlisting in Labour's army. For they do not have the strength to win themselves. They've signed up for political control of the police, for giving away our nuclear weapons, for high tax. They've so often put the rates up massively where they control the councils. And they pledge themselves to every kind of extra spending without telling you how in the world they'll raise the money. They've decided the best way to help Labour is to soft-pedal Labour policies whilst smiling to capture anti-Labour votes. We must make sure they don't let the Labour fox slip in through the hedge. It's no good saying after the event, 'I didn't mean *that* to happen.'

You will have seen reports of yesterday's economic debate in the House of Commons. Some people talk as if there were a simple choice: are you on the side of more public spending or are you on the side of tax cuts? People who put it that way assume that the national cake is always the same size, and that a bigger slice here means a smaller slice there. But that's just not true if the national cake is getting bigger. Indeed, this year the penny off income tax appeared in pay packets the same week as the Government announced more manpower for the police and a further £60 million for the Health Service. Of course we had set aside reserves for contingencies, so the extra was well within the total we had planned. That is only prudent.

But caring in its true sense is also about not overtaxing those who have to live on modest incomes. My concern is those people who are still paying too much income tax. Yes, I am proud of this Government's record on, for example, increasing the pay of nurses. But did you know that a nurse earning £150 a week has £41.60 deducted from her pay packet in tax and contributions? That a single person on £100 a week has £25 taken out of his or her pay packet? That a widow, trying to keep a family home going on a weekly income of £153, can find that £42 is taken away?

There are eighteen million people in this country whose

earnings are at, or below, average male earnings. These people look to the Conservative Government so that they can keep more of what they themselves have earned and saved. They can't look to anyone else and we have to keep faith with them. Moreover, by cutting income tax, people's take-home pay goes up without adding to industrial costs. That's vital when we have to compete against countries whose costs are rising more slowly than ours. What do people do with their extra take-home pay? It gives them an opportunity to improve their home: do up the kitchen, spend something on the children. And that in turn creates jobs. It means people can spend *their* money on what *they* want. Not on what somebody else thinks they should want. And if people decide to put their money into savings, that can help provide the finance for somebody else to borrow money to start up in business. That's good for jobs too. It's no coincidence that those countries – like the United States, Japan and Switzerland – which have lower personal taxes, also have more jobs and lower unemployment.

Tax cuts help the economy. They create the wealth to sustain our social services. And they help the family to build up savings; to own some property; to have a bit of independence. That brings a sense of security, and the satisfaction of being able to pass something on to your children, to give them a start in life. That's the kind of society we want to create.

Which is the better country for its citizens? One which trusts its people to be free, diverse, self-reliant, where the State is the servant of the people; or the one, of which Mrs Bonner spoke, where the people are subservient to the State? John Betjeman caught the whiff of State domination in his memorable lines:

> *Cut down that timber . . .*
> *Remove those cottages, a huddled throng! . . .*
>
> *I have a Vision of The Future, chum,*
>   *The workers' flats in fields of soya beans*
>   *Tower up like silver pencils, score on score:*
> *And Surging Millions hear the Challenge come*
>   *From microphones in communal canteens*
>   *'No Right! No Wrong! All's perfect, evermore.'*
>
>   *'The Planster's Vision'*

217

I saw it, I heard those microphones, as I stood and looked over the border at North Korea.

A few days ago one staunch headmistress, the President of the National Association of Head Teachers, spoke up about the responsibility of individuals and of parents. She said this: 'I firmly believe that the greatest crisis facing British education in 1986 is not the question of our budgets, the curriculum or the quality of our teachers. It is much more basic than that. In the 1980s it is all too easy for parents to abdicate their responsibilities. So many children enter school barely able to speak because parents haven't made time to talk to them. It is a generation of children who haven't been taught a single nursery rhyme.'

It's too easy trying to lay off your conscience with more and more public spending. But compassion can't be nationalized. It's individuals that count. A responsible society is one in which people do not leave it to the person next door to do the job. It is one in which people help each other, where parents put their children first and friends look out for the neighbours, and families for their elderly members. That is the starting point for care and support – the unsung efforts of millions of individuals, the selfless work of thousands upon thousands of volunteers. It is their spirit that helps to bind our society together. They've made Britain envied the world over for the strength of its voluntary contribution.

Caring isn't measured by what you say: it's expressed by what you do. It was Conservatives who cared enough about the problem of pensioners and others on fixed incomes to take on inflation and win. It was Conservative love of country that fought off those who would disarm us, and leave us empty-handed at the bargaining tables of the world. It was Conservative respect for families and their freedoms which has led us to return houses and shares to the people, broadening ownership beyond our fathers' wildest dreams. It was Conservative courage which met the trade union leaders and, by appealing to their members, brought in new rights for the working man.

This Government has fought many battles and won much

ground, ground which others feared to take. Our first duty is to defend and hold that ground against all-comers. That we shall do. But that is not enough to secure the Britain of the future. Yes, let us hold on to, and cherish, all that is dear to us. But the needs of a country are always changing and new occasions teach new duties.

Some say the time has come to relax. But success does not come to those who just want a bit of peace and quiet. That is not the way of this Government, or of any responsible Government. For Britain can never prosper through dodged decisions, fudged choices or lost direction.

Our young people have all the drive and all the initiative required to meet new challenges now and in the years to come.

The first challenge is the challenge of jobs. In the last three years nearly a million extra jobs have been created. But how do we generate more? Get bureaucracy out of the way of those who create jobs – and allow enterprise to flourish. Reform tax and benefits – and make it worth while to work. Harness the energies of private enterprise with Government – and revive our inner cities. Train and retrain our people – and equip them with the skills of tomorrow. Get ahead in technology – and build the new science-based industries. Fight for Britain in the tough markets of the world – and win the orders that bring the jobs.

It's successful business enterprise that creates new and lasting jobs; and only a Government which puts enterprise first offers real hope to those without work.

Then, there is the challenge of education. The pursuit of excellence in education has never been more vital: to get the best out of each and every pupil, all different, all equally important. That means helping teachers and parents to work together; giving children a good general education so that when, in their working life, one skill becomes obsolete, they can quickly learn another; sorting out teachers' pay, so that the better teachers are better paid; backing teachers who believe in maintaining discipline; and rejecting political indoctrination in favour of true learning.

Third is the challenge to our society from violence and

THE REVIVAL OF BRITAIN

intimidation. If order is not maintained, then all rights of the citizen are threatened. We deplore the humbug of some of our political opponents who, though they condemn violence, condone the tactics, the demonstrations, the picket lines which inevitably lead to violence, as they have done in Wapping. Having watched those terrible scenes on television, in which so many police were injured, what I can't stand are those detached discussions between armchair commentators as to who started it. Do they think we can't see the injuries to the police and the missiles thrown at them and their horses? Don't those who organize these demonstrations ever think of those who live nearby?

Our message is clear. In the fight against crime, lawlessness and intimidation, wc must give unswerving support to the police and the courts as they carry out their exacting duties. And in our party, we stand rock-firm in the fight against terrorism at home and abroad. Yet the Labour Party votes regularly against the Prevention of Terrorism Act. Worse still, an official prospective Labour parliamentary candidate [Mr Ken Livingstone] goes abroad to attack the British Army and British courts and to defend convicted IRA terrorists. Is he being expelled by Labour? No one dares.

The fourth challenge is of East–West relations. I hope that a second Summit *will* take place this year between President Reagan and Mr Gorbachev. I believe there is still time before that Summit to make progress on arms control agreements; particularly on chemical weapons where Britain has the chair in the current negotiations. I believe that in a world where there is no power to enforce international law, it is vital that treaties negotiated between the United States and the Soviet Union – like the ABM Treaty and the SALT Agreement – should be upheld.

But for a treaty to be valid *both sides* have to comply with it. The United States has just decided to dismantle two nuclear weapon submarines as required under SALT 2. The Soviet Union has a case to answer that she has not complied with the treaties as regards new missiles, new radars and by concealing information on new missile tests. So far she has failed to answer

220

the case against her on these matters. I hope that both Governments will comply with the treaty and will take steps to be *seen* to comply with it, and that the treaty will continue.

We shall tackle these four challenges with the same vigour as we tackled the challenges of seven years ago. Indeed, Conservative Government alone can manage the changes required to bring Britain free, prosperous and secure into the twenty-first century.

I began by referring to a single courageous woman, Yelena Bonner; and I conclude with Mrs Bonner. She symbolizes in an arresting, heart-warming way the indomitable spirit of the human individual even when confronted with the awesome power of a totalitarian State.

As I look round this hall today, at the many hundreds of Conservative women gathered together here, how can I be other than profoundly hopeful about the prospects for our country? For that same spirit which inspires the defiance of Mrs Bonner, which yearns in her for the happiness and security of her husband and family, would no less inspire us here – each one of us – if ever Britain were to slip into the thraldom of State domination.

You are the best guardians of our liberties. Continue with the Conservative Party to build on the great open site of human freedom: the homes, the families, the values, the enterprises – in a word, the good society. For it's that which can bring, as Yelena Bonner herself has testified, a little bit of Heaven on Earth.

The Conservative Party Conference

BLACKPOOL, 9 OCTOBER 1987

Thatcherism is a political creed which is constantly renewing and increasing its strength. Those who suggested in the mid-1980s that its momentum might be slowing got their answer at the 1987 election. The Conservative manifesto contained the most detailed and radical programme that any political party, seeking re-election for a third term, had ever produced. A new approach was promised on three key social issues: education, housing and local Government. And it was made clear that, by taking tough action in these three areas, the Government would make a decisive contribution to resolving the problems of the inner cities which had now moved to the top of the political agenda.

Mrs Thatcher explained how the new phase of Thatcherism would proceed in this speech – after first reminding her audience of the guiding principles on which it has always been based. The Times (10 October 1987) described the speech as 'the best she has made to a Conservative Conference' and went on to emphasize what was undoubtedly its central theme: 'the proposition that the nation's problems are now overridingly social and are capable of a moral solution'.

A lot has happened since we last met. There was, for instance, our election victory in June. They tell me that makes it three wins in a row. Just like Lord Liverpool. And he was Prime Minister for fifteen years. It's rather encouraging.

It was an historic victory. And I want to thank all those who did so much. Above all, our Chairman, Norman Tebbit. Norman and Margaret hold, and will always hold, a unique place in our esteem and affection. Thank you, too, Margaret.

And on 11 June we even won some nine seats we failed to gain in 1983. And we won back three we lost at by-elections. To the victors we say – congratulations. To our former colleagues who lost – come back soon. We miss you.

Just why did we win? I think it is because we knew what we stood for. We said what we stood for; and we stuck by what we stood for. Since the election, it sometimes seems we are the only party that does.

Twelve years ago, I first stood on this platform as Leader of the Conservative Party. Now one or two things have changed since 1975. In that year we were still groaning under Labour's so-called 'Social Contract'. People said we should never be able to govern again. Remember how we had all been lectured about political impossibility? You couldn't be a Conservative, and sound like a Conservative, and win an election – they said. And you certainly couldn't win an election and then act like a Conservative and win another election. And – this was absolutely beyond dispute – you couldn't win two elections and go on behaving like a Conservative, and yet win a third election. Don't you harbour just the faintest suspicion that somewhere along the line something went wrong with that theory?

Right up to 11 June the Labour Party, the Liberals and the SDP were busy saying that Conservatism doesn't work. Oddly enough, since 12 June, they've been saying that it does. And so our political opponents are now feverishly packaging their policies to look like ours. And it's interesting that no party now dares to say openly that it will take away from the people what we have given back to the people.

Labour's language may alter, their presentation may be slicker, but underneath, it's still the same old Socialism. Far be it from me to deride the sinner that repenteth. The trouble with Labour is they want the benefit of repentance without renouncing the original sin. No way!

And the so-called 'Alliance'? During the election campaign I used to wonder what the Alliance Leaders meant by consensus politics. I have a feeling that, if Dr Owen didn't know it before, he knows now: six inches of fraternal steel beneath the shoulder blades.

We are a successful party leading a successful nation. And I'm often asked what's the secret. It's really quite simple. What we have done is to re-establish at the heart of British politics a handful of simple truths.

First, no economy can thrive if Government debases the coinage. No society can be fair or stable when inflation eats up savings and devalues the pound in everyone's pocket. Inflation threatens democracy itself. We've always put its defeat at the top of our agenda. For it's a battle which never ends. It means keeping your budget on a sound financial footing. Not just one year, but every year, and that's why we need Nigel Lawson.

Second, men and women need the incentive that comes from keeping more of what they earn. No one can say that people aren't interested in their take-home pay. If that were true, a lot of trade union leaders would be out of a job. So, as economic growth has taken off, we've cut income tax. And as soon as we prudently can, we'll do it again.

Third, as people earn more, they want to own more. They value the security which comes from ownership – whether of shares or homes. Soon there will be more shareholders than trade unionists in this country. Of course, not all trade unionists are shareholders – yet. But I hope that before long they will be.

Home ownership too has soared. And to extend the right to council tenants, we had to fight the battle, as you know, the battle in Parliament every inch of the way – against Labour opposition, and against Liberal opposition. Does the Labour Leader now applaud what has happened? Does the Liberal Leader welcome it? Surely, now that it's proved so popular, it must be the sort of liberating measure of which even he would approve.

For years we Conservatives had talked about wanting to create a property-owning democracy. Looking back, I wonder whether we did as much as we should have done to achieve that

224

goal. But I don't believe that anyone will be able, in the years ahead, to make a similar charge against this Government. Indeed, extending ownership has been one of the achievements of which I am most proud.

Fourth, it is our passionate belief that free enterprise and competition are the engines of prosperity and the guardians of liberty. These ideas have shaped free political institutions and brought unimagined wealth to countries and continents. Just look at what we have achieved – low inflation; tax cuts; wider ownership; a revival of enterprise and, over the last year, unemployment has fallen at record speed by 400,000. And we want it to fall further. And with continued economic growth, it should.

Our economic success has enabled Britain to play a more prominent role in the world at large. We are now the second biggest investor in the world, and the very model of a stable economy. And that's why Nigel Lawson has been able to play a leading role in helping to tackle the world debt crisis. International bankers, the finance Ministers of other nations: they all listen to you a lot harder when they owe you money rather than the other way round.

The old Britain of the 1970s, with its strikes, poor productivity, low investment, winters of discontent, above all its gloom, its pessimism, its sheer defeatism – that Britain is gone. We now have a new Britain, confident, optimistic, sure of its economic strength – a Britain to which foreigners come to admire, to invest, yes and to imitate.

I have reminded you where the great political adventure began and where it has led. But is this where we pitch our tents? Is this where we dig in? Absolutely not. Our third election victory was only a staging post on a much longer journey. I know with every fibre of my being that it would be fatal for us just to stand where we are now. What would be our slogan for the 1990s if we did that?

Would 'consolidate' be the word that we stitch on our banners? Whose blood would run faster at the prospect of five years of consolidation? Of course, we secure what we've achieved. But we move on – applying our principles and beliefs to even more challenging ground.

For our purpose as Conservatives is to extend opportunity – and choice – to those who have so far been denied them.

Our most important task in this Parliament is to raise the quality of education. It's in the national interest. And it's in the individual interest of every parent and, above all, of every child. We want education to be part of the answer to Britain's problems, not part of the cause.

To compete successfully in tomorrow's world – against Japan, Germany and the United States – we need well-educated, well-trained, creative young people. Because if education is backward today, national performance will be backward tomorrow.

But it's the plight of individual boys and girls which worries me most. Too often, our children don't get the education they need – the education they deserve. And in the inner cities – where youngsters must have a decent education if they are to have a better future – that opportunity is all too often snatched from them by hard Left education authorities and extremist teachers. Children who need to be able to count and multiply are learning anti-racist mathematics – whatever that may be. Children who need to be able to express themselves in clear English are being taught political slogans. Children who need to be taught to respect traditional moral values are being taught that they have an inalienable right to be gay.

Children who need encouragement – and children do so much need encouragement – so many children – they are being taught that our society offers them no future. All of those children are being cheated of a sound start in life – yes, cheated.

Of course – in the country as a whole – there are plenty of excellent teachers and successful schools. And in every good school, and every good teacher, is a reminder of what too many young people are denied. I believe that Government must take the primary responsibility for setting standards for the education of our children. And that's why we are establishing a national curriculum for basic subjects.

It is vital that children master essential skills: reading, writing, spelling, grammar, arithmetic; and that they understand basic science and technology. And for good teachers this will provide a foundation on which they can build with their own creative skill and professionalism.

But the key to raising standards is to enlist the support of parents. The Labour Left – hard, soft and in-between – they hate the idea that people should be able to choose. In particular, they hate the idea that parents should be able to choose their children's education. The Conservative Party believes in parental choice. And we are now about to take two dramatic steps forward in extending choice in education.

First, we will allow popular schools to take in as many children as space will permit. And this will stop local authorities from putting artificially low limits on entry to good schools.

And second, we will give parents and governors the right to take their children's school out of the hands of the local authority and into the hands of their own governing body. This will create a new kind of school funded by the State, alongside the present State schools and the independent private schools.

These new schools will be independent State schools. They will bring a better education to many children because the school will be in the hands of those who care most for it and for its future.

There's no reason at all why local authorities should have a monopoly of free education. What principle suggests that this is right? What recent experience or practice suggests it is even sensible?

In these ways, we are furthering our Conservative tradition of extending opportunity more widely. This policy will be of the greatest advantage, not to those schools where the parents are already satisfied with their children's education, but to those schools where the parents are dissatisfied and believe that their children could do a lot better. Nowhere is this policy more needed than in what have come to be known as 'inner cities'. It will profit those people most.

Now the phrase 'inner cities' is a kind of convenient shorthand for a host of problems. Cities have risen and declined throughout history. They have risen by responding to the opportunities, the markets, the technologies of their day have

227

offered. And they declined when they clung to old, outdated ways and new markets passed them by. That is what has happened to many of our great cities.

Their decline was sometimes aggravated by the worst form of post-war town planning – a sort of social vandalism, carried out with the best of intentions but the worst of results. All too often, the planners cut the heart out of our cities. They swept aside the familiar city centres that had grown up over the centuries. They replaced them with a wedge of tower blocks and linking expressways, interspersed with token patches of grass and a few windswept piazzas, where pedestrians fear to tread.

The planners didn't think, 'Are we breaking the pattern of people's lives. Are we cutting them off from their friends, their neighbours?' They didn't wonder, 'Are we uprooting whole communities?' They didn't ask, 'Can children still play safely in the street?' They didn't consider any of these things. Nor did they consult the police about how to design an estate in which people could walk safe from muggers and vandals. They simply set the municipal bulldozer to work. What folly, what incredible folly.

And the people who didn't fit into this urban Utopia? They dispatched them to outlying estates without a pub or corner shop or anywhere to go.

Oh! the schemes won a number of architectural awards. But they were a nightmare for the people. They snuffed out any spark of local enterprise. And they made people entirely dependent on the local authorities and the services they chose to provide.

As if that were not enough, some of our cities have also been dominated by Labour councils implacably hostile to enterprise. So when industries left, they piled higher rates on those that remained. When old markets vanished, they sought not new markets but new subsidies. And they capitalized not on their strengths, but on their weaknesses. And in fact they accelerated decline.

So dying industries, soulless planning, municipal Socialism – these deprived the people of the most precious things in life: hope, confidence and belief in themselves. And that sapping of the spirit is at the very heart of urban decay.

To give back heart to our cities we must give back hope to the people. And it's beginning to happen. Because today Britain has a strong and growing economy. Oh yes, recovery has come faster in some parts of the country than others. But now it is taking root in our most depressed urban landscapes. We all applaud the organization 'Business in the Community' – it is over 300 major firms that have come together to assist in reviving the urban communities from which so many of them sprang.

So many of the amenities of our towns and cities – the parks and public gardens, the libraries and art galleries, the churches and schools – they had their origin in the philanthropy of men who made good themselves, and they wanted to do good for others. That impulse – that sense of obligation to the wider community – it is that we must enlist today.

I've seen the start of recovery for myself: on Teeside, in Gateshead, in Wolverhampton and the West Midlands. And in Glasgow, which is undergoing a remarkable revival, thanks largely to the work of George Younger and Malcolm Rifkind. I shall never forget one Glaswegian I met on my visit there. How do you do, I said. My name's Margaret Thatcher. Mine's Winston Churchill, he replied. And astonishingly enough it was. And he produced a document to prove it. Winston Harry Churchill, absolutely splendid person.

To speed up the process of recovery in these and other places, we have a whole battery of special measures and programmes – you heard about them from Kenneth Clarke [the Cabinet Minister then responsible for co-ordinating the Government's inner city initiatives]: special measures and programmes to clear derelict land, to renovate run-down council estates, to regenerate city centres, and to turn dereliction into development.

But by themselves these measures are not enough. We must also give people in the inner cities the opportunity to improve their own lives and the belief that they can do it.

The major reforms in our programme are of course designed for the whole country. But they will be of particular benefit to inner cities. We will free tenants from their dependence on council landlords. We will free parents to choose the schools they want for their children. We will free businesses in the urban development areas from irksome planning restrictions and controls. And with our rate reform legislation, Socialist councils will no longer be able to drive out small businesses and destroy employment by imposing sky-high rates. Above all, the community charge will make local councils far more accountable to all their voters.

With all these things taken together, these measures will greatly reduce the power of the local council over tenants, parents, pupils and businesses; and greatly increase the opportunities open to those very people. To coin a phrase it is an 'irreversible shift . . . of power . . . in favour of working people and their families'.*

The social problems of some inner cities are deep-seated. Quick and easy solutions are not possible. But the philosophy of enterprise and opportunity, which has put the spark back into our national economy – that is the way – and the only way – to rejuvenate our cities and restore their confidence and pride.

But our greatest concern, in inner cities and elsewhere, is to reverse the tide of crime which disfigures our lives. Crime invades homes; it breaks hearts; it drags down neighbourhoods; and it spreads fear. The Government is playing its full part in the fight against crime. We have strengthened the police. We have introduced tougher sentences. Violent crime concerns us, above all. It's not just that violent crime is worse than other crime. It's much worse. That's why we are now taking still tougher action against knives and against guns.

Even so, the feeling persists that some of the sentences passed by the courts have not measured up to the enormity of the crime. And so, as Douglas Hurd announced this week, we shall be introducing legislation to provide for an appeal against sentences which are too lenient. And may I point out it will be the second time this Government has brought a measure of this

*Labour's general election manifesto October 1974.

kind before Parliament. And I hope that this time it will receive a speedy passage on to the statute book.

But we shall make little progress in the drive against crime if we expect the police and the courts to take on the whole burden. When we are sick, we turn to the doctor; yet we accept responsibility for taking care of our health. When fire breaks out, we call in the fire brigade; yet we know it is up to us to take sensible precautions against fire. So it is with crime.

There is enormous scope for the public to help the police in what, after all, is a common duty: in neighbourhood watch; in business watch; in crime prevention; in prompt reporting of crime seen or suspected; and in readiness to give evidence. But even that is not enough. Civilized society doesn't just happen. It has to be sustained by standards widely accepted and upheld. We must draw on the moral energy of society. And we must draw on the values of family life.

For the family is, in the first place, where we learn those habits of mutual love, tolerance and service on which every healthy nation depends for its survival. It was Sir William Haley, the great editor of *The Times*, who, twenty years ago, said this, 'There are things which are bad and false and ugly and no amount of argument or specious casuistry will make them good or true or beautiful. It is time that these things were said.' And he said them.

But if we are to succeed today, all those in authority must recover that confidence and speak with a strong, emphatic and single voice. Because too often they speak in different and conflicting voices. The great majority of crimes are committed by young people, in their teens and early twenties. It is on such impressionable young people that anti-police propaganda and the glamorization of crime can have the most deadly effect. And when left-wing councils and left-wing teachers criticize the police, they give moral sanction to the criminally in-clined. When the broadcasters flout their own standards on violent television programmes, they risk a brutalizing effect on the morally unstable. When the Labour Party refuses to support the Prevention of Terrorism Act – an Act that saves lives – they weaken society, they weaken society's resistance

231

to the modern scourge of terrorism.

Local councils, teachers, broadcasters, politicians: all of us have a responsibility to uphold the civilized values which underpin the law. We owe it to society of which we are a part. And we owe it especially to future generations who will inherit the society that we create.

Our conference takes place at a time which could prove to be an historic turning point in world affairs. And we can say – with some pride – that Britain has played a major part in creating the opportunities which now open up before us.

It is, of course, a time of tension and even of danger in the Persian Gulf. But there, too, Britain is giving a strong lead. And I do indeed pay tribute to both Geoffrey Howe and you, Mr President [George Younger, Defence Secretary], for the lead which you have given. May I join you, Mr President, in speaking for this whole conference – and indeed for the people of this country – when I express our thanks and appreciation to the Merchant Officers and seamen who sail that vital waterway; and to the Royal Navy's Armilla Patrol and its minesweepers which protect them. We honour their dedication and their courage.

But today is also a time of hope. Indeed, there is no mistaking the bracing air of change in the Soviet Union. In my many hours of talking with Mr Gorbachev in Moscow earlier this year, his determination to bring about far-reaching reform was plain. The difficulties and obstacles confronting him are massive. But we must recognize that anything which increases human liberty, which extends the boundaries of discussion and which increases initiative and enterprise in the Soviet Union, is of fundamental importance in terms of human rights. And that's why we support it. That is why we have publicly welcomed and encouraged those aspects of Mr Gorbachev's reforms which do just this. They are genuinely courageous – not least in their admission that, after seventy years, the Socialist system has failed to produce the standard of life the Russian people want.

But we have yet to see that change carried through into the Soviet Union's policies towards the outside world. The traditional instruments of Soviet power – military strength, subversion, propaganda – are all being exercised as vigorously as ever. Afghanistan is still occupied. The Berlin Wall still stands, and Soviet weapons are still pouring into Third World countries which need food but not arms. They get the food from the free world and arms from the Soviet Union.

There is, however, hope in the agreement which now seems certain to be signed later this autumn, by the United States and the Soviet Union, to eliminate medium and shorter-range nuclear missiles. We welcome that agreement. Indeed Britain has contributed in a major way to its achievement. It's a success for the West – especially for the United States and President Reagan.

But let us remember one thing. If we had listened to the Labour Party and to CND – insofar as you can distinguish between the two – that agreement would never have been achieved. The Russians would have kept their 1,300 nuclear warheads, while the West would have given away its 300, for nothing in return. That lesson must never be forgotten. Reductions in nuclear weapons come about not from weakness, but from strength.

Our policies, Conservative policies, are bearing fruit and we have every reason to be pleased. But we must not let satisfaction turn to euphoria. We are ready for improved relations with the Soviet Union. But we can't afford to take anything on trust. Nor should we be deceived by changes in style rather than substance. We shall continue to judge the Soviet Union not by what they say but by what they do.

We believe that the strategic nuclear weapons of the United States and the Soviet Union could be reduced by 50 per cent without endangering Western security. But so long as the Soviet Union continues to enjoy massive superiority in chemical and conventional forces, we say that reductions in nuclear weapons in Europe have gone far enough. As the Supreme Allied Commander in Europe reminded us recently: it is not a nuclear-free Europe we want, it is a war-free Europe.

Nuclear weapons will continue to play a vital role in preventing war in Europe – as they have done for forty years. And that is why we will press ahead with Trident and the modernization of our independent deterrent, vital to our security.

The British people want peace. But it must be a peace with freedom and justice. And that peace is only maintained by keeping our defences strong, by resisting violence and intimidation at home, and by standing up to tyrants and terrorists abroad. That is the true spirit of the British people. That is the spirit which sustained us through two World Wars. And it guides us still.

You may perhaps have heard that I'm a faithful student of Rudyard Kipling. Occasionally, I've even been known to quote him. So it won't come as a complete surprise if I refer to his poem 'Recessional', in which he warned us to beware of boasting and to keep 'A humble and a contrite heart'. That's sound advice to any Government.

But may I say today we have both a right and a duty to remind the whole free world that, once more, Britain is confident, strong, trusted. Confident, because attitudes have changed. 'Can't be done' has given way to 'What's to stop us?' Strong, because our economy is enterprising, competitive and expanding. And trusted, because we are known to be a powerful ally and a faithful friend.

All this has been made possible by the national revival which we have carried through. And everyone in this hall, and millions outside it, can claim a share in that revival.

Now it has fallen to the Conservatives to lead the nation into the 1990s. Let us face that future with quiet confidence born of what we have accomplished in the last eight years. Britain's institutions are shaped by the character of her people. It's all that is gifted, just and fair in that character which reassures our friends and allies; and brings hope to those who have yet to know the liberty we take for granted.

Mr President, it is a great trust which has been placed in our care. May we never fail that trust.

The Scottish
Conservative Party Conference

PERTH, 13 MAY 1988

The Conservative Party was reduced to ten seats in Scotland at the 1987 Election, its worst result since 1910. Mrs Thatcher had to decide whether to modify her policies in Scotland, or whether to rebuild the Party by reaffirming in unambiguous terms the relevance of Thatcherism to Scotland (as to the rest of the United Kingdom). There was never any doubt about the course she would adopt. After all, as she pointed out in this speech, 'the Scots invented Thatcherism': its basic economic objectives had first been defined by the philosophers of the eighteenth-century Scottish Enlightenment.

Conservative policies, which drew on that Scottish tradition, had created a 'great surge of progress' from which the people of Scotland in particular had benefited – just as they would benefit from the great measures of social reform (described here in some detail) which were the central features of the Conservatives' third term. Above all, Mrs Thatcher emphasized that Scotland would not be governed on special terms which would alter its relationship with the rest of the United Kingdom. For the Conservative Party, the Union remained the only possible basis for the successful Government of Scotland. 'As long as I am Leader of this Party, we shall defend the Union and reject legislative devolution unequivocally.'

I am proud and delighted to speak once again from this platform at Perth. It was here that I made my first speech as Prime Minister. From here I launched the last two successful election campaigns. Today, I launch a third campaign: a campaign to strengthen the Union by winning back Scotland for the Conservative and Unionist cause.

The Conservative party is the oldest political party in Scotland. We have had our share of triumphs. We have been through challenging times – but we have never ceased to serve the interests of Scotland, indeed, of the whole United Kingdom.

Today, we have hard work ahead of us – to turn the electoral map of Scotland Conservative blue once more. But your lively and candid conference these last three days has confirmed that it is we in the Conservative Party who are doing the new thinking for the new Scotland.

It is Malcolm Rifkind and his team at the Scottish Office who are setting the policy agenda with style and conviction. It is Jim Goold, John MacKay and their colleagues at Central Office who are rebuilding the organization that will win our future victories. And it is Alec Home who has set a tradition of service to Scotland and the Conservative Party which is matchless.

I'm sometimes told that the Scots don't like Thatcherism. Well, I find that hard to believe – because the Scots *invented* Thatcherism, long before I was thought of.

It is more than 200 years since Adam Smith, David Hume, Adam Fergusson and others first set out their ideas of a world in which wealth would be generated and spread ever more widely. They saw that it's not Government which creates wealth – it's people. That people do best when they pursue their own vision. And that a wise Government will harness the efforts of individuals to improve the well-being of the whole community. So they proposed to restrain Government and to liberate men and women.

Those are the ideals I hold most dear. And they had their origins in the Scottish Enlightenment. They were ideas that changed the world. The Industrial Revolution, the expansion of British trade, the development of new nations, the spread of new goods, new technologies, right across the globe, benefiting millions of people who had never heard of Adam Smith, or

David Hume, or indeed of Scotland – that's the history of Scottish ideas in action.

It is also the history of Britain. The British Empire could never have flourished as it did if the Scots had not been there to build the roads, cure the sick, establish industries, promote trading links, and to map out the unknown territories.

Scotland herself flourished in the days when Glasgow was the second city of Empire, and a quarter of the world's ships were launched into the Clyde. But an economy in the forefront of the first Industrial Revolution was bound to face major problems adapting to the second.

When that challenge came, Governments failed Scotland – not by doing too little, but by promising too much. Successive Governments promised to insulate Scotland from the reality of industrial change. They told you: 'you don't need to worry. We'll protect you.' But they couldn't – and they didn't. Shipyards closed. Factories closed. Men lost their jobs. Whole areas turned to wasteland. And the money that might have been invested in new industries, new opportunities, went instead in trying to keep yesterday's jobs alive.

The result was that the economy fell faster, apathy and despair spread wider. And disillusion with Government grew deeper. It was as if the Scots concluded, 'if Government can't save us, what on earth can we do?'

What had happened to the enterprise of Carnegie, James Watt, John Macadam, Alexander Graham Bell? Where was the energy which had founded great Scottish companies along the banks of the Clyde? And the canniness which had made Edinburgh one of the first centres of international finance?

Today the Scots have answered those questions by their actions. Those qualities were always there – but they were buried by over-government. This Government has liberated the energies of the Scottish people. And Scotland is on the march again.

With the benefits of lower company taxes, growing market opportunities, and rising standards of living, new companies are springing up. Nearly 6,000 of them were registered in 1987 alone. Scotland is a world leader in the industries of tomorrow, in electronics, in computer sciences, in financial services. Over £80,000 million pounds of funds is managed and controlled within one square mile of the centre of Edinburgh. That's equal to two years' income tax for the whole United Kingdom. The situations vacant columns of Scottish newspapers are bursting at the seams – offering real jobs founded on real needs.

Who has benefited most from this great surge of progress? The Scottish people. Judged by cold statistics, Scots enjoy greater prosperity than anywhere in the United Kingdom outside the crowded, high-priced South-East. But no statistic can capture the benefits of living in a civilized city within five minutes of some of the finest scenery and fishing in the world – not to mention a handy golf course and a distillery or two. I am told they sometimes go together.

This Scottish miracle didn't happen by accident. Indeed, it could never have happened at all if the Government had been in the hands of the negative, bitter, class-ridden, and backward-looking Labour Party that Malcolm Rifkind and I face daily in the House of Commons. It happened because the Tory Government set the Scottish people free – free from Labour's controls on their wages; free from Labour's restrictions on enterprise; free from Labour's penalties on investment; free from Labour's punitive taxes on effort; free from all the shackles that Socialism had imposed on the work and imagination of the people.

As someone once said, the people had nothing to lose but their chains. They had a world to win. And they are winning it. Investment coming to Scotland has soared – but first we had to abolish exchange controls. Financial services have mushroomed in Edinburgh and Glasgow – but first we had to deregulate the industry. The unions are back in the hands of the moderate majority – but first we had to change the law to control the militants. Above all, the Scottish economy is now infused with the spirit of enterprise – but first we had to get taxes down.

If Labour's income tax rates were still in force, a Scotsman on average earnings would be paying nearly £15 a week more to the man in Whitehall than he is paying today. We believe in incentives to create wealth; the Labour Party believes in taxes to redistribute it. That is the great divide in politics.

Labour's high taxes don't redistribute income. They redistribute taxpayers – from high-tax countries to low-tax countries. They redistribute accountants – from improving efficiency to avoiding tax. They redistribute work – from honest employment to the black economy. And under every Labour Government since the war, high taxes have redistributed economic success from this country to West Germany, to Japan and the United States.

What we have done is to reverse that process. We have given everyone more incentive to work, to save and to invest. We have encouraged unskilled workers to try for a job and train in new techniques rather than be demoralized on the dole. We have persuaded the wealth-creators – the scientists, the business-men, the entertainers – to stay in this country and pay their taxes here – not to our competitors abroad. We have generated prosperity and, with prosperity, jobs.

In those difficult days of the early Eighties, I used to be asked: where will the new jobs come from? I had to tell people: Governments don't know what the jobs of tomorrow will be. And when they try to guess, they get it wrong. But what we do know is that when we get the conditions right, the jobs will follow. Today I can reply: look around you at the new factories, the new industries, the new signs of commerce and prosperity. The jobs of tomorrow are here.

A month ago, I visited IBM's plant in Greenock. In 1951 it employed ten people. On what? Assembling typewriters. Today, in 1988, it employs 2,500 people and supports 4,000 more. The day I was there, it produced its two-millionth personal computer. The same day I opened a new five-crown hotel in Dundee, built at a cost of £4 million and employing a staff of 120. And for good measure, I was able to announce up to another 300 new jobs at a new medical science centre at the nearby Technology Park. Scotland is changing before our eyes.

This Government has worked hard for that kind of prosperity. Scotland has worked hard for it too. And that is why I get pretty upset when it's thrown away. Scotland won Ford for Dundee. Labour lost it. And let that be a reminder – a reminder that Scotland's soundly-based, dynamic economic revival could never have happened under a Labour Government. Even out of power, the ghost of Labour stalks the industrial land-scape, frightening away foreign investment and chilling the prospects of growth.

As a great Glasgow journalist, Colm Brogan, once remarked, wherever a Labour Government attempts to increase human wealth and happiness, grass never grows again. And when Labour is presented with the evidence of Scotland's success in tomorrow's world, they shut their eyes to it. They don't want to know. And sometimes, the media shut *their* eyes as well. So perhaps I should take the opportunity to reassure them that news of Scotland's success is not covered by Section Two of the Official Secrets Act. Perhaps if we labelled it secret, it might make the front page.

No Tory ever forgets the vital importance of farming to a prosperous economy and a healthy society. Today, Scottish farmers have to compete in a world where trading conditions are tough and surpluses abound. Within the European Com-munity, we have had to put a limit on the Budget in order to reduce those surpluses and to bring supply more in line with demand. Otherwise the CAP would, quite simply, have run out of money. And the victims would have been farmers and farm workers alike. So Britain brought our European partners to face reality. They haven't always welcomed that.

But Scottish farmers have never been afraid to face reality. All they ask is that the competition be on fair terms. That's why this Government has repeatedly fought in Brussels for a fair deal for our farmers – in lamb, beef, cereals and much else. That's why we've reformed the tax laws so that the family farm can be passed on to the next generation – one of the best deals for farmers anywhere in the Community. That's why we have cut the rate of tax on small farmers. As a result, Scottish agriculture – never afraid to adapt to change – has established major export markets.

Speaking of exports, I must congratulate the Scotch whisky

industry, whose exports exceeded one billion pounds in 1986. I'm told it's Scotland's largest single export. And, as I told the Japanese Prime Minister last week, it could do still better if foreign countries didn't protect their pale imitations behind devices like tax discrimination – which leave a very nasty taste in the mouth.

At each of our last three conferences, you have sought assurances from me that we would abolish the domestic rating system. Nobody could tell the Scots that revaluation was fair. It wasn't. That's why you wanted a better system – and that's why we are replacing the old, outdated, arbitrary and unfair system of local rates with the Community Charge.

It is absurd that out of almost four million local electors in Scotland, only one million pay full rates, and two million pay no rates at all. Yet all four million use local services and benefit from the rates paid by their neighbours. What's fair about that? It is equally absurd that the same rate is levied on similar properties, however many people are living in them. Yet local services are used by people, not by houses. Why on earth should a retired widow living alone in the family home pay the same rates as four working adults next door? What's fair about that? There's nothing fair about that. A system of finance which totally separates local democracy from financial responsibility is wrong at the root.

If we are to have responsible and accountable local government, a clear link between the services provided and the charge levied is essential. That is the principle behind the Community Charge. The charge does not cover the whole of local spending. In Scotland, it will account for only one-seventh of the total. But it is designed to ensure that the same level of services, delivered with the same degree of efficiency, will result in the same Community Charge for every person in Scotland – subject to generous rebates for those who cannot afford to pay. And it will be the same system throughout England too.

Let us be clear. The local level of Community Charge is not set by the Government. It is set by local councils. An extravagant and inefficient council will have to charge more, and a prudent and responsible council will be able to charge less. So, when every local resident pays a Community Charge, the councils will have to justify their expenditure to the voters. Voters in Labour Edinburgh will want to know why on current figures their Community Charge would be £70 more than the charge in Tory Eastwood. Hard Left councils will no longer be able to hide the cost of their Socialist fads and anti-nuclear fancies by passing them on to business and the ratepaying minority. They will have to send the bill to everyone – and face the consequences at the next election.

Two bills are now going through Parliament which will radically change education. They will provide for parents to play a much greater role in the education of their children.

In Scotland there is a tradition of excellence in education which our opponents constantly threaten. Some of you may have heard of Paisley Grammar! That school and others like it were under threat from Labour because their values and traditions were resented. They were popular with parents. They had high academic standards. They enforced high standards of discipline.

We have given them a right of appeal. Labour hated it. The parents loved it. Let Labour be in no doubt about the message. We will defend the rights of parents and the education that *they* seek to attack.

Day after day, week after week, in the House of Commons and elsewhere, we have been treated to the sound of sanctimonious Opposition politicians loftily congratulating themselves on their superior compassion – with particular reference to the health and welfare services. Well, here are the facts. We are not spending less on these services, but more – a lot more – on both of them. On the NHS nearly £2,000 million more this year. And with this Conservative Government, the nurses and doctors have had the largest pay increases ever – something that has been greatly welcomed.

On social security also we are spending another £2,000 million more this year. In fact, for every three pounds that Labour spent on social benefits, we are spending four pounds – and that's after allowing for inflation. It's not a figure you will hear from Labour.

But in social security, it wasn't only a question of spending more. A number of problems had grown up over the years and they simply had to be dealt with. For example, the system of social benefits we inherited was telling young people that living on benefit was an acceptable substitute for being in work. So some young people were choosing to be idle. That was wrong – so we stopped it. For those who couldn't get a job, we offered training instead and we paid a training grant. That way they learn a skill for the future – and the habits of work and self-reliance. That was right and most parents and sensible people agreed.

Then some families on low wages with young children found that they were worse off if they worked harder and earned more. They lost benefit. That too was wrong. So we have introduced Family Credit – a new benefit. Overall, they now keep more when they earn more. That will help 400,000 people to keep the dignity and respect of working to provide for their own families. Another good and necessary reform.

Then we found that the cost of housing benefit was rising dramatically, from £1.5 billion pounds in 1979 to over £5 billion this year. It was going to an increasing number of households even in times of much greater prosperity. In fact, every two households not only have to keep themselves but also contribute to a third household. That is still so – even after the reforms which we have just brought in. This year expenditure will be £5.3 billion – but we had to take the steps we did to contain its growth in future years.

We have also tried to give special help to the long-term sick and disabled. But with something like twenty possible extra allowances, it's hardly surprising that some people didn't know where they were. Or what they could claim. So we have rolled them all into one benefit which covers almost all disabled people. All told, and in real terms, we spend 80 per cent more on this group than when we came to power.

All this is taking time to sort out. But the reform is a good one – a compassionate reform – a real Tory reform. And to people who are retired let me say this: It's not only a question of providing more for each pensioner, but providing for more

243

pensioners too: something like a million more since we took office. And while the number of pensioners will continue to increase over the next decade, the population of working age will decline. On top of that, the promises that had been made for the second pension – SERPS – were too great for future generations to bear.

We have honoured our pledge to protect the basic pension against rising prices. And now we have safeguarded pensions by putting them on a sound financial basis – one that is fair all round. And we have done other things to help the pensioner. We have slashed inflation, so your savings are safer with a Conservative Government; abolished the Investment Income Surcharge; and introduced an extra tax allowance for the over-eighties. Those who are now retiring can do so secure in the knowledge that they can look forward to a far better future than was ever imagined a few years ago.

That is the measure and purpose of the reforms you have heard so much about. They strike a balance between those in need and those who provide. Our purpose is to ensure that the recovery now taking place will benefit all the people. Yes, our reforms have cost more and they will go on costing more, but like our financial position as a whole, they are soundly based and will endure.

Since the Act of Union, Scotland has had a proud history as a distinctive nation within the United Kingdom. We in this party believe in a Scotland that continues to play a full part in the kingdom and on equal terms.

Now that every other party in Scotland is challenging that role, it is vital that we defend it. People say that we're not a Scottish party. But neither are we an English party, nor a Welsh party, nor an Irish party. We are a party of the whole United Kingdom. We are the Conservative and Unionist Party. And we will always be a Unionist party.

I am delighted that at this conference you resoundingly rejected the prospect of a second-class Scotland, cut off from the rest of the United Kingdom by tax barriers that would destroy her economy. For just stop to think for one moment how utterly inadequate and superficial the proposals for devolution from the Opposition parties really are. At least the Nationalists have the honesty to say that they want to break up the United Kingdom. Labour say they don't, but their policies say that they would. They want to establish a Scottish Assembly – another layer of Government – with the power to raise taxes. But why should companies want to invest in an area with higher taxes than the rest of the kingdom? And how could Scottish MPs continue to vote on English matters at Westminster if English MPs were excluded from consideration of Scottish issues? And who would foot the bill for the additional bureaucracy? How could Scotland possibly benefit from *losing* influence and representation in Whitehall and Westminster?

As long as I am Leader of this party, we shall defend the Union and reject legislative devolution unequivocally.

We have endorsed a very different policy – a policy far bolder and more imaginative than that of our opponents. Not devolution to politicians and bureaucrats, but devolution to the Scottish people themselves – devolution of housing, devolution of education, devolution of share-ownership and devolution of State-run industries to individuals.

It was a *Unionist* Government which gave council tenants in Scotland the right to buy their own homes. And over 113,000 Scots have done so.

It was a *Unionist* Government which gave people the opportunity to choose to which school they send their children. And over 100,000 Scots have done so.

And it was a *Unionist* Government which gave people the opportunity to buy shares in British industry. And today twice as many Scots own shares than was the case in 1979.

This policy of devolution to the people continues with our policy of Scottish privatization. Nationalization took companies out of Scottish hands and into Whitehall; privatization will hand them back to Scotland. It will create major new Scottish companies with vast assets, thousands of employees and a powerful presence in the Scottish economy – and give the Scottish public a new opportunity to acquire a major stake in the ownership of Scottish industry.

These are policies which give real power back to the people; policies which the people support. The challenge for us now is to turn support for our policies into support for our party.

This is a time of excitement and of hope in world affairs – and it gives Britain an unrivalled opportunity to use its traditional influence, now so much enhanced by our economic strength and the prestige we once again enjoy in the world.

We see a great debate going on in the Soviet Union over the future course of Communism: a debate caused by the admission that after seventy years the Communist system has failed to deliver the standards of living and the quality of life which the free, democratic societies of the West enjoy. We see the numbers of those permitted to leave the Soviet Union rising – not enough, but better than it was. Now, 1,000 years after Christianity first came to the Soviet Union, we hear it promised that Christians will at last be given full freedom of worship. We watch and pray that it will happen. The same restlessness is abroad in Eastern Europe where people understand that the doctrine that the State provides everything and controls everything is bankrupt. They want the prosperity which they see others enjoy in the West. They want the liberty which we have in the West. And they know these benefits can only be achieved by far-reaching reforms.

We must encourage these stirrings of reform, *not* in the sense of interfering in the affairs of these countries – we would find that just as unacceptable as they would – but by declaring where *we* stand. We stand for greater contacts between people in East and West; for greater human rights; for societies in which the individual can improve his own condition and that of his family by his own efforts.

We cannot yet say with confidence what the outcome of this debate will be. We hope it will lead to societies which are more free and more just. But the spectre of repression has not yet been finally banished. The military might of the Soviet Union remains formidable and far beyond what it requires for defensive purposes alone – indeed, it is that military might, not its economic or political weight, which makes it a world power.

We must therefore keep our own defences strong and up to date, knowing that whatever happens *our* defence is sure. That way we can welcome with confidence the changes which we see happening in the Soviet Union. They offer greater hope for the future than we have seen for many years. On Sunday we shall see the first Soviet soldiers begin their withdrawal from Afghanistan. They are leaving because the Afghan people fought for their liberty with the support of their friends including the United Kingdom, and because almost the whole world united in condemning the Soviet military occupation.

We are now on the verge of further progress here in Europe. By 1992 the European countries are committed to remove all the artificial barriers which hamper economic growth. That will give our firms a domestic market not just of fifty-five million people but of 320 million people. And by 1993 we shall have the Channel Tunnel – a project which you could say started in Scotland, for the machinery to bore the tunnel was made at Alexander Howden in Glasgow. Indeed, orders for the equipment and material have already brought Scotland over £40 million.

Thanks to Conservative policies, Britain is now well placed to take advantage of that huge European market. But the greatest advantage of all is that we now have a climate in this Britain in which business *wants* to succeed, *can* succeed and *is* succeeding. We are now in a position to lead Europe into the next century.

I have come here to encourage you to assert our party's place in the centre of Scotland's national life. I won't be discouraged by temporary setbacks. I didn't come into politics to take short cuts, or court easy popularity. My principles are not at the mercy of the opinion polls – neither, I am sure, are yours. Only the practical application of Tory principles has made the recovery of the Scottish economy possible. As Scotland regains its self-confidence, as more Scots realize that they have every right to be proud of Scotland's economic recovery, so our fortunes will revive.

Tory values are in tune with everything that is finest in the Scottish character and with the proudest moments in Scottish

247

history. Scottish values are Tory values – and vice versa. The values of hard work, self-reliance, thrift, enterprise – the relishing of challenges, the seizing of opportunities. That's what the Tory Party stands for – that's what Scotland stands for. And that will be our message to the people.

The General Assembly of the Church of Scotland

EDINBURGH, 21 MAY 1988

In this speech Mrs Thatcher returned to the question of the relationship between politics and religion which she had previously explored in her two lectures at St Lawrence Jewry (nos 6 and 11 in this collection). Her object on this occasion was to answer those churchmen and others who had criticized her for creating a society which, they maintained, appeared to encourage materialism and greed, and which neglected its responsibilities towards the poorest and most vulnerable members of the community (the previous month the Bishop of Durham had asserted that her policies were 'almost wicked').

The nub of her argument was that spiritual redemption and personal responsibility stand at the centre of the Christian faith. Each individual should be encouraged to devote adequate time to his daily work, and to help create wealth for the nation by the use of his talents. But, Mrs Thatcher stressed, a personal moral duty is imposed on each individual to dispose responsibly of his wealth, and in particular to use it for the good of others. As for the State, it had a permanent and binding obligation to relieve hardship and ensure that education and other vital social services are available to all, but its intervention should not be on such a scale as to undermine individual responsibility. In a key passage Mrs Thatcher said, 'It is not the creation of wealth that is wrong but the love of money for its own sake. The spiritual dimension comes in deciding what one does with one's wealth.' She concluded by reminding her audience of the abiding association between the Church and our entire national tradition, quoting

249

THE REVIVAL OF BRITAIN

Cecil Spring-Rice's magnificent hymn 'I vow to thee my country' whose words sum up some of the deepest sentiments of Toryism.

I am greatly honoured to have been invited to attend the opening of this 1988 General Assembly of the Church of Scotland; and I am deeply grateful that you have now asked me to address you.

I am very much aware of the historical continuity extending over four centuries, during which the position of the Church of Scotland has been recognized in constitutional law and confirmed by successive sovereigns. It sprang from the independence of mind and rigour of thought that have always been such powerful characteristics of the Scottish people. It has remained close to its roots and has inspired a commitment to service from *all* people.

I am therefore very sensible of the important influence which the Church of Scotland exercises in the life of the whole nation, both at the spiritual level and through the extensive caring services which are provided by your Church's department of social responsibility.

Perhaps it would be best if I began by speaking personally as a Christian, as well as a politician, about the way I see things. Reading recently, I came across the starkly simple phrase: 'Christianity is about spiritual redemption, not social reform.'

Sometimes the debate on these matters has become too polarized and gives the impression that the two are quite separate.

Most Christians would regard it as their personal Christian duty to help their fellow-men and women. They would regard the lives of children as a precious trust. These duties come not from any secular legislation passed by Parliament, but from being a Christian.

But there are a number of people who are not Christians who would also accept those responsibilities. What then are the distinctive marks of Christianity?

They stem not from the social but from the spiritual side of our lives. I would identify three beliefs in particular. First, that from the beginning man has been endowed by God with the

250

fundamental right to choose between good and evil. Second, that we were made in God's own image and therefore we are expected to use all our *own* power of thought and judgement in exercising that choice; and further, if we open our hearts to God, He has promised to work within us. And third, that Our Lord Jesus Christ, the Son of God, when faced with His terrible choice and lonely vigil *chose* to lay down His life that our sins may be forgiven. I remember very well a sermon on an Armistice Sunday when our preacher said, 'No one took away the life of Jesus, He chose to lay it down.'

I think back to many discussions in my early life when we all agreed that if you try to take the fruits of Christianity without its roots, the fruits will wither. And they will not come again unless you nurture the roots.

But we must not profess the Christian faith and go to church simply because we want social reforms and benefits, or a better standard of behaviour – but because we accept the sanctity of life, the responsibility that comes with freedom and the supreme sacrifice of Christ, expressed so well in the hymn:

> *When I survey the wondrous Cross*
> *On which the Prince of glory died,*
> *My richest gain I count but loss,*
> *And pour contempt on all my pride.*

May I also say a few words about my personal belief in the relevance of Christianity to public policy – to the things that are Caesar's?

The Old Testament lays down in Exodus the Ten Commandments as given to Moses, the injunction in Leviticus to love our neighbour as ourselves, and generally the importance of observing a strict code of law. The New Testament is a record of the Incarnation, the teachings of Christ and the establishment of the Kingdom of God. Again we have the emphasis on loving our neighbour as ourselves and to 'Do-as-you-would-be-done-by'. I believe that by taking together these key elements from the Old and New Testaments, we gain a view of the universe, a proper attitude to work, and principles to shape economic and social life.

THE REVIVAL OF BRITAIN

We are told we must work and use our talents to create wealth. 'If a man will not work he shall not eat,' wrote St Paul to the Thessalonians. Indeed, abundance rather than poverty has a legitimacy which derives from the very nature of Creation.

Nevertheless, the Tenth Commandment – Thou shalt not covet – recognizes that making money and owning things could become selfish activities. But it is not the creation of wealth that is wrong, but love of money for its own sake. The spiritual dimension comes in deciding what one does with the wealth. How could we respond to the many calls for help, or invest for the future, or support the wonderful artists and craftsmen whose work also glorifies God, unless we had first worked hard and used our talents to create the necessary wealth? And remember the woman with the alabaster jar of ointment.

I confess that I always had difficulty with interpreting the biblical precept to love our neighbours 'as ourselves' until I read some of the words of C. S. Lewis. He pointed out that we don't exactly love *ourselves* when we fall below the standards and beliefs we have accepted. Indeed, we might even *hate* ourselves for some unworthy deed.

None of this, of course, tells us exactly what kind of political and social institutions we should have. On this point, Christians will very often genuinely disagree, though it is a mark of Christian manners that they will do so with courtesy and mutual respect. What is certain, however, is that any set of social and economic arrangements which is not founded on the acceptance of individual responsibility will do nothing but harm. We are all responsible for our own actions. We cannot blame society if we disobey the law. We simply cannot delegate the exercise of mercy and generosity to others. The politicians and other secular powers should strive by their measures to bring out the good in people and to fight down the bad: but they can't create the one or abolish the other. They can only see that the laws encourage the best instincts and convictions of the people, instincts and convictions which I am convinced are far more deeply rooted than is often supposed.

Nowhere is this more evident than in the basic ties of the

family, which are at the heart of our society and are the very nursery of civic virtue. It is on the family that we in Government build our own policies for welfare, education and care. You recall that Timothy was warned by St Paul that anyone who neglects to provide for his own house (meaning his own family) has disowned the faith and is 'worse than an infidel'.

We must recognize that modern society is infinitely more complex than that of biblical times, and of course new occasions teach new duties. In our generation, the only way we can ensure that no one is left without sustenance, help or opportunity is to have laws to provide for health and education, pensions for the elderly, succour for the sick and disabled.

But intervention by the State must never become so great that it effectively removes personal responsibility. The same applies to taxation, for while you and I would work extremely hard whatever the circumstances, there are undoubtedly some who would not, unless the incentive was there. And we need *their* efforts too.

Moderator, recently there have been great debates about religious education. I believe strongly that politicians must see that religious education has a proper place in the school curriculum.

In Scotland, as in England, there is an historic connection expressed in our laws between Church and State. The two connections are of a somewhat different kind, but the arrangements in both countries are designed to give symbolic expression to the same crucial truth: that the Christian religion – which, of course, embodies many of the great spiritual and moral truths of Judaism – is a fundamental part of our national heritage. I believe it is the wish of the overwhelming majority of people that this heritage should be preserved and fostered. For centuries it has been our very life-blood. Indeed, we are a nation whose ideals are founded on the Bible.

Also, it is quite impossible to understand our history or literature without grasping this fact. *That* is the strong practical case for ensuring that children at school are given adequate instruction in the part which the Judaic-Christian tradition has played in moulding our laws, manners and institutions. How

253

can you make sense of Shakespeare and Sir Walter Scott, or of the constitutional conflicts of the seventeenth century in both Scotland and England, without some such fundamental knowledge?

But I go further than this. The truths of the Judaic-Christian tradition are infinitely precious, not only, as I believe, because they are true, but also because they provide the moral impulse which alone can lead to that peace, in the true meaning of the word, for which we all long.

To assert absolute moral values is not to claim perfection for ourselves. No true Christian could do that. What is more, one of the great principles of our Judaic-Christian inheritance is tolerance. People with other faiths and cultures have always been welcomed in our land, assured of equality under the law, of proper respect and of open friendship.

There is absolutely nothing incompatible between this and our desire to maintain the essence of our own identity. There is no place for racial or religious intolerance in our creed.

When Abraham Lincoln spoke in his famous Gettysburg speech of 1863 of 'government of the people, by the people, and for the people', he gave the world a neat definition of democracy which has since been widely and enthusiastically adopted. But what he enunciated as a form of Government was not in itself especially Christian, for nowhere in the Bible is the word democracy mentioned. Ideally, when Christians meet, as Christians, to take counsel together their purpose is not (or should not be) to ascertain what is the mind of the majority, but what is the mind of the Holy Spirit – something which may be quite different.

Nevertheless I am an enthusiast for democracy. And I take that position, not because I believe majority opinion is inevitably right or true – indeed, no majority can take away God-given human rights – but because I believe it most effectively safeguards the value of the individual and, more than any other system, restrains the abuse of power by the few. And that *is* a Christian concept.

But there is little hope for democracy if the hearts of men and women in democratic societies cannot be touched by a call to something greater than themselves. Political structures, State institutions, collective ideals are not enough. *We* Parliamentarians can legislate for the rule of law. *You*, the Church, can teach the life of faith.

For, when all is said and done, a politician's role is a humble one. I always think that the whole debate about the Church and the State has never yielded anything comparable in insight to that beautiful hymn 'I vow to thee my country'. It begins with a triumphant assertion of what might be described as secular patriotism, a noble thing indeed in a country like ours: 'I vow to thee my country all earthly things above; entire, whole and perfect the service of my love'. It goes on to speak of 'another country I heard of long ago' whose King cannot be seen and whose armies cannot be counted, but 'soul by soul and silently her shining bounds increase'. Not group by group, or party by party, or even church by church – but soul by soul – and each one counts.

That, members of the Assembly, is the country which you chiefly serve. You fight your cause under the banner of an historic Church. Your success matters greatly – as much to the temporal as to the spiritual welfare of the nation.

The College of Europe

BRUGES, 20 SEPTEMBER 1988

Immense interest and controversy were aroused by this speech, which was instantly recognized as one of the most significant pronouncements that had ever been made on the relationship between Britain and the rest of Europe – which, as Mrs Thatcher stressed, is not coterminous with the European Community. The speech brought into the sharpest possible focus the most crucial questions that have to be addressed as Britain develops its role in Europe. The vigorous debate which Mrs Thatcher has provoked is a testimony to the enduring importance of this speech.

First, may I thank you for giving me the opportunity to return to Bruges – and in very different circumstances from my last visit shortly after the Zeebrugge ferry disaster, when Belgian courage and the devotion of your doctors and nurses saved so many British lives.

Second, may I say what a pleasure it is to speak at the College of Europe under the distinguished leadership of its Rector, Professor Lukaszewski. The College plays a vital and increasingly important part in the life of the European Community.

Third, may I also thank you for inviting me to deliver my address in this magnificent hall. What better place to speak of Europe's future than in a building which so gloriously recalls the greatness that Europe had already achieved over 600 years ago?

Your city of Bruges has many other historical associations for us in Britain. Geoffrey Chaucer was a frequent visitor here. And the first book to be printed in the English language was produced here in Bruges by William Caxton.

Mr Chairman, you have invited me to speak on the subject of Britain and Europe. Perhaps I should congratulate you on your courage. If you believe some of the things said and written about my views on Europe, it must seem rather like inviting Genghis Khan to speak on the virtues of peaceful co-existence!

I want to start by disposing of some myths about my country, Britain, and its relationship with Europe. And to do that I must say something about the identity of Europe itself.

Europe is not the creation of the Treaty of Rome. Nor is the European idea the property of any group or institution. We British are as much heirs to the legacy of European culture as any other nation. Our links to the rest of Europe, the continent of Europe, have been the *dominant* factor in our history. For 300 years we were part of the Roman Empire and our maps still trace the straight lines of the roads the Romans built. Our ancestors – Celts, Saxons and Danes – came from the continent.

Our nation was – in that favourite Community word – 'restructured' under Norman and Angevin rule in the eleventh and twelfth centuries.

This year we celebrate the three hundredth anniversary of the Glorious Revolution in which the British crown passed to Prince William of Orange and Queen Mary.

Visit the great churches and cathedrals of Britain, read our literature and listen to our language: all bear witness to the cultural riches which we have drawn from Europe – and other Europeans from us.

We in Britain are rightly proud of the way in which, since Magna Carta in 1215, we have pioneered and developed representative institutions to stand as bastions of freedom. And proud too of the way in which for centuries Britain was a home for people from the rest of Europe who sought sanctuary from tyranny.

But we know that without the European legacy of political ideas we could not have achieved as much as we did. From classical and medieval thought we have borrowed that concept of the rule of law which marks out a civilized society from barbarism. And on that idea of Christendom – for long synonomous with Europe – with its recognition of the unique and spiritual nature of the individual, we still base our belief in personal liberty and other human rights.

Too often the history of Europe is described as a series of interminable wars and quarrels. Yet from our perspective today surely what strikes us most is our common experience. For instance, the story of how Europeans explored and colonized and – yes, without apology – civilized much of the world is an extraordinary tale of talent, skill and courage.

We British have in a special way contributed to Europe. Over the centuries we have fought to prevent Europe from falling under the dominance of a single power. We have fought and we have died for her freedom. Only miles from here in Belgium lie the bodies of 120,000 British soldiers who died in the First World War. Had it not been for that willingness to fight and to die, Europe *would* have been united long before now – but not in liberty, not in justice. It was British support to resistance movements throughout the last war that helped to keep alive the flame of liberty in so many countries until the day of liberation.

Tomorrow, King Baudouin will attend a service in Brussels to commemorate the many brave Belgians who gave their lives in service with the Royal Air Force – a sacrifice which we shall never forget.

It was from our island fortress that the liberation of Europe itself was mounted. And still today we stand together. Nearly 70,000 British servicemen are stationed on the mainland of Europe.

All these things alone are proof of our commitment to Europe's future.

The European Community is *one* manifestation of that European identity. But it is not the only one. We must never forget that east of the Iron Curtain peoples who once enjoyed a full share of European culture, freedom and identity have been cut off from their roots. We shall always look on Warsaw,

Prague and Budapest as great European cities.

Nor should we forget that European values have helped to make the United States of America into the valiant defender of freedom which she has become.

This is no arid chronicle of obscure facts from the dust-filled libraries of history. It is the record of nearly 2,000 years of British involvement *in* Europe, co-operation *with* Europe and contribution *to* Europe, a contribution which today is as valid and as strong as ever. Yes, we have looked also to wider horizons – as have others – and thank goodness for that, because Europe never would have prospered and never will prosper as a narrow-minded, inward-looking club.

The European Community belongs to *all* its members. It must reflect the traditions and aspirations of *all* its members.

And let me be quite clear. Britain does not dream of some cosy, isolated existence on the fringes of the European Community. Our destiny is in Europe, as part of the Community. That is not to say that our future lies *only* in Europe. But nor does that of France or Spain, or indeed any other member.

The Community is not an end in itself. Nor is it an institutional device to be constantly modified according to the dictates of some abstract intellectual concept. Nor must it be ossified by endless regulation.

The European Community is the practical means by which Europe can ensure the future prosperity and security of its people in a world in which there are many other powerful nations and groups of nations.

We Europeans cannot afford to waste our energies on internal disputes or arcane institutional debates. They are no substitute for effective action.

Europe has to be ready both to contribute in full measure to its own security and to compete commercially and industrially, in a world in which success goes to the countries which encourage individual initiative and enterprise, rather than to those which attempt to diminish them.

This evening I want to set out some guiding principles for the future which I believe will ensure that Europe *does* succeed, not just in economic and defence terms but also in the quality of life and the influence of its peoples.

My first guiding principle is this: willing and active co-operation between independent sovereign States is the best way to build a successful European Community.

To try to suppress nationhood and concentrate power at the centre of a European conglomerate would be highly damaging and would jeopardize the objectives we seek to achieve.

Europe will be stronger precisely because it has France as France, Spain as Spain, Britain as Britain, each with its own customs, traditions and identity. It would be folly to try to fit them into some sort of identikit European personality.

Some of the founding fathers of the Community thought that the United States of America might be its model.

But the whole history of America is quite different from Europe. People went there to get away from the intolerance and constraints of life in Europe. They sought liberty and opportunity; and their strong sense of purpose has, over two centuries, helped create a new unity and pride in being American – just as our pride lies in being British or Belgian or Dutch or German.

I am the first to say that on many great issues the countries of Europe should try to speak with a single voice. I want to see us work more closely on the things we can do better together than alone. Europe is stronger when we do so, whether it be in trade, in defence, or in our relations with the rest of the world.

But working more closely together does *not* require power to be centralized in Brussels or decisions to be taken by an appointed bureaucracy.

Indeed, it is ironic that just when those countries such as the Soviet Union, which have tried to run everything from the centre, are learning that success depends on dispersing power and decisions away from the centre, some in the Community seem to want to move in the opposite direction.

We have not successfully rolled back the frontiers of the State in Britain only to see them reimposed at a European level, with a European super-State exercising a new dominance from Brussels.

Certainly we want to see Europe more united and with a greater sense of common purpose. But it must be in a way which preserves the different traditions, parliamentary powers and sense of national pride in one's own country; for these have been the source of Europe's vitality through the centuries.

My second guiding principle is this: Community policies must tackle present problems in a *practical* way, however difficult that may be. If we cannot reform those Community policies which are patently wrong or ineffective and which are rightly causing public disquiet, then we shall not get the public's support for the Community's future development.

That is why the achievements of the European Council in Brussels last February are so important.

It wasn't right that half the total Community budget was being spent on storing and disposing of surplus food. Now those stocks are being sharply reduced.

It was absolutely right to decide that agriculture's share of the budget should be cut in order to free resources for other policies, such as helping the less well-off regions and training for jobs. It was right too to introduce tighter budgetary discipline to enforce these decisions and to bring total EC spending under better control.

Those who complained that the Community was spending so much time on financial detail missed the point. You cannot build on unsound foundations, financial or otherwise; and it was the fundamental reforms agreed last winter which paved the way for the remarkable progress which we have since made on the Single Market.

But we cannot rest on what we have achieved to date. For example, the task of reforming the Common Agricultural Policy is far from complete.

Certainly, Europe needs a stable and efficient farming industry. But the CAP has become unwieldy, inefficient and grossly expensive. Production of unwanted surpluses safeguards neither the income nor the future of farmers themselves.

We must continue to pursue policies which relate supply more closely to market requirements, and which will reduce overproduction and limit costs.

Of course, we must protect the villages and rural areas which are such an important part of our national life – but not by the

261

instrument of agricultural prices.

Tackling these problems requires political courage. The Community will only damage itself in the eyes of its own people and the outside world, if that courage is lacking.

My third guiding principle is the need for Community policies which encourage enterprise. If Europe is to flourish and create the jobs of the future, enterprise is the key.

The basic framework is there: the Treaty of Rome itself was intended as a Charter for Economic Liberty. But that is not how it has always been read, still less applied.

The lesson of the economic history of Europe in the 1970s and 1980s is that central planning and detailed control don't work, and that personal endeavour and initiative do; that a State-controlled economy is a recipe for low growth; and that free enterprise within a framework of law brings better results.

The aim of a Europe open to enterprise is the moving force behind the creation of the Single European Market by 1992. By getting rid of barriers, by making it possible for companies to operate on a Europe-wide scale, we can best compete with the United States, Japan and the other new economic powers emerging in Asia and elsewhere.

And that means action to *free* markets, action to *widen* choice, action to *reduce* Government intervention.

Our aim should *not* be more and more detailed regulation from the centre: it should be to deregulate and to remove the constraints on trade.

Britain has been in the lead in opening its markets to others.

The City of London has long welcomed financial institutions from all over the world, which is why it is the biggest and most successful financial centre in Europe.

We have opened our market for telecommunications equipment, introduced competition into the market for services and even into the network itself – steps which others in Europe are only now beginning to face.

In air transport, we have taken the lead in liberalization and seen the benefits in cheaper fares and wider choice.

Our coastal shipping trade is open to the merchant navies of

Europe. I wish I could say the same of many other Community members.

Regarding monetary matters, let me say this. The key issue is *not* whether there should be a European Central Bank. The immediate and practical requirements are: to implement the Community's commitment to free movement of capital – in Britain we have it – and to the abolition throughout the Community of the exchange controls – in Britain we abolished them in 1979; to establish a genuinely free market in financial services, in banking, insurance, investment; to make greater use of the ECU. Britain is this autumn issuing ECU-denominated Treasury bills, and hopes to see other Community Governments increasingly do the same.

These are the *real* requirements because they are what Community business and industry need, if they are to compete effectively in the wider world. And they are what the European consumer wants, for they will widen his choice and lower his costs.

It is to such basic practical steps that the Community's attention should be devoted.

When those have been achieved, and sustained over a period of time, we shall be in a better position to judge the next moves.

It is the same with the frontiers between our countries. Of course we must make it easier for goods to pass through frontiers. Of course we must make it easier for our people to travel throughout the Community. But it is a matter of plain common sense that we cannot totally abolish frontier controls if we are also to protect our citizens from crime and stop the movement of drugs, of terrorists, and of illegal immigrants.

That was underlined graphically only three weeks ago, when one brave German customs officer, doing his duty on the frontier between Holland and Germany, struck a major blow against the terrorists of the IRA.

And before I leave the subject of the Single Market, may I say that we certainly do not need new regulations which raise the cost of employment and make Europe's labour market less flexible and less competitive with overseas suppliers.

If we are to have a European Company Statute, it should contain the minimum regulations. And certainly we in Britain would fight attempts to introduce collectivism and corporatism at the European level – although what people wish to do in their own countries is a matter for them.

My fourth guiding principle is that Europe should not be protectionist. The expansion of the world economy requires us to continue the process of removing barriers to trade, and to do so in the multilateral negotiations in the GATT.

It would be a betrayal if, while breaking down constraints on trade within Europe, the Community were to erect greater external protection. We must ensure that our approach to world trade is consistent with the liberalization we preach at home.

We have a responsibility to give a lead on this, a responsibility which is particularly directed towards the less developed countries. They need not only aid; more than anything they need improved trading opportunities if they are to gain the dignity of growing economic strength and independence.

My last guiding principle concerns the most fundamental issue, the European countries' role in defence. Europe must continue to maintain a sure defence through NATO. There can be no question of relaxing our efforts even though it means taking difficult decisions and meeting heavy costs.

It is to NATO that we owe the peace that has been maintained over forty years. The fact is things *are* going our way: the democratic model of a free enterprise society *has* proved itself superior, freedom *is* on the offensive, a peaceful offensive, the world over for the first time in my lifetime. We must strive to maintain the United States' commitment to Europe's defence. That means recognizing the burden on their resources of the world role they undertake, and their point that their allies should play a full part in the defence of freedom, particularly as Europe grows wealthier. Increasingly they will look to Europe to play a part in out-of-area defence, as we have recently done in the Gulf.

NATO and the WEU have long recognized where the problems with Europe's defences lie, and have pointed out the solutions. The time has come when we must give substance to our declarations about a strong defence effort with better value for money.

It is not an institutional problem. It is not a problem of drafting. It is something at once simpler and more profound: it is a question of political will and political courage, of convincing people in all our countries that we cannot rely for ever on others for our defence, but that each member of the Alliance must shoulder a fair share of the burden.

We must keep up public support for nuclear deterrence, remembering that obsolete weapons do not deter; hence the need for modernization.

We must meet the requirements for effective conventional defence in Europe against Soviet forces which are constantly being modernized.

We should develop the WEU, not as an alternative to NATO, but as a means of strengthening Europe's contribution to the common defence of the West.

Above all, at a time of change and uncertainty in the Soviet Union and Eastern Europe, we must preserve Europe's unity and resolve, so that whatever may happen our defence is sure. At the same time, we must negotiate on arms control and keep the door wide open to co-operation on all the other issues covered by the Helsinki Accords.

But let us never forget that our way of life, our vision, and all that we hope to achieve is secured not by the rightness of our cause but by the strength of our defence. On this we must never falter, never fail.

I believe it is not enough just to talk in general terms about a European vision or ideal. If we believe in it, we must chart the way ahead and identify the next steps. That is what I tried to do this evening.

This approach does not require new documents: they are all there, the North Atlantic Treaty, the Revised Brussels Treaty, and the Treaty of Rome, texts written by far-sighted men, a remarkable Belgian – Paul Henri Spaak – among them.

However far we may want to go, the truth is that we can only get there one step at a time.

THE REVIVAL OF BRITAIN

What we need now is to take decisions on the next steps forward rather than let ourselves be distracted by Utopian goals. Utopia never comes, because we know we should not like it if it did.

Let Europe be a family of nations, understanding each other better, appreciating each other more, doing more together but relishing our national identity no less than our common European endeavour.

Let us have a Europe which plays its full part in the wider world, which looks outward not inward, and which preserves that Atlantic Community – that Europe on both sides of the Atlantic – which is our noblest inheritance and our greatest strength.

May I thank you for the privilege of delivering this lecture in this great hall to this great College.

The Conservative Party Conference

BRIGHTON, 14 OCTOBER 1988

Thatcherism is constantly evolving in order to ensure that Britain is fully prepared to meet the challenges of the 1990s. In this speech Mrs Thatcher stressed that the Conservative Party alone had the capacity, the ideas and the policies to equip Britain successfully for the next decade. She said, 'The Conservative Party occupies the common ground of British politics. Indeed, we staked out that ground. It is where the great majority of the British people have pitched their tents. And so it has fallen to us to lead Britain into the 1990s. And, who knows, beyond.' This speech makes clear the kind of society that Mrs Thatcher hopes to bequeath to her successors, and it contains a ringing reaffirmation of the great Tory principles which she has adapted and refined to provide the basis for the revival of Britain.

Four years have passed since we last came to Brighton for our conference. We all have memories of that week: memories sad and memories brave. But the human spirit is indomitable. And today we take inspiration from those of our friends, many of them here in this hall, friends who survived to rededicate themselves to the cause of freedom.

All elections matter. But some matter more than others. Some elections are not just part of history. They make history. And such was our Conservative victory in 1979. After a series of Socialist Governments that said 'we can't', Britain wanted a Government that said 'we can'. And it got one.

THE REVIVAL OF BRITAIN

Nearly ten years in Government – how much energy and commitment we have all put into the battle. And no one more so than the great friend and colleague we are delighted to have with us today – Willie Whitelaw. Just like old times. Nearly ten years in Government – and a resurgence of freedom and prosperity without parallel. Nearly ten years – yet it's still we Conservatives who set the pace, generate the ideas, and have the vision.

Alone among the political parties, we hold fast to our convictions. But next year's tenth anniversary is no time to rest on our laurels. It marks the start of our next ten. We are all too young to put our feet up.

I'm not so sure, though, about our political opponents. They don't seem to have had too good a summer.

After the two platoons of the old Alliance went their separate ways, they popped up last month at Torquay and Blackpool respectively. The second called the first one names, but seemed to have some difficulty knowing what name to call themselves. All those initials are so confusing, aren't they? I suggested SOS – but clearly things have gone too far for that. In the end, I think they decided to be one thing in the country and whatever they felt like in the House of Commons. Or was it the other way round?

As for Labour's goings-on at Blackpool, for half an hour or so it seemed that their Leader had seen the light and would shortly be calling his memoirs *I Did it Her Way*. Whatever happened to Socialism? I began to compose a gracious little tribute to get the new session off to a bright start. Alas for high hopes. Was Labour about to shake off its union shackles and go it alone? Not on your Todd – and that, Madam President, is positively the last Todd joke at this conference.

So it's back to square one for the Socialists. The Labour leopard can't change its spots – even if it sometimes thinks wistfully of a blue rinse.

Nearly ten years into this Conservative Government and everybody knows that our policies work and that Labour's don't; and that our policies have produced a standard of living undreamed of by our parents and the highest standard of social services this country has ever known. The Japanese call it Britain's economic miracle – and who are we to argue?

I'm proud that with a Conservative Government people are better off than they've ever been before. But an odd thing has happened recently. Because we strive to increase the prosperity of the nation and its citizens, we're accused of materialism. It's a curious charge. For years one of the main arguments in British politics was how to secure economic growth. Now we've done that, now we've halted and reversed the years of decline over which Labour presided, we are told that all we care about is 'Loadsamoney'.

Because we give people the chance to better themselves, they accuse us of encouraging selfishness and greed. What nonsense. Does someone's natural desire to do well for himself, to build a better life for his family and provide opportunities for his children, does all this make him a materialist? Of course it doesn't. It makes him a decent human being, committed to his family and his community, *and* prepared to take responsibility on his own shoulders.

The truth is that what we are actually encouraging is the best in human nature. The prosperity brought about by our policies offers a wider choice to more people than ever before. Yes, our children can travel to see the treasures and wonders of the world. Yes, older people can enjoy greater comfort and pursue their own interest. Yes, culture and the arts are thriving. Yes, people can expect to enjoy these things. And if that is the charge, I plead guilty.

There's another reply to Labour's charge of materialism. Our approach has meant more to spend on the social services, more on the Health Service, more on the disabled. Indeed, if you measure community concern by community spending – as Labour does – we win hands down every time.

Now, of course we don't expect the Labour Party to have anything good to say about us. After all, they have hardly anything good to say about each other. But it's time we took the credit for some of the things we have achieved: for example the eight million patients treated in hospitals each year; the 80 per cent increase in spending on benefits for the disabled; and an increase in *real* terms of *45 per cent* in nurses' pay.

It's not for Labour, who cut nurses' pay, and cut hospital building, to lecture Conservatives on care and compassion. Our Government has made enormous increases in the amount spent on social welfare to help the less fortunate – and so have individuals.

As prosperity has increased, so the fundamental generosity of our people has prompted *far* more personal giving. Of course, there will always be a minority whose sole concern is themselves. But those who care, and they are the great majority of us, now have the means to give. And they are giving in full measure: over £1,500 million a year to boost charities, rebuild churches, help medical research and feed the hungry. That's a marvellous record. And it doesn't stop at individuals. Many businesses are now giving a percentage of their profits to help the community in which they are situated.

Is this materialism? Is this the selfish society? Are these the hallmarks of greed? The fact is that prosperity has created not the selfish society but the generous society. Madam President, Labour's charge is absurd.

So our critics come up with a new charge. They say the individual gains success only at the expense of the community. That's wrong, too. Personal effort doesn't undermine the community; it enhances the community. When individual talents are held back, the community is held back too. Encourage the individual and the community benefits. A parent's success is shared by his family, a pupil's success by his school, a soldier's by his regiment. A man may climb Everest for himself, but at the summit he plants his country's flag.

We can only build a responsible, independent community with responsible, independent people. That's why Conservative policies have given more and more of them the chance to buy their own homes, to build up capital, to acquire shares in their companies.

But there are some people – such as those living on housing estates controlled by hard Left councils or parents with children going to inadequate schools – who, by the time of the last election, had not benefited from our policies as much as we'd like. And our last manifesto had those people especially in mind. And that's why we're giving council tenants new rights in housing. We believe that where families have a bigger say in their own home, the whole street looks up. In some areas, it's already happening. And we're giving parents more say in their children's education. We believe that if parents help to run schools, we'll get the best schools not just for their children, but for all children.

But it's not enough to pass new laws at Westminster. We have to see that the benefits reach the people for whom they were intended. And we have to do that. We have to help those families. Otherwise they'll be browbeaten by Socialist councillors and bombarded by Socialist propaganda calculated to deny them the opportunities we have provided.

Greater responsibility gives more dignity to the individual and more strength to the community. That belief is at the heart of Conservatism. And we must make it live.

When we were returned at that historic election in 1979 we were faced with the overriding threat of inflation. It was inflation that had redistributed wealth from the thrifty to the fly-by-night. It was inflation that had undermined confidence, first in the currency, then in savings, then in investment, and finally in our country's future. To salvage our economy, we had first to defeat inflation and only then could the great revival of the British economy begin.

Today we are in our eighth year of growth. Our unemployment figures are below the Community average. We have created more jobs than they have. And other countries come to our shores to see what we do and go home to copy. Since we took office we have handed eighteen State enterprises back to the British people – eighteen, so far, more to come. We have encouraged ownership at home and ownership at work. We have turned small business from an endangered species into a vital and rapidly growing part of our economy. The habits of hard work, enterprise and inventiveness that made us great are with us again.

But however firmly rooted our new-found strength, you can't steer an economy on automatic pilot. Success doesn't look after

THE REVIVAL OF BRITAIN

itself. You have to work at it. In economics, there are no final victories. At home, the fast pace of economic growth has put more money into people's pockets and more money into industry's profits. Some has been invested, but with rapid growth in consumption, imports have grown faster than exports, leaving us with a substantial trade deficit. And too much buying has been paid for by too much borrowing. And so to encourage people to spend less and save more, the Chancellor has had to raise interest rates. It's never popular to push them up – except perhaps with savers – but popular or not, the Chancellor has done the right thing, as you'd expect of him.

The right thing is to make sure that we continue to grow steadily, if less fast than in recent months. Too much borrowing has also meant that inflation today is too high. Make no mistake. We intend to bring inflation down again. That's not an expression of hope. It's a statement of intent. And I think the country knows us well enough by now to recognize that we say what we mean and we mean what we say.

As you know, there are always pressures on Government to spend more than the country can afford. We're not going down that road – not this year, not next, not any year. We'll continue to keep a firm grip on public spending. And I look forward to those who so roundly condemn extravagance with private money giving their whole-hearted enthusiastic support to our prudence in handling the public's money.

There is nothing new or unusual about the Tory commitment to protect the environment. The last thing we want is to leave environmental debts for our children to clear up – slag, grime, acid rain and pollution.

For too much of human history, man assumed that whatever he did, he could take his natural world for granted. Today we know that simply isn't true.

In the last century or so, we have seen an unprecedented increase in the pace of change – quite unprecedented – because of the growth in population, the spread of industry, the dramatically increased use of oil, gas and coal, and the cutting down of forests. And these have created new and daunting problems. You know them: acid rain, and the greenhouse effect

272

– a kind of global heat trap and its consequences for the world's climate.

In the past, science has solved many of the problems which at the time seemed quite insuperable. It can do so again.

We are far too sensible to think that in 1988 we can turn the clock back to a pre-industrial world where Adam delved and Eve span. The Garden of Eden had a population of two. Our world has a population of five billion, going on six. And it has more than doubled in my own lifetime. Those people need to cook meals, heat homes, clothe themselves, find work. They need factories, roads and power stations. All these things are part of our lives today and the ambition of the Third World tomorrow.

The choice facing us is not industrial development or a clean environment. To *survive* we *need* both. Industry is part of our habitat; economic growth is one of the systems that sustain human life today.

Pride in these islands – our countryside, our seas and rivers – runs like a thread through our history and literature. Sometimes, it seems a perverse pride. 'Fog, fog everywhere' begins one of Dickens's greatest novels. That was still true in London when I first went to work there. But the Clean Air Act of 1956 – passed by a Conservative Government – banished smog from the air we breathe. The Thames is now the cleanest metropolitan estuary in the world and £4 billion is now being spent on the Mersey. I want to see the industrial rivers of the North and Midlands – and of Europe – as clean as the Thames.

We have led Europe in banning the dumping of harmful industrial waste in the North Sea. And, given our record, we are well placed to take the lead with other Governments in practical efforts to protect the wider world. We will work with them to end the destruction of the world's forests. We shall direct more of our overseas aid to help poor countries to protect their trees and plant new ones. We will join with others to seek further protection of the ozone layer – that global skin which protects life itself from ultraviolet radiation. We will work to cut down the use of fossil fuels, a cause of both acid rain and the greenhouse effect. But that means a policy for safe, sensible and balanced use of nuclear power.

It's we Conservatives who are not merely friends of the Earth – we are its guardians and trustees for generations to come. The core of Tory philosophy and the case for protecting the environment are the same. No generation has a freehold on this Earth. All we have is a life tenancy – with a full repairing lease. And this Government intends to meet the terms of that lease in full.

Year in, year out, this Conservative Government has taken action against crime – action on police numbers, on police powers, on firearms, on fraud, on prison buildings, on compensation for victims, on stiffer penalties. And action against football hooligans and those who carry knives and firearms. And there is more to come. Witness, for example, the new Criminal Justice Act. That is the action we have consistently taken.

I hope that the courts will continue to take account of the strong public support for tough penalties against violent criminals. I am sure they will pay the most careful attention to the longer sentences that are now available to them. Anyone who mugs an old lady leaving the post office with her pension, anyone who rapes a teenager walking home from an evening with friends, anyone who commits violence against a child should have no shred of doubt about the severity of the sentence for that sort of brutality.

Violent crime is a blight on too many lives. And its reduction has a claim not only on the political energy of the Government, but on the moral energy of the people. We are not spectators in the battle between the police and criminals. We are all involved. To witness a crime and say nothing about it hinders the police and helps the criminal. To protect our own home from burglary hinders the criminal and helps the police.

There's a breed of left-wing politicians who excuse violence on the grounds that it's not the criminal who is guilty – but the rest of us. That's a specious argument left over from the Sixties. In effect it excuses, indeed even encourages, crime by absolving the criminal of guilt in advance. Weasel words can never justify the actions of the robber, the thug or the hooligan.

Conservatives need no sermons from Socialists on the rule of law. We proposed tougher sentences for criminals who carry guns: they opposed them. We proposed that over-lenient sentences should be referred to the appeal court: Labour voted against. We condemned violence on the picket line: they equivocated. And, year after year, they will not support the Prevention of Terrorism Act – an Act which is vital to the defeat of the IRA and which has saved so very many lives. I find that very hard to forgive.

In this country and in other democracies, the enemies of civilization and freedom have turned to the gun and the bomb to destroy those they can't persuade. The terrorist threat to freedom is worldwide. It can never be met by appeasement. Give in to the terrorist and you breed more terrorism.

At home and abroad our message is the same. We will not bargain, nor compromise, nor bend the knee to terrorists. In our United Kingdom, the main terrorist threat has come from the IRA. Their minds twisted by hatred and fanaticism, they have tried to bomb and murder their way to their objective of tearing more than a million citizens out of the United Kingdom. The truth is that the whole IRA campaign is based on crushing democracy and smashing anyone who doesn't agree with them.

To all those who have suffered so much at their hands – to the Northern Ireland policemen, prison officers and their families, to the soldiers, the judges, the Civil Servants and their families – we offer our deepest admiration and thanks for defending democracy and our thanks for facing danger while keeping within the rule of law – unlike the terrorist who skulks in the shadows and shoots to kill.

We thank too the security forces who had the guts to go to Gibraltar to give evidence to the inquest, demonstrating conclusively that they acted at all times within the law and to save lives – the lives of countless people who would have been killed had the IRA fulfilled their murderous purpose. What a pity it is that there are still some in this country not prepared to accept the verdict of the jury, so great is their prejudice against the security forces. What comfort that must be to the terrorists.

We will work to increase co-operation in security between

the sovereign Governments in London and Dublin. We will work to involve both Protestants and Catholics fully and fairly in the economic and political life of Northern Ireland. But we will never give up the search for more effective ways of defeating the IRA. And if the IRA think they can weary us or frighten us, they have made a terrible miscalculation.

People sometimes say that it's wrong to use the word 'never' in politics. I disagree. Some things are of such fundamental importance that no other word is appropriate. So I say once again today that this Government will *never* surrender to the IRA. *Never*.

Madam President, great changes are taking place in world affairs, no less momentous, no less decisive for our future than those which followed the Second World War. But there is a crucial difference. This time liberty is gaining ground the world over; Communism is in retreat. Democracy and free enterprise are showing that only they can meet the real needs of people.

Britain's resurgence and our close relationship with the United States under President Reagan's strong leadership have put us right at the forefront of these great events. And once again we are playing the part which history and our instincts demand. President Reagan has rebuilt the strength and confidence of the West – not without a little help – and he has inspired the democracies to go out and win the battle of ideas. It's vital that Britain and America should always stand together. So the next President of the United States will have the United Kingdom as a staunch ally. The need for strong leadership in America and in Britain will be no less in the period ahead.

Perhaps one day the exciting developments taking place in the Soviet Union will lead to a freer society and less expansionist aims. Let us hope so. But hope is no basis for a defence policy. For all the bold reforms, the Soviet Union remains a one-party State, in which the Communist Party is supreme, and Soviet forces remain far in excess of what they need for defence alone. So we have to keep our sense of perspective and our defences in good repair.

The old dangers persist and we also have to be alert to new

dangers. Even as relations with the Soviet Union become more hopeful, some other countries have already acquired chemical weapons and missiles. And what's more, some seek nuclear weapons. It's in the nature of democracies to relax at the first sign of hope. *This we must not do.* For great change is also a time of great uncertainty, especially in the countries of Eastern Europe.

Now, more than ever before, the West must be united and prepared. NATO's purpose is to prevent not only nuclear war but all war. And its strategy recognizes that conventional weapons alone can't provide an adequate and effective deterrent against either nuclear threat or the massive conventional and chemical weapons of the Warsaw Pact.

Yet last week in Blackpool, Labour reduced the defence of the realm to a farce. Their new secret weapon for Britain's defence was revealed. It was a form of words. Labour's leadership proposed a composite resolution embracing unilateral disarmament, bilateral disarmament and multilateral disarmament, all at the same time – not to defend Britain against her enemies, but to defend the Labour Leader against his. And like all forms of appeasement it failed.

The Labour conference passed a resolution reaffirming Labor's commitment to one-sided disarment. But the only resolution that matters is the unswerving resolution of *this* Conservative Government. The British people know that it is our strength which keeps us safe.

As you know, I spoke recently in Bruges about Britain's views on Europe. It caused a bit of a stir. Indeed, from some of the reactions you would have thought I had reopened the Hundred Years War. And from the avalanche of support, you'd have thought I'd won it single-handed.

And why all the fuss? Because I reminded people that Europe was not created by the Treaty of Rome? Because I said that willing and active co-operation between independent sovereign States is the best way to build a successful European Community? Because I said that to try to suppress nationhood and concentrate power at the centre of a European conglomerate would be highly damaging and would jeopardize the objectives we seek to achieve?

Of course, that wasn't at all convenient for those who want to bring about a federal Europe by stealth. They don't like having these points aired publicly. That was evident from their confusion. First they argued that national identity is *not* threatened by Brussels. Then they said that the whole idea of nationhood is old-fashioned and out of date. Well, they can't have it both ways!

But I welcomed the debate, because it's brought into the open an equally fundamental question – the choice between two kinds of Europe: a Europe based on the widest possible freedom for enterprise; or a Europe governed by Socialist methods of centralized control and regulation.

There's no doubt what the Community's founders intended. The Treaty of Rome is a charter for economic liberty, which they knew was the essential condition for personal and political liberty. Today that founding concept is under attack from those who see European unity as a vehicle for spreading Socialism. Well, we haven't worked all these years to free Britain from the paralysis of Socialism only to see it creep in through the back door of central control and bureaucracy from Brussels.

That wasn't what we joined the European Community for. *Ours* is the true European ideal. It is that ideal which will fire our campaign in the European elections. That's why we must win every possible seat in the European Parliament for the Conservative cause.

We shall point out that Britain has taken the lead in tackling practical issues in Europe which are of real benefit to people – reform of the Common Agricultural Policy, completion of the Single Market, the fight against terrorism and drugs; that Britain continues to make the second largest financial contribution to Europe; and that Britain stations more forces beyond its borders – nearly 70,000 of them – than any other European country, in defence of freedom. With these sort of credentials *no one* should doubt Britain's whole-hearted commitment to Europe.

Every year the press tells us in advance that Conservative conferences are dull affairs in which everyone agrees with everyone else. And every year we have a debate on law and order. Still, the press is right in one respect. Everyone can see, through all the cut-and-thrust of debate, that this party is united on the great fundamentals of politics.

We believe: that individuals have a right to liberty that no State can take away; that Government is the servant of the people, not its master; that the role of Government is to *strengthen* our freedom, not deny it; that the economic role of Government is to establish a climate in which enterprise can flourish, not to elbow enterprise out of the way; that a wise Government will spread opportunities, but that individuals must seize them; that citizens who are protected by the law have a duty to assist in maintaining the law; that freedom entails responsibilities, first to the family, then to neighbours, then to the nation – and beyond; and that a strong Britain is the surest guarantor of peace. As well as these grand themes, we have always believed in what is small and precious, in the value of what is local and familiar, in the patchworks of voluntary groups and associations, each with its own purpose, but all pursuing the common purpose of making the country a better and more civilized place.

These are the beliefs which sustain us. Other parties may discard their principles along with their names or seek to conceal their beliefs in order to win power. We hold by the principles we know to be right – not right because they serve our interests; not even right just because they work; but right because they express all that is best in human nature.

Nothing less would have sustained us through the difficult early days of this Government. Nothing less would have ensured the loyalty of our supporters and the trust of the British people when the going wasn't so good. But we had – and we have – the great assurance that our beliefs are not lofty abstractions confined to philosophy lectures. They are the common sense of the British people. They are what ordinary men and women agree on instinctively.

The Conservative Party occupies the common ground of British politics. Indeed, we staked out that ground. And it is where the great mass of the British people have pitched their tents. And so it has fallen to us to lead Britain into the 1990s. And, who knows, beyond.

There will be new challenges, new problems, new tests. For there are no final victories in politics either. But we will meet them strengthened by our belief in this country. In the talents and wisdom of its people. In their tolerance and fairness. In their decency and kindness. And in their confidence and their courage.